20 juin

Avec toute mon am
Irène et Leonard

THE
POLITICS
OF THE
CROSS

THE POLITICS OF THE CROSS

The Theology and Social Ethics
of John Howard Yoder

Craig A. Carter

Brazos Press

A Division of Baker Book House Co
Grand Rapids, Michigan 49516

Published by Brazos Press
a division of Baker Book House Company
P.O. Box 6287, Grand Rapids, MI 49516-6287

Printed in the United States of America

Library of Congress Cataloging-in-Publication Data

Carter, Craig A.
  The Politics of the cross : the theology and social ethics of John Howard Yoder / Craig A. Carter.
    p.   cm.
  Includes bibliographical references (p.   ).
  ISBN 1-58743-010-X (pbk.)
  1. Yoder, John Howard.   I. Title.
BX8143.Y59 C37 2001
241'.0443—dc21   00-067613

For current information about all releases from Brazos Press, visit our web site:
http://www.brazospress.com

For Bonnie

Contents

Foreword

Do we need a book on the work of John Howard Yoder? I certainly think we do, particularly if it is a book as good as *The Politics of the Cross*. However, I think it serves some purpose to ask why a book on Yoder's work is needed. I have a friend, for example, who is a very well known philosopher. I recently asked him about a book that involved a very favorable account of his work. He, however, was not happy about the book, observing "If you understand me, then you ought to write about what I care about rather than writing about me." Does the same rule pertain concerning Yoder's work?

I do not think so, because I think my friend is wrong about those that write about what he has written. Of course, some should write about what my friend or Yoder cares about; but one of the ways we learn to write about what they cares about is by writing about them. People who teach us to think differently, people who challenge our habits of speech and thought, people who change our questions—that is, people like John Howard Yoder—are hard to understand. Learning to understand them requires we submit not only to what they have to say but how they have to say it. One of the ways that kind of retraining can occur is by not only reading what they write but writing about them after them.

Certainly that is what Craig Carter has done in this wonderful book on Yoder's work. Hopefully this will be one of many books written on Yoder, but it is surely the case that subsequent books on Yoder will have to begin with what Carter has done, for at the very least he has provided the first comprehensive account of Yoder's logically rigorous but diverse work. He has, moreover, helped us see the ecumenical significance of Yoder's work just to the extent he shows that Yoder's understanding of as well as commitment to Nicea and Chalcedon is inseparable from his defense of nonviolence. That Yoder maintained that peace is at the heart of the gospel and enshrined in the creeds of orthodox Christianity, of course, is one of the reasons that he remains so misunderstood. Yoder, as Carter demonstrates, challenges the assumption that the distinction between theology and ethics, between theory and practice, makes sense. To think with Yoder requires a willingness to begin again—a hard and difficult requirement for those well-schooled in the theological habits of liberal or conservative forms of the Christian faith.

One of the great virtues of Carter's study of Yoder's thought is to help us understand not only Yoder's Mennonite conversation partners, but also Yoder's relation to Barth and the work of Hans Frei. Indeed Carter spells out how Barth may have shaped Yoder's work in a manner that Yoder never saw the necessity to make specific. I think Carter may well be right that Barth's later understanding of the church and its relation to "the state" (*Church Dogmatics* IV/3.2) came very close to resembling Yoder's eschatological understanding of the relation of church and world. Carter rightly also suggests that a fruitful conversation needs to take place between those who have been influenced by the work of Hans Frei and Yoder's way of doing Christology. My hunch is that such a conversation will require that we simply forget the distinction between so-called low and high Christologies. Even more important, if "post-liberals" came to understand Yoder, they might see that their "antifoundationalism" is better understood as a rejection of Constantinianism.

A "foreword" is not an appropriate context for a polemical defense of my work, but Carter does make a suggestion on which I expect the readers of this book (which I hope will be many) would expect me at least to comment. Carter observes that one of the biggest problems in Yoder interpretation is me. I do not think he means I have done Yoder an intentional disservice. Rather, it seems because I am better known than Yoder and I credit Yoder's influence on my work, some only read Yoder through the grid of my work. If it is true my work is better known than Yoder's, I certainly regret that state of affairs. Even more I regret that some may come to have misunderstand Yoder because of my work.

So let me say as clearly as I can that if there is in fact a difference—which may even amount to a disagreement—between Yoder and me, no one should be tempted to side with me. For example, I share with Yoder (and Barth) the kind of theological realism Carter attributes to them but worries I may lack. I may have not made my position in that respect as clear as I should, but I cannot imagine any serious Christian theology that is not "realist." As far as I am concerned it is never a question if God exists. The question is whether and how we exist.

Of course, I wish I could be as competent a scriptural reasoner as Yoder was. I simply lack the formation he received from his Mennonite mentors. I also, of course, lack Yoder's extraordinary intelligence. But I thank God that God made me a Texan, which means I was just ornery enough to think that Yoder could not be dismissed simply because what he has to say is so challenging to those of us who prefer to think the way things are is the way things have to be. So if I have any ambition about my own work, it is that having read me, someone may be led to read Yoder. I can, therefore, give no higher praise to Carter's good book than to suggest that I can imagine no one reading this book who will not be led to read Yoder, and even more, to become, as Carter desires, a "skillful reader" of John Howard Yoder's demanding work. May such readers multiply.

Stanley Hauerwas
Gilbert T. Rowe Professor of Theological Ethics
The Divinity School
Duke University

Preface

I believe that the work of John Howard Yoder has a great deal to teach us about doing theology after Christendom, and I hope that this book contributes in some small way to the clarification and appreciation of the significance of his thought for the church in the twenty-first century. Yoder's work also has a lot to teach us about living as faithful Christians in a society in which our faith is not accepted by the majority of those who rule us. All of us, as fallen creatures, fail to live up to what we know, and John Howard Yoder was no exception to the rule. But some among us have been gifted with a much deeper understanding of the truth of the mystery of the Lamb who was slain and yet reigns, and I would put John Howard Yoder into that category. He had a lot to live up to and his legacy gives all of us a lot to live up to as well.

This book has been a little over ten years in the making. During that time I have incurred significant indebtedness to a number of people whom I would like to thank publicly. This book began as a doctoral thesis in the Toronto School of Theology, and I am grateful for the many outstanding professors and fellow students with whom I studied there. In particular, however, I want to express my deep appreciation for my advisor, John Webster, formerly professor of systematic theology at Wycliffe College, University of Toronto, and now Lady Margaret Professor of Divinity at the University of Oxford. John taught me to appreciate the theology of Karl Barth, and even more importantly, he modeled what it is to do theology in conscious awareness of the reality of God. He could be a stern taskmaster, but he worked harder than any of his students and gave prompt, sage, and insightful advice every step of the way. If this book achieves any success whatsoever, it will be mostly due to his mentoring.

I also want to thank James Reimer, who helped me immensely with understanding the Mennonite historical context out of which Yoder emerged and for his aid in finding important research materials. Even though we come to significantly different interpretations of Yoder's

13

thought at certain points, he has helped me avoid mistakes on many issues. I am also grateful to him for arranging an interview for me with John Howard Yoder in 1997, less than ten months, it turned out, before Yoder's death late in December of 1997. Another person who helped with the research was Mark Thiessen Nation, who has made a crucial contribution to Yoder research with his comprehensive bibliography of Yoder's writings. He also graciously read my thesis and recommended it to Stanley Hauerwas. I want to thank Stanley Hauerwas for reading the thesis and giving me such gracious and insightful feedback and encouragement at a crucial point. I also appreciate his willingness to provide a foreword to this book. My former administrative assistant, Diane Trail, went above and beyond the call of duty in helping me with the manuscript. I also want to thank my editor, Rodney Clapp, who has believed in this project from the first time he heard about it, and who was willing to take a chance on publishing a first-time author. The whole staff at Brazos has been extremely helpful and professional.

Finally, I want to thank my family most of all. Rebecca, Elizabeth, and Stephen have practically grown up with their father working on this project, and I am grateful for their support. The person who is most responsible for this project coming to fruition, however, is my wife Bonnie. No one (including me) has sacrificed as much for this project as she has, and no one I know lives the Christian life of discipleship described in this book more completely than she does.

Introduction

Why a Book on Yoder?

The social-ethical thought of John Howard Yoder represents a major contribution to Christian theological ethics in the second half of the twentieth century, but it has not yet been taken with the seriousness it deserves at the level of disciplined scholarship. Yoder's impact can be seen in the influence that his thought has had on the increasingly vocal left wing of North American evangelicalism[1] and on mainline Protestants who have grown weary of liberalism and are developing various nonfundamentalist ways of being postliberal.[2] Ten years after the publication of Yoder's most important book, *The Politics of Jesus*,[3] Edward Leroy Long Jr. stated that it "has become as frequently cited in discussions of social ethics as Paul Ramsey's *Deeds and Rules* in the discussion of norm and context."[4] An indication of the interest in Yoder's thought in American gradu-

1. Yoder has contributed to *Sojourners* magazine and has influenced groups like Sojourners, Church of the Saviour, and the group that publishes *The Other Side*. Yoder gave a keynote address at the founding meeting of Evangelicals for Social Action in Chicago in 1973. See a revised version of this address, "The Biblical Mandate for Evangelical Social Action," in *For the Nations: Essays Public and Evangelical* (Grand Rapids: Eerdmans, 1997), 180–98. Philip Thorne describes Yoder as a "New Evangelical" who, as one of the few Anabaptist evangelicals to have interacted seriously with Karl Barth, has exerted an important influence on the North American evangelical tradition. See Thorne's *Evangelicalism and Karl Barth: His Reception and Influence in North American Evangelical Theology* (Allison Park, Pa.: Pickwick Publications, 1995), 171. See also Dale Brown, "Communal Ecclesiology: The Power of the Anabaptist Vision," *Theology Today* 36 (April 1979): 22–29.

2. Stanley Hauerwas writes of the influence Yoder has had on him in *The Peaceable Kingdom: A Primer in Christian Ethics* (Notre Dame, Ind.: University of Notre Dame Press, 1983), xxiv.

3. *The Politics of Jesus: Vicit Agnus Noster,* 2d ed. (Grand Rapids: Eerdmans, 1994). All future references to this work will be to the second edition except where specified. The first edition, published in 1972, sold over 75,000 copies and was translated into at least nine other languages. The second edition sold over 11,000 copies between 1994 and April 1998. See Mark Thiessen Nation, "John Howard Yoder: Ecumenical Anabaptist: A Biographical Sketch" in *The Wisdom of the Cross: Essays in Honor of John Howard Yoder,* ed. S. Hauerwas et. al. (Grand Rapids: Eerdmans 1999), 21.

4. Edward Leroy Long Jr., *A Survey of Recent Christian Ethics* (New York: Oxford University Press, 1982), 90, as cited by Mark Thiessen Nation, "A Comprehensive Bibliography of the Writings of John Howard Yoder," *Mennonite Quarterly Review* 71 (January 1997): 93.

ate schools can be seen in the fact that, in North America between 1984 and 1997, twelve doctoral dissertations were completed that deal, at least in part, with Yoder's thought in a substantial way.[5] Marlin VanElderen, in the World Council of Churches' magazine *One World,* said that *The Politics of Jesus* was one of the most influential North American theological works of the 1970s and spoke of how it had provided the theological underpinnings for renewed social engagement among a large number of evangelicals. He also credited the book with opening up dialogue between Anabaptists and representatives of the mainline Protestant groups.[6] Paul Ramsey stated that Yoder is "widely recognized as the leading contemporary American exponent of Christian pacifism."[7] The late James McClendon has noted that Yoder's lifework remains a serious but unanswered challenge to Christian thinkers and has called Yoder a "largely unsung American theologian."[8]

Stanley Hauerwas states, in a comment on the back cover of the second edition of *The Politics of Jesus,* that he is convinced that, when the history of theology in the twentieth century is written, Yoder's work will be seen as marking a new beginning. I agree with this comment, but many readers may find themselves puzzled as to what it is about Yoder's work that might cause Hauerwas or me to say this. Speaking for myself, I think that the most significant and original aspect of Yoder's thought is that he models a way of doing theology that is appropriate for the twenty-first century. He shows us how to remain faithful in a post-Constantinian and post-Enlightenment cultural situation in which Christians are no longer in control of most cultural institutions.[9] Yoder does theology from a minority position, but he does it with a concern for dialogue with those from other positions.

---

5. These dissertations are all available from University Microfilms International, Ann Arbor, Michigan, and will be referred to at appropriate points in this book. They were completed at Boston University (2), Duke University (2), Southern Baptist Theological Seminary (2), Baylor University, Catholic University of America, University of Chicago, Claremont Graduate School, Northwestern University, and the University of Virginia.

6. "On Studying War . . .," *One World* (October 1985): 18, quoted by Beulah Stauffer Hostetler, "Nonresistance and Social Responsibility: Mennonites and Mainline Peace Emphasis, ca. 1950 to 1985," *Mennonite Quarterly Review* 64 (January 1990): 70.

7. Paul Ramsey, *Speak Up for Just War or Pacifism: A Critique of the United Methodist Bishops' Pastoral Letter "In Defense of Creation"* (University Park: Pennsylvania State University Press, 1988), 96.

8. James Wm. McClendon Jr., "Commentary: John Howard Yoder, 1927–1997," *Books and Culture* 4 (May–June 1998): 7.

9. By *post-Constantinian,* I refer to the current period of Western culture in which the alliance of church and state, which has made Christianity the official or unofficial religion of the West, has ended. By *post-Enlightenment,* I refer to the period of Western culture in which the dominance of eighteenth-century rationalistic philosophy and the emphases on science, democracy, and objective truth have passed. For more on these two terms, see chapter 6.

He also does theology in a rational, but not rationalistic, manner, rejecting the foundationalist epistemology of the Enlightenment without compromising the truth claims of the gospel. Yoder makes historic Christian orthodoxy powerfully relevant for our day by his imaginative rereading of the Bible and classical orthodoxy from a nonestablishment, minority perspective.

In order to appreciate Yoder's true significance, we need to understand that he is a serious Christian theologian, not simply a member of a somewhat eccentric religious group that espouses an unrealistic, though in many ways admirable, pacifism. I want to show that, for Yoder, pacifism is not the point; Jesus is the point. Not only is Jesus the point, but protecting, declaring, and unpacking the claims of classical Christology is what Yoder is about. The persecution and killing of the Anabaptists in the sixteenth century prevented Anabaptist theologians from doing the kind of long-term, patient, nuanced scholarship that we find in Calvin's *Institutes*. When one reads Calvin, there is no question that his thought is deeply rooted in the Christian tradition as well as in the Scriptures. He is no iconoclast recklessly tossing over the side centuries of faith, reflection, and wisdom. The Anabaptists and their descendants, however, are often portrayed as doing precisely that. After Yoder, this can never be done legitimately again. Here is a thinker who is steeped in the writings of the church fathers and the Reformers, who has a firm grasp of the history of Christianity, and who has a deep respect for the creeds and historic Christian orthodoxy. The subversive and disconcerting thing about Yoder's challenge to the church is the way in which he argues from the Bible and classical trinitarian and christological creedal orthodoxy for his radical position. His is not a Mennonite theology, but a Christian theology, and his social ethics is deeply rooted in his theology. We may not agree with Yoder, and that is our right, but we must deal with the fact that he is basing his challenging arguments on beliefs that he and those of us who confess Jesus to be the Christ all hold in common.

The Purpose of This Book

The scholarly neglect of Yoder, bemoaned by James McClendon above, has occurred for several reasons. First, Yoder's recent death has only now made it possible to survey the impact of his lifework as a whole and to assess it objectively. We are still in the early stages of assessing the overall and permanent contribution of this highly original thinker. Much research into his thought needs to be done, and a great deal of debate needs to go on concerning the importance of his ideas. In this book, I attempt to make a contribution to both of these tasks.

Second, Yoder wrote no major systematic treatise in which the comprehensiveness, logical rigor, and originality of his theology could be readily ascertained.[10] One must read a large number of his essays, which are scattered in various journals and books and which are uneven in terms of style and vocabulary, before one begins to grasp just how powerful his analysis is and how coherent his overall system is. Yoder himself had substantive reasons for using the essay format as his primary vehicle for communication, reasons that will become clear in the course of this book as integral to his epistemology, his concept of his role as a writer, and his style of ecumenical dialogue.[11] Although Yoder considered the possibility of writing a basic introduction to ethics or to his thought as a whole, he rejected the idea as being inconsistent with his firm rejection of foundationalism or methodologism.[12] Yoder could acknowledge the educational value of an introduction to a subject, but he points out that one must have a clear picture of the student in mind; in other words, one must begin where the potential reader is and work from there.[13] This type of conversational and occasional writing is what Yoder did throughout his career.

Even though Yoder himself rejected the shaping of his thought into a system, he was nevertheless a very logical and systematic thinker. The coherence of his essays written over a period of a lifetime is extremely impressive.[14] It is, therefore, necessary that scholars carefully reflect on his work as a whole in order to make a complete, accurate, and fair as-

10. Yoder's most famous work, *The Politics of Jesus*, is not really an exception, although it comes closest to being a systematic presentation of his position.

11. Yoder, *For the Nations*, 9.

12. See Yoder's "Walk and Word: The Alternatives to Methodologism," in *Theology without Foundations: Religious Practice and the Future of Theological Truth*, ed. S. Hauerwas, N. Murphy, and M. Thiessen Nation (Nashville: Abingdon, 1994), 77–90. Yoder says that he cannot write a book from "scratch" because, in his opinion, there is no "scratch" from which to begin (*For the Nations*, 10). The terms *foundationalism* and *methodologism* will be defined and discussed in more detail in chapter 6, in the context of the discussion of the charge of sectarianism, which is often made against Yoder. For now, let it simply be noted that Yoder is quite suspicious of modernity's exaltation of method and sees it as being rooted in discredited rationalist epistemologies and linked to Western imperialist pretensions.

13. Yoder, *For the Nations*, 10.

14. See, for example, *The Royal Priesthood: Essays Ecclesiological and Ecumenical*, ed. Michael Cartwright (Grand Rapids: Eerdmans, 1994), which includes essays written between 1954 and 1990. The excellent introductory essay, "Radical Reform, Radical Catholicity: John Howard Yoder's Vision of the Faithful Church," by Michael Cartwright, cites no major examples of inconsistency of thought or self-contradiction. In fact, Cartwright affirms that one of the purposes of this collection of essays is to show the "substantial unity of Yoder's work over the past four decades" (3). This does not mean that Yoder's thought never evolved, but the differences in emphasis are mostly explicable by the situations of the various essays, and they do not entail a fundamental reversal of a prior position.

sessment of it. The danger inherent in attempting to facilitate this task is that I will turn Yoder's thought into a "system" that can easily be refuted by attacking its "axioms." I do not intend to do that; rather, I intend to help the reader of this book to become a skillful reader of Yoder's work by giving something more like a guided tour than an abstract analysis.[15]

Third, Yoder has often been pigeonholed as a representative of one (extreme) type of Christianity that needs to have a place at the ecumenical discussion table (to show how open we are) but that is known in advance to have the specific function of representing the extreme end of the spectrum and therefore not a viable option for mainstream Christianity. In other words, the value of the Mennonite/Anabaptist (or radical-reformation or believers' church) perspective that Yoder is taken to represent is not that it can be taken seriously as a debating partner but that it defines a sectarian extreme that rounds out the spectrum of positions under consideration.[16]

This attitude is alluded to by James Gustafson in his *Ethics in Theocentric Perspective,* where he says of Yoder's social ethics:

> It is patronizing to say that it is useful, in the mix of Christian communities and views of morality, to have this stringent tradition alive, just as it might be seen to be useful to have Marxists around to remind the exponents of the free market that there are some matters that seem lost in the outlook of the capitalist. Such a view assumes that that value of a position is its contribution to discourse on a moral plane, that the reason for interest in the position is that it represents a moral ideal which wiser persons know is "unrealistic" but nonetheless need to be reminded of from time to time. The issue that has to be joined is theological, not simply ethical. *Theological integrity more than moral distinctiveness is the challenge of the traditional radical Protestant view.... My conviction is that all constructive theology in the*

15. It could be argued that to turn Yoder's thought into an ahistorical system of ethics is to distort it seriously; as an interpreter first and critic second, one must be very sensitive to this concern. For this reason, my exposition is preceded by introductory chapters that seek to situate Yoder historically, that is, within his denominational and intellectual context. It is not possible to understand the thought of such a conversational theologian without keeping in mind who he was conversing with, reacting to, debating, and learning from while writing his essays.

16. Yoder expressed his frustration at being misinterpreted as a "pure type" by others who could then use that as their foil. See *The Priestly Kingdom: Social Ethics As Gospel* (Notre Dame, Ind.: University of Notre Dame Press, 1984), 1. Criticisms of Yoder's position range from reasonable concerns expressed in moderate tones about issues such as reductionism, sectarianism, responsibility, and balance to rather extreme accusations often tossed out without attempts at documentation and supported by *ad hominem* arguments. For example, Yoder has been accused of legalism, perfectionism, Marcionism, secularism, unitarianism, and politicizing a spiritual gospel. For the sake of ecumenical dialogue, these accusations need to be examined calmly and in light of Yoder's entire corpus of writings.

Christian tradition needs to be defined to some extent in relation to this radical option.[17]

My intention in this book is to take up the challenge laid out here by Gustafson: to expound, analyze, and critique Yoder's theology as a serious option for constructive Christian ethics today. It is interesting to note that, even though Gustafson admits that Yoder's theological ethics constitutes one of the most cogent challenges to his own approach, he himself does not engage Yoder's thought extensively in his book. This seems inconsistent of Gustafson, but it is typical of the way that the position represented by Yoder has been treated over the centuries. Some grudging respect is expressed and a bit of verbal praise is given; nevertheless, it remained possible to write one's *magnum opus* on Christian theological ethics in the 1980s without refuting Yoder's position in detail.

Yoder's Calvinist dialogue partner Richard Mouw makes an interesting observation in his foreword to Yoder's collection of essays on ecclesiology, *The Royal Priesthood.* After renouncing, like Gustafson, the attitude that treats the Anabaptist perspective as "a series of compensatory emphases whose ecumenical usefulness lies in their ability to modify other theological schemes," he then points out that the Anabaptists "have often left themselves open to this kind of treatment" because they have neglected systematic theology in favor of biblical and historical studies.[18] This neglect has meant that others do not have to deal with the Anabaptist perspective as a systematic challenge to their own dogmatics. Mouw praises Yoder for having led the way in setting forth the systematic challenge. But, as we have seen above, the type of writings Yoder has produced does not focus this challenge as sharply as they could have if his position were expressed more systematically. As an aid to informed ecumenical debate, therefore, my goal in this book is to expound the logic and depth of Yoder's theological social ethics in such a way that, in the future, refuting Yoder's position will be seen as a task to be undertaken by those who disagree with him and ignoring his position will not be seen as a viable option for those who wish to engage in serious Christian social-ethical debate.

In evaluating Yoder's thought it is necessary to distinguish between two perspectives from which an evaluation could be carried out: the external and the internal. The external critique is often carried out by those mentioned above who use Yoder as a foil or as a representative of a type.

---

17. James Gustafson, *Theology and Ethics,* vol. 1 of *Ethics in Theocentric Perspective* (Chicago: University of Chicago Press, 1981), 75 (emphasis added). This type of attitude to pacifism was advocated by Reinhold Niebuhr. Yoder discussed Niebuhr's views in his article "Reinhold Niebuhr and Christian Pacifism," *Mennonite Quarterly Review* 29 (April, 1955): 101ff. See chapter 1 of this book for further discussion of Yoder and Reinhold Niebuhr.

18. Richard Mouw, foreword to *The Royal Priesthood,* viii.

They employ axioms derived from elsewhere than Yoder or the radical-reformation (or believers' church or Anabaptist) tradition to use in testing the adequacy of his formulations. They cannot be blamed for using whatever axioms they believe to be correct to evaluate the thought of other ethicists, but neither can they claim thereby to have demonstrated the logical inconsistency or incoherence of Yoder's thought. In order to do that, they would have to employ an internal critique, which is what I attempt to do in this book. By situating Yoder in his denominational and intellectual context and then examining the logic of his response to that context as expressed in the total corpus of his writings, I hope to develop a balanced and nuanced evaluation of his importance as a twentieth-century Christian ethicist.[19]

A Brief Overview of Yoder's Life and Writings

Yoder was a significant figure in Mennonite studies, in ecumenical discussions, and in Christian ethics in Europe and North America for over forty years. He entered into significant dialogue with evangelicals, Catholics, the World Council of Churches, Latin American liberationists, Christian Realists, conservative Calvinists and Jewish theologians, including such figures as Karl Barth, Reinhold and H. Richard Niebuhr, Paul Ramsey, Albert Outler, Jose Miguez Bonino, Richard Mouw, James Turner Johnson, Michael Walzer, and Rabbi Steven S. Schwarzschild.[20] He lived for a number of years each in France and Switzerland, as well as spending a year each in Argentina and Israel. Yoder was a polyglot, being fluent in several languages besides English, reading yet others, and delivering lectures in languages other than English on many occasions.[21]

19. This book should be regarded as a preliminary step in the evaluation of Yoder's thought, since understanding a thinker as fully as possible must precede evaluation. It may be that Yoder's thought turns out, on the basis of an internal critique, to be strongly argued (in the sense of logical consistency), very coherent (in the sense of systematic consistency), and highly comprehensive (in the sense of taking into account all the relevant data), and yet one would still not be justified in declaring Yoder's position to be true. Two different systems of thought may both exhibit all of these internal characteristics and yet arise from vastly different foundational assumptions or worldviews. In order to choose between such alternatives, a person must make a decision about the worldviews or the foundational assumptions at the root of the two systems. The best way to facilitate such a choice, however, is to display the system as fully as possible, exploring its own inner logic.

20. For discussion of this aspect of Yoder's work, see Michael Cartwright, "Radical Reform, Radical Catholicity," 15–23, and Mark Thiessen Nation's "He Came Preaching Peace: The Ecumenical Peace Witness of John Howard Yoder," *Conrad Grebel Review* 16 (Spring 1998): 65–76.

21. John Howard Yoder, "How to Be Read by the Bible" (A Shalom Desktop Publication, 1996), 7.

His *Politics of Jesus* was the work that first brought his thought to the attention of most ethicists and theologians generally. Although his doctoral work was in historical theology,[22] he demonstrated enough competence in biblical studies and ethics to engage scholars in those fields in serious debate. The breadth of his scholarly endeavors is quite impressive. Although he was involved in the editing and translation of historical texts, the teaching of historical and systematic theology, ethics, and missiology, as well as mission-board and seminary administration, Yoder's primary contribution to scholarship probably was in the area of ethical methodology.

After World War II, Yoder was one of a group of young Mennonites who went to Europe to work in refugee relief ministry with the Mennonite Central Committee. While in Europe, he participated in various ecumenical discussions as a representative of the Mennonite tradition and studied at the University of Basel. He eventually obtained his Doctor of Theology degree in historical theology, specializing in sixteenth-century Reformation

22. His doctoral dissertation at Basel was published as *Täufertum und Reformation in der Schweiz: 1. De Gespräche zwischen Täufern und Reformatoren 1523–1538* (Karlsruhe: H. Schneider, 1962). See also *Täufertum und Reformation im Gespräch: Dogmengeschichtliche Untersuchung der frühen Gespräche zwischen Schweizerischen Täufern und Reformatoren* (Zurich: EVZ-Verlag, 1968). Yoder also translated and edited *The Legacy of Michael Stattler,* Classics of the Radical Reformation 1 (Scottdale, Pa.: Herald, 1973) and, with H. Wayne Pipkin, *Balthasar Hubmaier: Theologian of Anabaptism,* Classics of the Radical Reformation 5 (Scottdale, Pa.: Herald, 1989). He also translated and edited *The Schleitheim Confession* (Scottdale, Pa.: Herald, 1977) and translated other monographs and wrote many essays on the radical reformation and historiography. Furthermore, he also produced two large collections of class lectures on Christology and on war, peace, and revolution, consisting of over nine hundred pages of historical theology (*Preface to Theology: Christology and Theological Method* and *Christian Attitudes to War, Peace and Revolution: A Companion to Bainton*). Unfortunately, these two works have only been informally published at this point in time, although *Preface to Theology* is scheduled for publication in 2002 (Brazos Press). Another important work in historical theology, *Nevertheless: The Varieties and Shortcomings of Religious Pacifism,* revised and expanded edition (Scottdale, Pa.: Herald, 1992) is much more readily available. Readers of Yoder who only consult *The Politics of Jesus* and the three main books of essays, *The Priestly Kingdom, The Royal Priesthood,* and *For the Nations,* can certainly ascertain the main points of Yoder's thought. However, much of the background, rationale, and working out of the implications of his thought are found only in the one thousand plus pages of historical theology in the works mentioned above, especially in the unpublished class notes. Any serious interpreter or critic of Yoder must come to grips with this material and let it temper rash conclusions about Yoder's theology being not well thought out, heretical, one-sided, unrealistic, and the like. For example, the critic tempted to jump to the conclusion that Yoder is Manichean and totally negative toward the state would be well-advised to discipline his or her criticism by showing how it does justice to Yoder's discussion of William Penn and the Quaker experiment in colonial Pennsylvania. Or again, the critic tempted to conclude that Yoder is preaching an unrealistic form of perfectionist legalism would be well-advised to try and reconcile that view with Yoder's balanced, sober, and nuanced account of the rise of various forms of sectarian dissent in sixteenth-century Europe. The point is not that Yoder is beyond criticism or right on every point but that he has developed a case for pacifism that has unprecedented and unparalleled historical and theological depth and that, therefore, cannot be dismissed lightly.

studies. He also studied with Karl Barth and was drawn to Barth's ecclesiology and to his theological ethics in general.[23]

Yoder returned to North America in 1957 and spent a number of years working for the Mennonite Board of Missions. After taking up a full-time teaching post at Goshen Biblical Seminary in 1965, Yoder completed a book on Barth's view of war, which contains one of the best early expositions of Barth's ethics available in English.[24] Yoder's classic, *The Politics of Jesus*, was published in 1972. During the next quarter century Yoder emerged as the leading spokesperson in North America for the Anabaptist (or believers' church) vision of Christianity and for Christian pacifism in particular. From 1967 (part-time; full-time beginning in 1984) until his death in late 1997, Yoder taught at the University of Notre Dame. In 1988 he served as the president of the Society of Christian Ethics.

The Central Thesis of This Book

At the heart of this book lies the conviction that Yoder's work shows us how the trinitarian and christological orthodoxy of the fourth and fifth centuries contains the key to the survival and flourishing of the church's witness to Jesus Christ in the post-Christendom era that is now dawning. The central thesis I wish to defend is that Yoder creatively unites aspects of his Anabaptist theological heritage with the theological method and major themes of Karl Barth's thought to create a distinctive postliberal[25] alternative to Christian Realism, liberation theology, and privatized evangelical religion. Yoder's pacifism of the messianic community is not only a development of Barth's theology but also the most adequate account of social ethics to emerge thus far in the brief history of postliberalism. Furthermore, as Gustafson was noted as saying above, it is also the most important alternative to the revisionist theology that currently dominates many parts of the modern Western academy.

The theology of Karl Barth, once "widely dismissed by American theologians in the 1960s as a remnant of a discredited neo-orthodoxy,"[26] has

23. See John Howard Yoder, "Karl Barth: How His Mind Kept Changing," in *How Karl Barth Changed My Mind*, ed. D. McKim (Grand Rapids, Eerdmans: 1976), 166–71, and idem, "Karl Barth, Post-Christendom Theologian" (unpublished paper presented to the Karl Barth Society, Elmhurst, Ill., June 8, 1995). Many other references to Barth, scattered throughout Yoder's writings, will be noted at many points in this book.

24. John Howard Yoder, *Karl Barth and the Problem of War* (Nashville: Abingdon, 1970).

25. I am using the term *postliberal* here in a somewhat broader sense than simply as a reference to the so-called Yale School. I could easily have said "postmodern" or "post-Enlightenment" here instead of "postliberal." I clarify the relationship of Yoder to the Yale School below.

26. Mary Kathleen Cunningham, *What Is Theological Exegesis? Interpretation and Use of Scripture in Barth's Doctrine of Election* (Valley Forge, Pa.: Trinity Press International, 1995), 9.

recently come to light as the inspiration for a whole new generation of "postliberal" scholars who have in common an opposition to what they term "revisionism."[27] Centered in the work of a number of scholars associated with Yale University over the past thirty years, postliberalism has become a significant force on the current theological scene. Yale professors George Lindbeck and Hans Frei[28] and many of their former students, including William Placher, George Hunsinger, Ronald Thiemann, and Stanley Hauerwas, have been identified with this approach to theology. Influences on the genesis and development of this approach make for an eclectic list, including such diverse figures as Gilbert Ryle, Ludwig Wittgenstein, Thomas Kuhn, Clifford Geertz, Peter Berger, and Erich Auerbach, as well as a number of other figures at Yale, such as Brevard Childs, Wayne Meeks, Paul Holmer, William Christian, and David Kelsey. It would be misleading to overstate the degree of unity among this group of theologians. What is clear, however, is that the work of Karl Barth stands in the background and has been a major factor in making this new mood in theology possible.[29]

This book will interpret the thought of Yoder as "postliberal" in the sense of constituting a rejection of theological liberalism[30] and in the sense of having been influenced greatly by the theology of Karl Barth, but

27. See William Placher, "Postliberal Theology," in *The Modern Theologians*, vol. 2, ed. D. F. Ford (Oxford: Blackwell, 1989), 115–28; and idem, "Revisionist and Postliberal Theologies and the Public Character of Theology," *The Thomist* 49 (1985): 392–416.

28. George Lindbeck made the term *postliberalism* central in contemporary theological discussion in his book, *The Nature of Doctrine: Religion and Theology in a Postliberal Age* (Philadelphia: Westminster/John Knox, 1984). His colleague, the late Hans Frei, was also central in the development of this approach to doing Christian theology. Especially important are his books: *The Eclipse of Biblical Narrative* (New Haven: Yale University Press, 1974); *The Identity of Jesus Christ: The Hermeneutical Bases of Dogmatic Theology* (Philadelphia: Fortress, 1975); and *Types of Christian Theology*, ed. G. Hunsinger and W. C. Placher (New Haven: Yale University Press, 1992).

29. William Placher, "Postliberal Theology," 115–17.

30. "Liberalism," as used in this sentence, means both classical and contemporary liberal theology. Nineteenth-century "culture Protestantism," as expressed in the thought of Troeltsch, Ritschl, Harnack, and, in North America, the social gospel movement, was highly optimistic about human potential and used idealistic philosophy as a way to express the progress that it saw in history as Western culture moved toward the kingdom of God. It saw a correlation between Christian teachings, on the one hand, and secular science and the best insights of culture in general, on the other. Twentieth-century liberalism has been greatly chastened by the horrific events of this century (world wars, genocide, nuclear weapons, ecological threats) and has abandoned the assumption of progress and renounced undue optimism concerning all forms of utopia. Revisionism is chastened liberalism, still concerned to correlate Christian belief with the highest wisdom of secular culture, but largely purged of shallow optimism and inclined to take the reality of sin far more seriously. Twentieth-century liberalism is more inclined to look to existential, rather than idealistic, philosophy and views liberation as a more realistic metaphor for the goal of Christian social ethics than Christianizing the social order or bringing in the kingdom of God.

not in the sense of having been influenced by the "Yale theology." One of the differences between Yoder's thought and that of Frei and Lindbeck is that Yoder has engaged biblical texts more extensively than they have, even though postliberals tend to criticize revisionists for becoming pre-occupied with prolegomena and strongly advocate the constructive engagement of Scripture.[31] Another key difference is the prominence given to pacifism in Yoder's thought.[32] A third key difference between Yoder, on the one hand, and the Yale theologians, on the other, is that Yoder's theological realism is much more clear cut.[33] Yoder's nonfoundationalist approach to epistemology does not lead him to a relativist position when it comes to affirming the ontological reality of God; this book attempts to show why and how this is so. Yoder studied with Barth in the 1950s and published a book on Barth's ethics in the early 1970s, which makes him a rough contemporary of Lindbeck and Frei. However, there appears to be little, if any, evidence of influence either way in the early development of their respective positions.[34]

31. William Placher urges contemporary theologians to abandon their preoccupation with methodology and to get on with constructive theology—in the preface to a book on method! (*Unapologetic Theology: A Christian Voice in a Pluralistic Conversation* [Louisville: Westminster/John Knox, 1989], 7). It is interesting to note that the Yale theology has developed as discussion of method first and is only beginning to be applied in the construction of theology. This focus on method may well be due to the influence of Karl Barth's theological corpus, which fits in the background of postliberal theology. Since the 1960s, postliberal theologians have only gradually come to terms with the massive challenge to modernity presented by Barth as they have reflected on methodological moves which are more implicit than explicit in the *Church Dogmatics*. It is significant to remember that Frei's doctoral dissertation was written on Barth. What Frei wrote about Schleiermacher and Barth remains true: "A great man condemns the rest of us to the task of understanding his thought" ("Eberhard Busch's Biography of Karl Barth," in *Types of Christian Theology*, 147).

32. Of course, the major exception here is Stanley Hauerwas, who has embraced pacifism and made it central to his work. George Hunsinger has also written in support of pacifism but has not thus far produced major writings in which pacifism plays a central role. See Douglas Gwyn, George Hunsinger, Eugene Roop, and John H. Yoder, *A Declaration of Peace: In God's People the Renewal of the World Has Begun* (Scottdale, Pa.: Herald, 1991). Pacifism does not appear to play a role in the thought of Lindbeck or Frei.

33. This is not to say that the Yale theologians are not theological realists. This is a point on which it is hard to generalize. Hunsinger's commitment to realism seems to be clear, while that of Lindbeck and Frei is less so. That of Hauerwas is still more ambiguous. All that is being claimed here is that Yoder's commitment to theological realism is more straightforward than that of most of the theologians associated with postliberalism from Yale.

34. In the few references to Lindbeck I have noted in Yoder's work, Yoder refers positively to him: "The reason it is so hard for critics from within these foundationalist games to be fair to 'realism' is that they assume, as it does not, the need to justify one's recourse to Scripture by appeal to some other criterion outside it. For my 'straightforward' posture (and intrinsically for the account given by George Lindbeck, and the similar one presupposed without much analytical argument by Brevard Childs, or the one given with enormous analytical argument but less content by Alasdair MacIntyre) the presence of the

Stanley Hauerwas is the only other major ethicist thus far to have written extensively from a postliberal perspective, and he claims to have been greatly influenced by Yoder's thought.[35] Thus, it is natural that many commentators tend to assume that both Hauerwas and Yoder can be interpreted together as "narrative ethicists."[36] Of course, there are many significant points of similarity. However, there are some important differences between Hauerwas and Yoder as well that need to be taken into account in any discussion of the relationship of their respective positions. For now, some of these differences will be listed without comment. They will be documented in the course of this book. First, Yoder engages the text of Scripture to a much greater degree than Hauerwas. Second, Yoder takes history much more seriously than Hauerwas does in his theology. Third, Yoder does not share Hauerwas's interest in character; his doctrine of the imitation of Jesus is sharply focused on the cross. Fourth, it is questionable as to whether or not Hauerwas shares Yoder's Biblical Realism.[37] There are other differences in areas such as ecclesiology, but this list surely can serve to make the point that the two thinkers simply cannot be lumped together. Nor can Yoder be interpreted through the grid of Hauerwas.

Yoder makes what many of us today think of as "stuffy old orthodoxy" as fresh and relevant as the latest, trendy theological fad. It is fascinating to observe that, unlike many who derive a conservative social ethic from a conservative theology and many others who derive a radical ethic from an unorthodox theology, Yoder derives a very radical social ethic, centered on pacifism, from a classically orthodox Christology. In this book, I will present an interpretation of Yoder's thought as containing a highly coherent theological social ethic that has a contribution to make to Christian faith and practice in the coming century. Yoder's "disavowal of Constantine" allows him to develop a christocentric eschatology that views the church as an eschatological community that participates both in the old age of the fallen creation and in the new, messianic age inaugurated by Jesus. The Christian community is distinguished from the world

---

text within the community is an inseparable part of the community's being itself. It would be a denial of the community's being itself if it were to grant a need for appeal beyond itself to some archimedean point to justify it" (see Yoder's "How to Be Read by the Bible," 65, cf. 28). In a 1992 article ("On Not Being Ashamed of the Gospel: Particularity, Pluralism, and Validation," *Faith and Philosophy* 9 [1992]: 285–300), Yoder defends Lindbeck's position against Gustafson's charges of sectarianism. I am not aware of any references to Yoder in the work of Frei or Lindbeck.

35. See Hauerwas's comments on Yoder's influence in *The Peaceable Kingdom*, xxiv–xxvi. Hauerwas credits Yoder with having converted him to pacifism.

36. See, for example, J. Philip Wogaman, *Christian Ethics: A Historical Introduction* (Louisville: Westminster/John Knox, 1983), 234; and James Wm. McClendon Jr., *Ethics*, vol. 1 of *Systematic Theology* (Nashville: Abingdon, 1986), 328.

37. See chapter 2, note 10 of this book for Yoder's understanding of the term *Biblical Realism*.

by its confession of Jesus Christ and thereby is a foretaste of the coming age. The pacifism of the messianic community allows it to bear witness to the Lamb who was slain but who, nevertheless, reigns in heaven.

An Overview of the Argument of This Book

This book is divided into four parts, each consisting of two chapters, plus an introduction and a conclusion. In part I, I sketch the background necessary for understanding Yoder's theological method. In the first chapter, I focus on the Mennonite struggle for self-definition, which has been intricately connected to the scholarly reexamination of the histori- cal roots of Anabaptism during this century. Yoder has also been influ- enced in significant ways by the theology of Karl Barth, so the second chapter seeks to summarize the important areas of similarity and agree- ment between their respective positions. In particular, I explore the way in which Yoder creatively appropriated much of Barth's thought and combined it with his own Anabaptist heritage.

In parts II, III, and IV, I expound the source, context, and shape of Yo- der's social ethics. A major criticism of Yoder's thought is considered in detail in each part. In part II, I describe Yoder's Christology as the *source* of his social ethics. This is done first by examining, in chapter 3, his read- ing of New Testament Christology and the New Testament teaching on discipleship as the ethical meaning of Christology. Then, in chapter 4, I focus on Yoder's reading of the historical development of classical Chris- tology and contrast his understanding of the doctrine of the Trinity with that of H. R. Niebuhr. I show that Yoder's Barthian interpretation of the doctrine of the Trinity contrasts sharply with H. R. Niebuhr's liberal ap- proach and then build on this reading of Yoder to refute the charge that Yoder's theology is reductionistic. I argue not only that Yoder affirms clas- sical, orthodox Christology, rather than reducing Christology to ethics and spirituality to politics, but also that such a catholic affirmation is ab- solutely essential to the logic of his overall position.

In part III, I describe Yoder's eschatology as the *context* for his social eth- ics. In chapter 5, I show how Yoder attempts to derive his eschatology from the New Testament as interpreted in the light of the canonical thrust of Old Testament Scripture. Yoder deals creatively with the "problem of the escha- tological Jesus" in a way that is different from both Albert Schweitzer and Reinhold Niebuhr. He describes biblical eschatology as being both par- tially realized and future oriented. This chapter sets the stage for the dis- cussion of Constantinianism as an eschatological heresy in chapter 6. Yoder argues that Constantinianism is a reversal of New Testament escha- tology, a reversal that is rooted in a significant misreading of the Old Testa- ment. I show in this chapter how Yoder turns the charge of sectarianism back upon his critics by portraying Constantinianism as an abandonment of true Christian universality for a sectarian captivity to the Roman Empire (and Western Christendom). I defend a reading of Yoder as a radically catholic, ecumenical theologian and examine the political and epistemological implications of the charge of sectarianism. This reading of Yoder makes it clear that his theology is not denominational apologetics but a radical critique of the praxis (and the theory) of all denominations (including his own) that is based on, and rooted in, the historical mission of the church as Yoder understands it. That mission is incomprehensible apart from the understanding of history that governs Yoder's eschatology and the christological foundation of Yoder's eschatology.

In part IV, I describe Yoder's ecclesiology as the *shape* of his social ethics. I do so, in chapter 7, by expounding Yoder's view of the believers' church as the most faithful form of the New Testament view of the church and by contrasting it to the theocratic and spiritualist types of ecclesiology. The ecumenical potential of Yoder's believers' church ecclesiology is also explored, and the practices of the Christian community that enable it to build up and maintain unity are described. The believers' church vision involves viewing the church as the new humanity, a foretaste of the kingdom of God. In chapter 8, I consider the charge that Yoder's social ethics promotes the withdrawal of the Christian from society and makes the church irrelevant and ineffective in terms of social change. In response to this charge, I sketch a reading of Yoder as unfolding a coherent, though deliberately *ad hoc,* vision of social witness. Yoder's critique of, and alternative to, H. R. Niebuhr's model for "Christ transforming culture" is reviewed, and Yoder's believers' church vision is described as an alternative to strategies that compromise a faithful witness to Jesus Christ in the hopes of short-term effectiveness in terms of social change.

In the conclusion, I assess the coherence of the theological basis for Yoder's social ethics and suggest how the interpretation of Yoder's thought presented in this book is relevant for the contemporary Christian church. The overall interpretation of Yoder's thought is summarized, and a new profile of this much misunderstood thinker is sketched. The conclusion also assesses the validity of various criticisms of Yoder's social ethics and makes a few suggestions regarding how his thought could be developed further to address these criticisms.

Part I

The Historical Context of Yoder's Thought

*The Anabaptist-Mennonite tradition, theologically under-
stood, is seen to represent not simply a branch of Protestantism with a particular "talent," but a historical incarnation of
an entirely different view of the Christian life, of the work and
nature of the church, and fundamentally also of the meaning
of redemption.*

John Howard Yoder
"The Anabaptist Dissent:
The Logic of the Place
of the Disciple in Society," 1954

*"Barth is affirming for the first time in mainstream Protestant
theology since Constantine the theological legitimacy of
admitting, about a set of social structures, that those who participate in them cannot be presumed to be addressable from
the perspective of Christian confession. . . . Thus Barth is
beginning to develop an approach for which the technical
term in Anglo-Saxon sociology of religion since Troeltsch is
"sectarian."*

John Howard Yoder
"Why Ecclesiology is Social Ethics:
Gospel Ethics Versus
the Wider Wisdom," 1980

1

Yoder and the Recovery
of the Anabaptist Vision

In this chapter and the one that follows, I want to place Yoder's thought in its proper historical context so that his theological method can be discerned clearly and his occasional and conversational writings can be interpreted more accurately. In this chapter, I look at Yoder's Anabaptist and Mennonite roots and, in particular, his role in the Mennonite identity debate that has taken place during the second half of this century as a result of factors such as the "recovery of the Anabaptist vision" and the critique of pacifism mounted by Reinhold Niebuhr between the world wars. In the next chapter, I examine Yoder's relationship to Karl Barth. The surprisingly numerous, and profoundly significant, similarities between the theological method of the Swiss Reformed theologian and that of the American Mennonite ethicist are elucidated, and Yoder's "Barthian" method is proposed as a second key to understanding his thought, along with his Anabaptist roots. These two chapters thus set the stage for the systematic exposition of Yoder's thought in the next six chapters.

Of course, there were many other influences on Yoder's theology that could be considered. The impact of his years in Europe, from 1949 to 1957, was significant in many ways.[1] Yoder's role as spokesperson for Mennonites in ecumenical discussion, for example, led him into contact

1. See Mark Thiessen Nation, "John Howard Yoder, Ecumenical Neo-Anabaptist: A Biographical Sketch," in *The Wisdom of the Cross: Essays in Honor of John Howard Yoder*, ed. S. Hauerwas et al. (Grand Rapids: Eerdmans, 1999), 14–15, for these dates and generally for biographical details of Yoder's life.

with the leaders of the World Council of Churches. Midcentury European Protestant theology, however, was dominated by the influence of Karl Barth, and that, combined with the fact that Yoder was so sympathetically inclined to the theology of Barth, whom he saw as moving in a free-church direction during the 1950s, makes Barth by far the most important influence to consider from that period. Yoder was also significantly influenced by the movement called "Biblical Realism," which flourished mostly in Europe and which overlapped with what Brevard Childs would later label "the Biblical Theology Movement."[2] Yoder saw Biblical Realism as an extension of Karl Barth's attitude toward the Bible as the source of Christian theology and as a way of expressing loyalty to the authority of Scripture without adopting scholastic theories of inspiration.

Yoder also could be interpreted in the wider context of North American Protestant social ethics. He interacted intensively with the thought of Reinhold and H. Richard Niebuhr, Paul Ramsey, James Gustafson, and Stanley Hauerwas, and he also was involved with evangelical groups such as Sojourners, Evangelicals for Social Action, and Regent College. Finally, of course, Yoder taught at Notre Dame for many years and so, inevitably, was shaped by the experience of dialogue with Catholic ethicists and theologians. But Yoder's primary source of identity was never mainline Protestantism, evangelicalism, or Roman Catholicism. He very consciously and deliberately identified himself with the "Anabaptist vision" and attempted from that perspective to critique all expressions of Christianity, including the actual state of his own Mennonite denomination. His doctoral studies in the origins of Swiss Anabaptism constituted not only an academic vocation but were also a successful search for spiritual roots. He consciously spoke for a certain tradition of Christianity and took very seriously the responsibility for doing so. Therefore, understanding Yoder's role in the "recovery of the Anabaptist vision" and the resulting Mennonite identity debate of the second half of the twentieth century is crucial for understanding his position.

Yoder's sabbatical year in Israel at the Tantur Institute in 1976 stimulated his thinking on the Jewish roots of the Anabaptist vision. His deepening appreciation of the Jewish roots of the free-church vision meshed with his interpretation of the biblical foundations of his social ethic and affected his thought at the level of helping to shape his biblical exegesis.[3] But Yoder did not synthesize his own position with anything derived from his study of Judaism; rather, he felt that the study of Judaism between the exile and the New Testament served to clarify the proper interpretation of the trajectory of biblical revelation.

2. Brevard Childs, *Biblical Theology in Crisis* (Philadelphia: Westminster, 1970).

3. Much of the fruit of this study can be found in Yoder's *For the Nations: Essays Public and Evangelical* (Grand Rapids: Eerdmans, 1997).

Yoder's year of teaching and lecturing in Argentina (1970–1971), where he encountered Latin American liberation theology firsthand, led him to a new appreciation of liberation theology and similarities between it and his own thought. Yoder certainly expressed more appreciation for many aspects of liberation theology than most evangelical scholars did in the 1970s.[4] When one reads his writings on liberation theology, however, one gets the same impression as from reading his writings on Christian Realism, evangelicalism, and Roman Catholicism, namely, that of a thinker consciously and carefully drawing lines and making comparisons between his own well-thought-out position and the positions of other traditions. One never receives the impression that Yoder is synthesizing Christian Realism, evangelicalism, or liberation theology with his own thought, at least not to any great extent.

On the one hand, then, we have what might be called formative influences on Yoder's thinking: the Anabaptist vision, Karl Barth, and Biblical Realism. On the other hand, we have what could be termed major dialogue partners or even debating partners: Christian Realism, Latin American liberation theology, and North American evangelicalism. It would be an understatement to say that, when one mentions Karl Barth's theology or the Anabaptist vision, the other does not immediately pop into one's mind. How, then, did Yoder put these two influences together coherently? I hope that by the end of chapter 2 the outline of an answer to this question will be clear.

Yoder's relationship to his own Mennonite denomination was complex. On the one hand, he was probably the foremost spokesperson for the Mennonite position on pacifism in the twentieth century. However, he was also iconoclastic and critical of his own denomination in ways that offended some people. At times, the position Yoder stood for appeared to be an embarrassment to academically upwardly mobile, young Mennonites because of his unrepentant biblicism and his persistent defense of pacifism in the ecumenical and academic world. On the other hand, Yoder's social activism and his strong critique of the Mennonite tradition seemed less than helpful to sociologically conservative Mennonites, who were in the process of being drawn into mainstream North American society and therefore were preoccupied with the problems of holding on to their youth.[5] In order to understand Yoder's complex relationship with his own denomination, we begin with an examination of

4. For Yoder's evaluation of liberation theology, see his "The Wider Setting of Liberation Theology," *Review of Politics* 52 (Spring 1990): 285–96; and chapter 22, "Ecumenical Theologies of Revolution and Liberation," in *Christian Attitudes to War, Peace and Revolution: A Companion to Bainton* (Elkhart, Ind.: distributed by Co-op Bookstore, 1983), 511–38.

5. See James Wm. McClendon Jr., *Ethics*, vol. 1 of *Systematic Theology* (Nashville: Abingdon, 1986), 74.

the development of Anabaptist historiography and the debate over identity that it sparked among twentieth-century Mennonites.

The Development of Anabaptist Historiography

The development of historical scholarship on the left wing of the Reformation, the Anabaptist movement, can be divided into four periods.[6] The first period (1525–1850) was the age of Roman Catholic and Protestant vilification of Anabaptism, on the one hand, and Anabaptist hagiography, on the other. In the context of the heated polemics and polarization of positions characteristic of the Reformation and post-Reformation eras, scholarship was pressed into the service of denominational apologetics. Although the original Anabaptists preferred to be called simply "brethren," their enemies used the term *anabaptist* (rebaptizer) to identify them with the ancient Donatist heresy, which had been condemned by imperial law to create a legal basis for the death penalty.[7] The Belgic Confession required its adherents to "detest the Anabaptists and other seditious people."[8] On the other hand, works such as Thieleman van Braght's *Martyr's Mirror* and the *Hutterite Grand Chronicle* held up a very different interpretation of the meaning of the Anabaptist movement as the history of saints and martyrs.

The second period of historiography (1850–1925) saw the publication of many archival source materials, which allowed the Anabaptists to speak for themselves through confessions, court records, and other primary sources. At this point, at least four different approaches to understanding the Anabaptist movement emerged: (1) a continuation of the older denominational apologetics that continued to see Anabaptists as "fanatical heretics"; (2) minority apologetic interpretations that saw Anabaptism as the continuation of certain medieval traditions such as the

6. In this section, I follow the work of Arnold Snyder, *Anabaptist History and Theology: An Introduction* (Kitchner, Ont.: Pandora, 1995). See the appendix, "A Review of Anabaptist Historiography," 397–408. See also Yoder's "The Recovery of the Anabaptist Vision" (*Concern* 18 [July 1971]: 5–23, esp. 7) for his comments on the development of Anabaptist historiography up to the early 1970s.

7. The Donatists were an ethically rigorous group of Christians in North Africa who refused to recognize the validity of baptisms performed by certain bishops who had disgraced themselves. These bishops had avoided persecution during the last great wave of Roman persecution of the church during the latter third century by handing over copies of the sacred writings to the Roman persecutors. The Donatist schism greatly troubled Augustine of Hippo, to the point that he called on the Roman authorities to force compliance with the majority church. The persecution of the Donatists was the first, but unfortunately not the last, time Christians endorsed the use of the state's coercive power to force compliance with "orthodoxy."

8. See Richard Mouw's comments on this fact in his foreword to *The Royal Priesthood: Essays Ecclesiological and Ecumenical,* ed. Michael Cartwright (Grand Rapids: Eerdmans, 1994), vii.

Waldensians, the mystical and spiritualist traditions, or the radical Franciscans; (3) socialist historiography (e.g., Friedrich Engels), which saw in Anabaptism the beginnings of a proletarian, revolutionary consciousness; and (4) sociological historiography (e.g., Max Weber and Ernst Troeltsch), which labeled Anabaptism as a "sect type" as opposed to more "churchly" and "spiritualist" types of religion. The most influential of these schools in North America was the fourth, which was adopted by mainline Protestants and Roman Catholics, on the one hand, and by Mennonite historians themselves, on the other. Mennonite historians found it useful to identify themselves as a sect type of Christian denomination as they attempted to counter the continuing Lutheran "spiritualist fanatics" stereotype.

The third period of historiography (1925–1975) was initiated by a flurry of Mennonite historical writing, beginning in the 1920s, which seemed all out of proportion to the size of this tiny group. The leading figure in what came to be called "the recovery of the Anabaptist vision" was Harold S. Bender (1897–1962), church historian and founder of the *Mennonite Quarterly Review*. In a presidential address to the American Society of Church History in 1943, entitled "The Anabaptist Vision," Bender presented Anabaptism as "the fulfillment of the original vision of Luther and Zwingli" and as a "consistent evangelical Protestantism seeking to recreate without compromise the original New Testament church, the vision of Christ and the apostles."[9] Bender excluded from his definition of Anabaptism Thomas Müntzer and the Peasants War, the Münsterites, and other "aberrations." He identified as Anabaptism's central theological themes the Christian life as discipleship, the church as a brotherhood, and a new ethic of love and nonresistance. Bender was joined by historians such as Roland Bainton[10] of Yale and George Williams[11] of Harvard in the task of classifying and distinguishing between different kinds of sixteenth-century dissent. Williams's classification of the "radical reformation" as including Anabaptists, spiritualists, and evangelical rationalists became standard.[12]

The fourth period of historiography (1975–present) is characterized by Arnold Snyder as a move from monogenesis to polygenesis in terms of the understanding of Anabaptist origins.[13] Bender's view of Anabaptism as beginning in Switzerland and spreading from there (sometimes being corrupted in the process) has been challenged by numerous scholars (es-

9. Harold S. Bender, *The Anabaptist Vision* (Scottdale, Pa.: Herald, 1944), 13.
10. See Bainton's influential article, "The Left Wing of the Reformation," *Journal of Religion* 21 (1941): 124–34.
11. See George H. Williams, *The Radical Reformation*, 3d ed. (Kirksville, Mo.: Sixteenth Century Journal Publishers, 1992).
12. Ibid.
13. Snyder, *Anabaptist History and Theology*, 402–3.

pecially in Europe) who now see multiple points of origin for the movement.[14] Also, many scholars in North America (both Anabaptist and other) have challenged the picture of Anabaptism as Protestantism taken to its logical conclusion. Many of them would interpret it, in the words of Walter Klassen, as "neither Catholic nor Protestant."[15] In 1979, Werner Packull proclaimed the demise of the normative Anabaptist vision.[16] Current trends in Anabaptist research include the search for pan-Anabaptist commonalities in such areas as economic principles and apocalyptic expectation. But such discussions are carried on without losing sight of the amazing variety and vitality of the various radical reformation movements in the sixteenth century and later.[17]

The "Anabaptist Vision" and Mennonite Identity

The relationship between Yoder and Bender was complex. Yoder agreed with Bender's use of the Anabaptist vision as the hermeneutical key to the interpretation of Mennonite history because he believed, in the words of Rodney Sawatsky, that "Anabaptism caught the essence of Jesus like no Christian movement did in the centuries before or since."[18] Yoder completed his doctoral research on the origins of the Swiss Brethren and has written on Michael Sattler, a key figure in the movement leading to the Schleitheim Confession.[19] According to Sawatsky, Yoder was even more conservative (perhaps "radical" would be a better word?) than Bender in his interpretation of Anabaptism insofar as Yoder was less open than Bender to "the grafting of Anabaptist ideas onto Protestant polity to produce modern, denominational Mennonitism."[20] Yoder stated that nineteenth- and twentieth-century Mennonites received much of their identity from sources other than the sixteenth-century Anabaptists, and he interpreted the twentieth-century renewal of interest in Anabaptists as "an institutional and psy-

14. In an article entitled "From Monogenesis to Polygenesis: The Historical Discussion of Anabaptist Origins" (*Mennonite Quarterly Review* 49 [April, 1975]: 83–122), James Stayer, Werner Packull, and Kaus Depperman posit three movements with distinct origins: the Swiss, the South German/Austrian, and the North German/Dutch.

15. This phrase comes from the title of a book by Walter Klassen, *Anabaptism: Neither Catholic nor Protestant* (Waterloo, Ont.: Conrad, 1973).

16. Werner Packull, "Some Reflections on the State of Anabaptist History: The Demise of a Normative Vision," *Studies in Religion* 8 (Summer 1979): 313–23.

17. Snyder's book, mentioned above as the source of the material in this section, is an excellent example of this type of scholarship.

18. Rodney Sawatsky, "The Quest for a Mennonite Hermeneutic," *Conrad Grebel Review* 11 (Winter 1993): 1. See Yoder, "Recovery of the Anabaptist Vision," 9, where he refers to the Swiss Brethren as "mainstream Anabaptism."

19. See n. 22 in the introduction.

20. Sawatsky, "Quest," 1–2.

chological rallying cry," as opposed to a study of the actual history of the Mennonite denomination.[21]

During the late nineteenth and early twentieth centuries, North American Mennonites began to emerge from their immigrant enclaves and interact with the wider culture. During this period, the "fundamentalist-modernist controversy" came to a head, and its effects were felt within Mennonite circles in the form of the identification of most Mennonites with fundamentalist concerns.[22] Scholars who followed Bender in embracing the "outside influences" of the late nineteenth and early twentieth centuries, such as revivalism, Sunday schools, mission boards, church colleges and periodicals, and conference bureaucracies, included John C. Wenger and William W. Dean.[23] This process resulted in what can be termed the "denominationalization" of the several branches of the Mennonites (with the exception of those who followed the Old Order strategy). The Mennonite move from an "ethnic sectarian" identity to an American denominational identity can be understood as an adaptation to the North American cultural situation. Bender termed this an "awakening," promoted it as a *via media* between sectarianism and liberalism, and used all his influence to make his conception of "evangelical Anabaptism" the normative center.[24]

For Yoder, however, the ideal of Anabaptism stands in judgment on modern, denominational Mennonitism. He contends that Mennonitism in the seventeenth to nineteenth centuries, by ceasing to be missionary, became a "mass church" itself.[25] It became a church made up of all those of a certain ethnic background, as opposed to being a church made up of individuals who consciously choose to follow Jesus by identifying with his church. Today, it is common to identify being Mennonite with being of a certain ethnic background. Moreover, Yoder argues, as the Mennonites emerged from cultural isolation in this century (the process of denominationalism), the movement lost much of its true identity. He goes

21. Yoder, *Christian Attitudes to War*, 168.

22. Yoder, "Recovery of the Anabaptist Vision," 5. A minority of Mennonites, however, adopted a more liberal stance.

23. Sawatsky, "Quest," 4.

24. Bender editorialized about the Swiss Brethren of 1525 as the "purest and most original form of Anabaptism" and as "consistent biblicists, evangelical, soundly moderate and practical, free from fanaticism or doctrinal aberration" (editorials in *Mennonite Quarterly Review* 5 [April 1931]: 85; and *Mennonite Quarterly Review* 5 [January 1931]: 5, quoted by Sawatsky, "Quest," 6). It is noteworthy to observe how similar his description of the Anabaptist norm is to the "evangelical" movement that would emerge out of American fundamentalism in the 1940s.

25. Yoder, "Recovery of the Anabaptist Vision," 23. By "mass church" I mean that it ceased to be an outreach-oriented church that grows mainly by adult conversion and instead took on many of the characteristics of state churches, such as recruiting almost all new members from its own children, being identified with a certain ethnic or linguistic group, and elevating some of its own traditions to the level of the gospel.

so far as to say that, out of faithfulness to the Anabaptist vision, the Mennonite denomination should cease to exist as a denomination.[26]

But how can Yoder presume to make such claims? I have outlined above the development of Anabaptist historiography and the end result of that process of "relativizing historiography,"[27] namely, the disappearance of a single, monolithic "Anabaptism." The problem is not just the current state of Anabaptist historiography but the nature of historical study itself. Sawatsky puts the question precisely:

> How can one moment in history which is the product of the cultural relativities of agents and interpreters stand in judgment upon another moment in history similarly shaped? Must not such moments in history assume the category of revelation to become normative of history?[28]

The Anabaptists of the sixteenth century were only fallible human beings and sinners like us. Within history, the church has never been perfect yet and never will be perfect. So how can Yoder use the Anabaptist vision as a standard to which the contemporary church can be held? The answer to this question is quite complex, involving a description of Yoder's hermeneutic, which includes both his understanding of history and his way of reading Scripture. Since he develops his hermeneutic in the context of the Anabaptist identity debate, we need to extend our understanding of this debate in the next three sections before coming back, at the end of this section on Yoder and the Anabaptist-Mennonite tradition, to the crucial question raised by Sawatsky as to how Yoder can possibly hope to avoid the relativizing effects of historiography in developing a norm by which contemporary Mennonitism can be critiqued.

The *Concern* Movement

The article by Yoder cited above was published in the journal *Concern,* an "independent pamphlet series dealing with questions of Christian renewal."[29] This publication venture arose out of a meeting of young Mennonites held in Amsterdam in 1952. This group of conscientious objectors, who were performing denominational relief work in Europe after World War II as well as studying in European universities, met for two weeks "to gain a better understanding of their own Mennonite experi-

26. Ibid.
27. This phrase is applied to the situation by Arnold Snyder, "Reflections on Mennonite Uses of Anabaptist History," in *Mennonite Peace Theology: A Panorama of Types,* ed. John C. Burkholder and Barbara Nelson Gingerich (Akron, Pa.: Mennonite Central Committee Peace Office, 1991), 84, quoted by Sawatsky, "Quest," 15.
28. Sawatsky, "Quest," 11.
29. The publication's self-description is taken from the inside cover of *Concern* 18 (July 1971).

ences and current theological issues."[30] They were all young, well educated, and anxious to relate their Mennonite heritage to the wider Christian heritage of Western culture. They all had been inspired by Harold Bender's Anabaptist vision and were concerned to bring that norm to bear as a critique both of Western Christianity *and* their own Mennonite denomination. This group read papers to each other during this retreat and then began to publish *Concern,* a venture that lasted into the early 1970s before breaking up.

The themes of two of the papers presented at that original retreat give an idea of the tone and spirit of the group. Paul Peachey's "Toward an Understanding of the Decline of the West"[31] criticized the Protestant Reformation for failing to repudiate the *corpus christianum* ideal. This failure led to the assimilation of the church rather than to a prophetic critique of the world and, thus, contributed to the secularization of the humanist tradition and ultimately of Western culture itself. The post-Christendom situation of postwar Europe offered a second chance for the church to develop a radically different social ethic. Orley Swartzentruber's paper, "An Estimate of Current American Mennonitism," offered a severe criticism of the home church as having become a little *corpus christianum* all its own.[32]

Yoder's contribution was "The Anabaptist Dissent: The Logic of the Place of the Disciple in Society,"[33] in which he attempted to "elaborate a doctrine of social responsibility logically consistent with the concept of discipleship as understood and interpreted within the Anabaptist-Mennonite tradition."[34] The goal of the *Concern* movement was to call Mennonites to take their Anabaptist heritage seriously in order to be prepared to engage the wider world more effectively.[35] Yoder's contribution in this context, typically for him, was to undergird the critiques of Protestantism and Mennonitism as given in the two papers mentioned above with a biblical basis.[36]

30. Paul Toews, "The Concern Movement: Its Origins and Early History," *Conrad Grebel Review* 8 (Spring 1990): 109.

31. Paul Peachey, "Toward an Understanding of the Decline of the West," *Concern* 1 (June 1954), 8–44.

32. This paper was never published, but a copy is in the Guy F. Hershberger papers, box 16, folder 2, Archives of the Mennonite Church in Goshen, Indiana. It is described by Toews, in "The Concern Movement," 111.

33. John Howard Yoder, "The Anabaptist Dissent: The Logic of the Place of the Disciple in Society," *Concern* 1 (June 1954): 45–68.

34. Ibid., 45.

35. Mark Thiessen Nation, "He Came Preaching Peace: The Ecumenical Peace Witness of John Howard Yoder" *Conrad Grebel Review* 16 (Spring 1998): 69. Paul Toews points out that they were concerned for theological, not sociological, boundaries. Just as sixteenth-century Anabaptists sought to evangelize outsiders, the members of the *Concern* group felt that a movement that remained withdrawn in its own ethnic enclave was not being a faithful witness ("The Concern Movement," 122–23).

36. Thiessen Nation, "He Came Preaching Peace," 69. Thiessen Nation notes that over the years Yoder contributed more to *Concern* than anyone else.

Yoder's essay (and his position as a whole) is open to two misinterpretations by those who do not approach it in context. He could be misread as engaging in denominational apologetics, that is, defending the Mennonite denomination as true Christianity over against other denominations, especially given his use of the term "Mennonite" synonymously with the term "Anabaptist"[37] and his critique of Roman Catholicism, Luther, and Calvin.[38] But to read his essay as a whole, in the context of his thought as a whole, leads to a different interpretation. What Yoder is doing here is critiquing both his own denomination and all Western Christianity by means of a standard drawn ultimately from the Bible, not from the sixteenth century. Yoder is interpreted by many commentators as promoting "sectarianism," and this is taken as a descriptive, not necessarily pejorative, fact.[39] However, Yoder is actually extremely critical of sectarianism. In another early article, "Biblicism and the Church," Yoder includes a section called "The Denominational Problem" in which he uses the New Testament (specifically 1 Corinthians 1 and 2) to reject both sectarianism and denominationalism.[40] Part of the confusion over this issue arises from a failure to distinguish between ecclesiastical and political sectarianism. Too often, in a Constantinian framework, no distinction is made, and one is thought automatically to imply the other. But Yoder, while eschewing ecclesiastical sectarianism, views political sectarianism as a good thing. In other words, Yoder is arguing that Christians ought to seek to be unified with other Christians, but not at the cost of supporting such things as militarism, racism, and the routine use of violence to achieve the economic goals of the nation-state.[41]

A second misinterpretation would be to read too much into Yoder's endorsement of the language of perfectionism in this article. He writes: "Biblical perfectionism affirms not a simple possibility of achieving love in history, but a crucial possibility of participating in the victory of Christ over the effects of sin in the world."[42] Yoder is contrasting what he takes to be the biblical position with the ethics of responsibility, in which the love norm becomes an unrealizable ideal, thus rendering Christian witness invisible. What Yoder calls the "perfectionism of the cross" means being empowered by the Holy Spirit in the context of the resurrection of Christ to take up one's cross and bear witness to Christ. The issue here is not whether the Christian life can be perfect in the

37. Ibid. See, for example, Yoder's reference to "the Mennonite view" in "The Anabaptist Dissent," 51.

38. Ibid., 51–54.

39. See, for example, a critic as friendly as Sawatsky, "Quest," 16.

40. John Howard Yoder and David Shank, "Biblicism and the Church" *Concern* 2 (1955): 56.

41. This issue will be discussed more fully in chapter 6 of this book.

42. Yoder, "The Anabaptist Dissent," 59.

sense of being completely free of sin but whether or not a Christian witness can become visible in history. Yoder goes on in this article to reject legalism explicitly. He notes that two significantly different definitions are often given to legalism: first, the belief that "by observing a set of rules, which in principle are within human possibilities, we will be just in the sight of God," and second, "the belief that it is possible, as a guide to discipleship and discipline for Christians, to know adequately what God demands of those who have received His grace." Yoder calls the first view "unscriptural" and incompatible with "the sin in even the Christian's heart."[43] Yet, he goes on to note, critics of his position often use the term *legalism* in both senses at once in order to condemn the second definition along with the first. To do that, says Yoder, is to advocate what Paul calls sinning "that grace may abound" and what Bonhoeffer referred to as "cheap grace."[44]

Yoder actually is advocating here, and continued to advocate throughout his career, a third way between the extremes of the doctrine of the invisible church and the doctrine of sectarian perfectionism. He argues for a church that, despite its imperfections, is enabled by grace to make visible a true witness to Jesus Christ. He is not really writing here as a "Mennonite," nor is he ultimately writing as an "Anabaptist." The best description of Yoder's stance, though it too can be misinterpreted, is "ecumenically biblicist" or, in Cartwright's term, "radically catholic."[45] Further justification of this interpretation of Yoder, however, must await further examination of Yoder's thought in the context of the debate over Mennonite identity after World War II.

Reinhold Niebuhr's Critique of Pacifism

The theoretical justification of withdrawal and separation from social-ethical engagement with the wider culture, which the *Concern* group found necessary to critique in the Mennonite tradition in which they had been raised, goes back to developments that took place between the two world wars and, in particular, the critique of pacifism by Reinhold Niebuhr in the late 1930s. Until World War I, Reinhold Niebuhr was a typical liberal pacifist. He abandoned pacifism to join in Woodrow Wilson's crusade, "the war to end all wars," but swung back to his former pacifism after the war, when the stupidity and futility of the whole enterprise became clear to everyone. But it was the failure of liberal pacifists to find an

43. Ibid., 62.
44. Ibid., 60.
45. See Michael Cartwright, "Radical Reform, Radical Catholicity: John Howard Yoder's Vision of the Faithful Church," an essay that introduces a collection of Yoder's writings in *Royal Priesthood*.

adequate way to respond to Hitler in the 1930s that drove Niebuhr to abandon pacifism decisively once and for all.[46]

By World War II, Niebuhr was what he would remain for the rest of his life, "an Augustinian liberal."[47] He had made peace with the necessity of war and, in the process, worked out his overall theology. His mature theology was basically a "chastened liberalism," that is, the liberalism of the social gospel corrected by a doctrine of original sin informed by Augustine and Luther, a doctrine that recent events in Western culture had once again made relevant. Yoder notes that Niebuhr's major work in systematic theology, *The Nature and Destiny of Man*,[48] was an exercise in applied anthropology and says of this work, "All the great themes in the classic tradition are transposed into ways of saying something about human nature or human hope."[49]

In a pamphlet originally published in 1939, Niebuhr attacked the liberal pacifism that he himself had formerly embraced.[50] His thesis in this essay is that "the refusal of the Christian Church to espouse pacifism is not apostasy and that most modern forms of pacifism are heretical."[51] Niebuhr distinguishes between heretical and nonheretical kinds of pacifism. The heretical kind is the liberal humanist type, the "secularized and moralistic versions of Christianity," which deny the Christian doctrine of sin and labor under the "utopian illusion" that "there is some fairly simple way out of the sinfulness of human history."[52] This type of pacifism is dangerous because it never stops war but only delays and hinders defense preparations that could prevent war. What is worse, by failing to discriminate between tyranny and democracy, it inevitably gives a "morally perverse preference" to tyranny.[53]

46. See Yoder, *Christian Attitudes to War*, 343–69, for a brief summary. A recent interpretation of Niebuhr by one of his students is Ronald Stone, *Professor Reinhold Niebuhr: Mentor to the Twentieth Century* (Louisville: Westminster/John Knox, 1992). This book builds on Stone's earlier work, *Reinhold Niebuhr: Prophet to Politicians* (Nashville: Abingdon, 1972). Unfortunately, the later work's only reference to Yoder (104–5) merely repeats word for word his brief assessment of Yoder's early pamphlet on Niebuhr in Stone's previous work (78–79). No account is taken of Yoder's challenge to Niebuhr in *The Politics of Jesus*, an omission that was understandable in a work published in 1972 but inexcusable in a work published in 1992.

47. Stone, *Professor Reinhold Niebuhr*, xiii. Yoder agrees with the view of Niebuhr as a liberal (*Christian Attitudes to War*, 344–45).

48. Reinhold Niebuhr, *The Nature and Destiny of Man*, 2 vols. (New York: Charles Scribner's Sons, 1941, 1943).

49. Yoder, *Christian Attitudes to War*, 345.

50. See Reinhold Niebuhr, "Why the Christian Church Is Not Pacifist," in *War in the Twentieth Century: Sources in Theological Ethics*, ed. R. B. Miller (Louisville: Westminster/John Knox, 1992), 28–46.

51. Niebuhr, "Why the Christian Church Is Not Pacifist," 32.

52. Ibid., 29.

53. Ibid., 36.

On the other hand, Niebuhr states, there is another type of pacifism, "a version of Christian perfectionism," that arises out of "a genuine impulse in the heart of Christianity, the impulse to take the law of Christ seriously and not to allow the political strategies, which the sinful character of man makes necessary, to become final forms."[54] This type of pacifism can be seen in medieval ascetic perfectionism and Protestant sectarianism of the type of Menno Simons. In this type of pacifism, according to Niebuhr, "the effort to achieve a standard of perfect love in individual life was not presented as a political alternative." Instead, "it was content to set up the most perfect and unselfish individual life as a symbol of the Kingdom of God."[55]

This "apolitical"[56] type of pacifism is not heretical, according to Niebuhr, because it does not call the whole church to embody the ideal of pacifism, even though Niebuhr is adamant that nonviolence is both the teaching of Jesus and the ultimate norm of Christian faith. He writes: "It is very foolish to deny that the ethic of Jesus is an absolute and uncompromising ethic."[57] But "human egotism makes large scale cooperation on a purely voluntary basis impossible," so human society requires coercion. Thus, "the collective life of man undoubtedly stands on a lower moral plane than the life of individuals."[58] This is precisely why it is important to have a reminder of the ultimate norm of love among us in the form of individuals who choose the higher way. As "a principle of indiscriminate criticism upon all forms of justice," the law of love reminds us that there is sin in us as well as in the enemy, and it can help us come as close to the ideal as possible within history.[59]

Yoder's Response to Niebuhr

Yoder assesses Niebuhr's critique of pacifism in a pamphlet entitled *Reinhold Niebuhr and Christian Pacifism*,[60] and he discusses the effect of Niebuhr's critique on Mennonites in his *Christian Attitudes to War, Peace, and Revolution: A Companion to Bainton*.[61] I want first to look at his critique of Niebuhr's position and then to examine Yoder's discussion of the effect this critique had on Mennonites.

Yoder's critique of Niebuhr's thought is presented on four levels, with the fourth being the most significant. The first level responds to Niebuhr's ethical reasoning by which he justifies war as the lesser evil. Yoder

---

54. Ibid., 30.
55. Ibid.
56. This is Yoder's term. See Yoder, *Christian Attitudes to War*, 365ff.
57. Niebuhr, "Why the Christian Church Is Not Pacifist," 32.
58. Ibid., 35.
59. Ibid., 40.
60. John Howard Yoder, "Reinhold Niebuhr and Christian Pacifism," *Mennonite Quarterly Review* 29 (April, 1955): 101ff. See also Yoder, *Christian Attitudes to War*, 319–55.
61. See Yoder, *Christian Attitudes to War*, 356–420.

sees two fallacies here: a factual one (the false judgment that modern war is actually less harmful to civilization than tyranny) and a moral one (the failure to distinguish between agents, in which Niebuhr fails to take account of the position that it may be better to suffer than to inflict injustice). The second level concerns unexamined presuppositions of Niebuhr's ethical reasoning, such as the notions of "impossibility," "necessity," and "responsibility." In Niebuhr's thought, Yoder argues, responsibility becomes an "inherent duty to take charge of the social order," a duty that is dictated not by love but by the social order itself. Thus responsibility becomes an "autonomous moral absolute" that overrules the law of love.[62] The third level of Yoder's critique proceeds from this analysis to note three errors in Niebuhr's ethical reasoning. First, Niebuhr makes the mistake of deriving an "ought" from an "is." The fact that all are sinners is not a justification for sinning. Second, Niebuhr's approach does not define the good; rather, it "finds grounds for calling good any policy which was chosen for other reasons." Third, this kind of ethical pluralism presupposes that God's will for all cannot be known, so both pacifism and nonpacifism are equally valid. Yoder says, "This must presuppose that there is no one knowable good."[63] Similarly, many contemporary liberals, acknowledging the failure of society to agree on the nature of the good for human beings, have renounced the search for a common good and have advocated a form of political and social structure in which individuals are free to pursue their own visions of the good to the greatest extent that is compatible with the freedom of other individuals to do the same.[64]

But Yoder's deepest critique of Niebuhr's position, the fourth level, is a theological critique. Zeroing in on Niebuhr's supposed strongest point, Yoder argues that Niebuhr's doctrine of sin "is not the Bible's." Despite the use of biblical language and the appeal to classical Christian sources, Niebuhr "derives his ethics from the fact of man's predicament, and the Bible derives not only ethics, but everything, from the fact of God's redemption."[65] Yoder points to four key biblical doctrines that are missing in Niebuhr's theology. First, whereas the New Testament never speaks of the cross except in the light of the resurrection, Niebuhr does so repeatedly. For Niebuhr, the resurrection is merely "a mythological symbol" for "the superhistorical triumph of the good."[66] Second, Niebuhr has no doctrine of the church, and this makes the nation-state, by default, the

62. Yoder, "Reinhold Niebuhr and Christian Pacifism," 118–19. Yoder offers a similar analysis of the concepts of "impossibility" and "necessity."

63. Ibid., 19–20.

64. Alasdair MacIntyre, *Whose Justice? Which Rationality?* (Notre Dame, Ind.: University of Notre Dame Press, 1988), 367.

65. Yoder, "Reinhold Niebuhr and Christian Pacifism," 121.

66. Ibid.

bearer of the meaning of history for Niebuhr. Yoder argues that Niebuhr fails to consider the church, which "differs from other social bodies in that it is not less moral than its individual members"; "[t]hus the thesis of *Moral Man and Immoral Society* falls down in the crucial case, the only one which is really decisive for Christian ethics."[67] Yoder's point here is that, whereas being a loyal American might well cause a person to have to break a command of Jesus, being a loyal member of the Christian church would never do that. Of course, that is only true historically insofar as the historical church itself is obedient to Christ in practice. But that does not disturb Yoder's point that being a member of the body of Christ, in principle (that is, when the ethical implications of being a member of the church are fully and properly understood), does not require a person to adopt a lower form of morality than that which is commanded by the Lord Jesus Christ. Third, Yoder points to the biblical doctrine of regeneration, which implies a change in the sinner so basic as to be called a new birth. Niebuhr's theology views the sinner as basically unchanged by Christian profession, at least as far as ethical performance is concerned. Fourth, the common denominator of the three doctrinal omissions mentioned so far is that they are all works of the Holy Spirit, but Niebuhr has no doctrine of the Holy Spirit. Yoder points out that, in the New Testament, the coming of the Holy Spirit means the imparting of power, and that power is "a working reality within history."[68]

We are now in a position to understand the root of the difference between Yoder's and Niebuhr's theological ethics. Niebuhr's student, Ronald Stone, says that Niebuhr "had learned from Ernst Troeltsch that a final Christian ethic is not achievable. . . . The ideal of love could not be realized in human history."[69] This is exactly the point at which Yoder challenges both Niebuhr and Troeltsch. The ideal of love has been realized in human history in the man Jesus and, because of the power of his resurrection flowing into the church through the ministry of the Holy Spirit, it is possible for admittedly sinful and imperfect people to bear a visible witness to the ideal of love, not in their individual piety or goodness, but insofar as they covenant themselves together into an alternative community that lives (and suffers) without resorting to violence. Yoder's critique of Niebuhr thus ultimately constitutes a critique of the authenticity of Niebuhr's commitment to key Christian doctrines.

Turning from Yoder's response to Niebuhr to his discussion of the effect of Niebuhr's critique on Mennonites, we find Yoder contending that it was Niebuhr's critique of pacifism that provided the theoretical justification for social withdrawal and apoliticism for Mennonites during World War II. It drove a wedge between those who accepted vocational

---

67. Ibid., 21.
68. Ibid., 22.
69. Stone, *Professor Reinhold Niebuhr,* 106.

pacifism and irrelevance, on the one hand, and those who believed they should try to make the world more peaceful, on the other.[70] World War II brought these issues to a head in a number of ways. For one thing, it shattered the peace movement in the Anglo-Saxon world[71] and gave liberal pacifism a bad odor from which Mennonites naturally wanted to distance themselves. For another, it joined "the issue of what kind of pacifists Mennonites wanted to be" to the larger issue of "what kind of Americans and what kind of Christians Mennonites were becoming."[72] Niebuhr's offer of a respectable place in the grand scheme of things could not help but be attractive to Mennonites. By embracing a Niebuhrian dualism, they could affirm that war was wrong for them but not really wrong for the state or for the majority of Christians outside the historic peace churches. For many Mennonites, a conservative, patriotic, pro-America stance was totally compatible with their pacifism. One is reminded of Origen's argument that Christians were more valuable to the state by praying for victory than if they actually fought in war.[73]

Mennonites from across the theological spectrum found Niebuhr's "deal" attractive. Donovan Smucker, for example, was a well-educated Mennonite who had worked for the "Fellowship of Reconciliation" before losing faith in liberal pacifism, along with so many others, in the 1930s. He wrote an article entitled "A Mennonite Critique of the Pacifist Movement,"[74] in which he presented four basic criticisms of the modern peace movement, to which he had come after a restudy of the Bible and Mennonite history. First, true peace can only be the fruit of the Christian gospel, so the first priority is to bring individuals to Christ.[75] Second, the modern peace movement is too optimistic about the possibility of genuine world peace.[76] Third, modern pacifism compromises with coercion by trying to effect nonviolent change. For this reason, it is different from biblical nonresistance.[77] Fourth, the modern peace movement gets involved in politics and tries to Christianize the social order using all means short of violence, but this is inconsistent. Christians should withdraw from politics because the state is no more than a "necessary evil" to prevent anarchy among those who do not accept the gospel.[78] Smucker

70. Yoder, *Christian Attitudes to War*, 412. See also chapter 16, "The Nonpacifist Resistance of the Mennonite Second Wind," *Nevertheless: The Varieties and Shortcomings of Religious Pacifism* (Scottdale, Pa.: Herald, 1992), 107–14.

71. Yoder, *Christian Attitudes to War*, 357.

72. Ibid., 412.

73. See Yoder's discussion of Origen in ibid., 31.

74. Donovan Smucker, "A Mennonite Critique of the Pacifist Movement," *Mennonite Quarterly Review* 20 (January 1946): 388–95.

75. Ibid., 389.

76. Ibid., 391.

77. Ibid., 392.

78. Ibid., 394.

thus accepts an apolitical stance of withdrawal as the only means of being faithful to the gospel.

On the other end of the Mennonite theological spectrum, John Mumaw, a long-time president of Eastern Mennonite College, which was the most sociologically and theologically conservative of the Mennonite colleges at the time, wrote a pamphlet in which he defined nonresistance as biblical, realistic, and the historic Mennonite position and then contrasted it to pacifism, which he defined as heretical, utopian, and modernist.[79] Whereas Smucker came from a liberal perspective to embrace Niebuhr's dualism, Mumaw came from the conservative perspective to do the same thing. Yoder comments:

> the Mennonite dualism which says we can't do anything in the wider world because we want to be different from those pacifists who are naive about the possibilities of good, was not learned so much from four centuries of minority history as it was by accommodation to Reinhold Niebuhr . . . so our theology of separation in its most current formulation was derived from a professor of Applied Christianity in Union Theological Seminary.[80]

Yoder here is making the point as forcefully as possible that Niebuhr's dualism is not historic Mennonite theology. From Yoder's theological critique of Niebuhr, we can see that he believes that Niebuhr's dualism is not compatible with biblical, historic, Christian doctrine either. Yoder's rejection of Niebuhr's critique of pacifism and his rejection of Niebuhr's liberal theology are integrally related, just as his positive restatement of pacifism and its rootedness in historic orthodoxy are integrally related, as I shall attempt to demonstrate in the following chapters. We now turn to the contemporary Mennonite identity debate, having sketched enough of its background to be able to see where the various sides are coming from historically.

The Contemporary Mennonite Identity Debate

Contemporary Mennonites are involved in a debate over which direction the Mennonite tradition should take in the coming century, and their evaluations of Yoder's thought vary immensely. Should Mennonites embrace both theological and political liberalism and join the mainstream as the culmination of the process of emerging from their cultural enclaves over the past century? In other words, should the Dutch Mennonite experience become a model for the North American Mennonite experience? Or should Mennonites attempt to maintain their sectarian-

79. John Mumaw, "Nonresistance and Pacifism" (1944), as reproduced in Yoder, *Christian Attitudes to War*, 372–87.

80. Yoder, *Christian Attitudes to War*, 360.

ism, accepting it as the price of preserving a viable link with their past history? Even if this is the preferred choice, is not this type of sociological isolation already a lost cause, given the high degree of influence already being exerted on Mennonite youth by the majority culture? It can be argued cogently that Mennonites are already so assimilated that the time is past when this choice could be made. A third option would be for Mennonites to attempt to engage the modern world critically, moving into the mainstream of Christianity as a denomination that eschews both liberalism and isolation. Can such a delicate balance be maintained, and what will happen to the Mennonite peace witness in the process?

Scholars such as J. Lawrence Burkholder, Gordon Kaufmann, and John W. Miller could be labeled "Mennonite revisionists" because they believe that the Mennonite denomination must be revised in more or less fundamental ways in order that Mennonites might join the mainstream.[81] The interpretation of Yoder that emerges from this group tends to be negative, labeling Yoder's thought as "sectarian," "perfectionist," and "premodern." Theologians such as J. Denny Weaver and Mark Thiessen Nation, on the other hand, could be labeled as "peace witness advocates" because they believe that the emphasis on peace must continue to be emphasized, even if that results in a continuing minority stance for Mennonites. The interpretation of Yoder emerging from this group tends to be positive, regarding Yoder's thought as a major contribution. The difference between Thiessen Nation and Weaver, however, is that Thiessen Nation (in conjunction with such non-Mennonite scholars as James McClendon, Nancey Murphy, Michael Cartwright, and Stanley Hauerwas) would view Yoder's thought as a major contribution to ecumenical Christian thought, whereas Weaver would tend to see it as more of an alternative to the theology of Constantinian Christianity. Scholars such as Ronald Sawatsky, Walter Klassen, James Reimer, and Arnold Snyder could be called "classically orthodox Mennonites" because they believe that the Mennonite tradition needs to be moved toward the mainstream of classical, orthodox Christianity.[82] Each of these scholars would want to appropriate the Mennonite heritage in a critical way and to engage the mainstream of Christianity in a critical way as well. Some, like Sawatsky, would agree with Bender that Mennonites should move toward evangelical Protestantism, while others, notably Reimer, would look more to the Catholic/Eastern traditions. Klassen would be reluctant to see Mennonites as either Catholic or Protestant.

81. It should be noted that this diverse group of scholars would not agree on precisely which features of the Mennonite beliefs and/or practice need to be revised. But for all of them, the revision would be major, not merely shifting emphases.

82. This would be the group that would most closely represent the spirit of Harold Bender's approach. The other two groups obviously represent the trends to the right and to the left of Bender's approach, trends about which he worried so much and tried so hard to head off in the interest of denominational unity.

In this book, I have implicitly entered this debate insofar as my interpretation of Yoder's thought as ecumenical and biblical aligns him with strands of all three of these approaches to the interpretation of Yoder's thought. Yoder was a revisionist in his own way, yet his goal was not to turn Mennonites into either Catholics or Protestants, and certainly not into liberal Catholics or liberal Protestants. I am attempting to bring the work of non-Mennonite scholars such as Stanley Hauerwas, James Mc-Clendon, Nancey Murphy, Richard Hays, and Michael Cartwright, who appreciate the value of Yoder's thought for the wider church, into dialogue with the Mennonite interpreters of Yoder by suggesting that the ecumenical significance of Yoder's work is not that he articulates a peace witness on behalf of a small denomination but rather that he presents a strong case for peace being at the heart of the biblical gospel as it is enshrined in the creeds of orthodox Christianity. If I am right, then the significance of Yoder's thought for the church as a whole is obvious. We now turn to an examination of some of the key issues raised by these various approaches to Yoder interpretation.

First, we need to consider the "revisionists." Some of these scholars have questioned not only Yoder's thought, but also the Mennonite movement itself. Most (such as John W. Miller[83] and J. Lawrence Burkholder[84]) have gone so far as to question the viability of a continued emphasis on pacifism as more than the vocational calling of the minority in the modern world, and some (such as original *Concern* member, Orley Swartzentruber[85]) have even left the denomination itself. We will examine briefly the position of John W. Miller as one representative of this general approach.[86]

83. See John W. Miller, "Schleitheim Pacifism and Modernity," *Conrad Grebel Review* 3 (Spring 1985): 155–63; idem, "Concern Reflections: John W. Miller," *Conrad Grebel Review* 8 (Spring 1990): 139–54; and idem, "In the Footsteps of Marcion: Notes toward an Understanding of John Yoder's Theology," *Conrad Grebel Review* 16 (Spring 1998): 82–92.

84. See Burkholder's *The Problem of Social Responsibility from the Perspective of the Mennonite Church* (Elkhart, Ind.: Institute of Mennonite Studies, 1989).

85. Since his *Concern* days, Swartzentruber has moved out of the Mennonite denomination to become an Episcopal priest. He explains his perspective on the Anabaptist movement he has chosen to leave in terms of a coming to a wider vision of the church. For him, the best description of the Swiss Anabaptism in which he was raised is "a form of married monasticism in the Benedictine tradition." He argues that where the Anabaptists went wrong was claiming to be the "The True Church" instead of seeing themselves as voluntary communities within the broader church, distinguished by a more disciplined life but in fellowship with the wider church. This approach is one way of understanding the essence of what Reinhold Niebuhr was proposing for the historic peace churches, as was described above. See A. Orley Swartzentruber, "Concern Reflections: A. Orley Swartzentruber," *Conrad Grebel Review* 8 (Spring 1990): 193–200.

86. Miller's work will be described in the following paragraphs. For a brief discussion of Kaufmann and Burkholder, see Beulah Stauffer Hostetler, "Nonresistance and Social Responsibility: Mennonites and Mainline Peace Emphasis, ca. 1950–1985," *Mennonite Quarterly Review* 64 (January 1990): 55–57.

Miller expresses a desire to "bring the Mennonite pacifist posture more into line with current modes of theological and historical-critical awareness"[87] because the defense of Schleitheim pacifism mounted by such people as Yoder is unconvincing to all but a "tiny circle of the already convinced."[88] He calls for a shift away from the insistence that "our pacifist theology is what Jesus taught" to an "awareness that our thinking . . . only partially derives from the first century Gospels."[89] This relativizing of the peace witness would not only allow Mennonites to view pacifism as their particular heritage and calling but also enable them to see those who choose the nonpacifist way as not being "outside the perfection of Christ."

In a recent article, Miller paints Yoder as a Marcionite who has a "monotheism of the Son" and who downplays the Old Testament with "supersessionist beliefs and attitudes toward Israel's story, Israel's Scriptures and Israel's God."[90] It is not clear what point Miller is trying to make by driving a wedge between Yoder and the Old Testament. Is he implying that Yoder does not do justice to the full range of biblical revelation? Does he mean to claim that a more respectful approach to the Old Testament portion of the canon would require Yoder to moderate his pacifist imperative? Marcion's rejection of the Old Testament was rooted in his assessment that the vengeful deity of the Old Testament could not be the loving God and Father of our Lord Jesus Christ. But Yoder's point is that Jesus is the Messiah, the fulfillment of the Old Testament promises, and that when Jesus is interpreted in any other context his significance is distorted.[91] Yoder's rejection of Constantinian Christianity is rooted in the

87. Miller, "Schleitheim Pacifism," 157.

88. Ibid., 156. As an outsider to the "Historic Peace Church" tradition who has found Yoder's defense of Schleitheim pacifism extremely convincing, I must confess to reading this comment with a combination of puzzlement and sadness.

89. Ibid., 163.

90. Miller, "In the Footsteps of Marcion," 89.

91. See Yoder's "War As a Moral Problem in the Early Church: The Historian's Hermeneutical Assumptions," in *The Pacifist Impulse in Historical Perspective*, ed. H. L. Dyck (Toronto: University of Toronto Press, 1996), 90–110, esp. 95–96, where he points to the Jewish-Christian worldview as basic to understanding the pacifism of the early church. Also see his "Jeremianic" reading of the Old Testament in "See How They Go with Their Face to the Sun," *For the Nations*, 51–78. If Miller wants to pin an early Christian heresy on Yoder, he might have better luck trying Ebionitism, given Yoder's strongly Jewish-Christian emphasis, although that would fail to do justice to Yoder's high Christology. Yoder goes so far as to identify the beginning of the fall of the church with the church's abandonment of its Jewish character: "It is with the beginning of an apologetic approach to the wisdom of the Gentile world, that the meaning of the Christian mission had been radically shifted. . . . The apologetes are missionary in that they try to show the Gentiles that they can have the God of the Jews without the Jews. That shift, somewhere between the New Testament canon and the middle of the next century is the real change in character in the Christian community, the sell-out to Greek or Roman provincialism instead of Hebrew universality. This is then what we would have to call the Fall of the Church" ("Tertium Datur: Refocusing the Jewish-Christian Schism" [paper read before the Notre

Old Testament; the call of Abraham is the beginning of God's work in creating a separate people to be a light to the nations.[92] For Yoder, Constantinianism is nothing more than a revival of the "Solomonic temptation," which had already been condemned by the Old Testament prophets.[93] Ironically, it may be Miller who is closer to Marcion at this point insofar as the church condemned Marcion, not for his attempt to create a canon, but for his attempt to drive a wedge between the God of the Old Testament and the God revealed in Jesus Christ.[94]

The "revisionist" approach involves a series of variations on the Niebuhrian theme of viewing vocational pacifism as tolerable for a minority but regarding a call to the whole church to follow Jesus in the way of peace as intolerable. Mennonites who place a high priority on being part of the Constantinian, wider church in the future will find a place under the ecumenical tent, but they should not delude themselves about their witness having any wider appeal or greater degree of logical power to nonpacifist Christians. The most important question with which those who accept some version or other of vocational pacifism will have to wrestle is whether or not they are actually maintaining a clear witness to Jesus as Jesus calls his disciples to do.

The "peace witness advocates" tend to interpret Yoder as standing up for the Mennonite tradition and express puzzlement when other Mennonites feel such a strong need to criticize Yoder. Mark Thiessen Nation, for example, says that he is used to hearing non-Mennonites criticize Yoder's thought as sectarian but finds it "startling" to hear such accusations coming from Mennonites. He says that he gets the impression that some Mennonite scholars "believe we have outgrown Yoder."[95] Thiessen Nation depicts Yoder as seeking to work out a theology of peace in a faithful way and as engaging in extensive ecumenical dialogue throughout his career. He quotes Jim Wallis, who said: "John Yoder inspired a whole generation of Christians to follow the way of Jesus into social action and peacemaking."[96]

Dame Graduate Union, October 13, 1977], 3, quoted by Gayle Gerber Koontz, "Confessional Theology in a Pluralistic Context: A Study of the Theological Ethics of H. Richard Niebuhr and John H. Yoder" [unpublished Ph.D. diss., Boston University, 1985], 218).

92. John Howard Yoder, *The Original Revolution: Essays on Christian Pacifism* (Scottdale, Pa.: Herald, 1971), 27–28.

93. See Yoder's "The Power Equation, the Place of Jesus, and the Politics of King," *For the Nations*, 141–42, and "How to Be Read by the Bible" (A Shalom Desktop Publication, 1996), 59.

94. On the other hand, it may not be accurate to speak of Miller believing that God is revealed in Jesus Christ in any kind of decisive sense at all, given his remarks about having been "released" from having to believe in "so-called 'high' Christologies" and his adoption of a "theocentric" Christology ("Concern Reflections," 149).

95. Thiessen Nation, "He Came Preaching Peace," 66.

96. Jim Wallis, "Lives of Peacemaking," *Sojourners* 27 (March–April 1988): 8, quoted by Thiessen Nation, "He Came Preaching Peace," 73.

J. Denny Weaver, in an article entitled "Peace-Shaped Theology,"[97] eschews a defensive posture of trying to justify the orthodoxy of the Mennonite tradition to the wider church. Instead, he goes on the offensive and argues that classic doctrines like Christology and atonement, which developed after the church had reached its accommodation with war, need to be reformed in accordance with the norm of Jesus Christ. For example, Weaver says that the formula of Chalcedon is not wrong in affirming that Jesus Christ is true God and true man, but such ways of speaking of Jesus' humanity and the ethical content of discipleship are extremely "thin." Weaver's real complaint boils down to a concern that "Jesus' life and teaching is not affirmed to be normative for Christian ethics" in classical Christology. Similarly, with respect to the doctrine of atonement, the highly influential satisfaction theory "separates salvation from ethics."[98] Weaver does not accept the relegation of the "normativeness of Jesus and rejection of the sword" to the status of a denominational distinctive; he considers them to be part of the core of the Christian faith.[99] He suggests that theologians writing systematic theology for peace churches should rethink the classic doctrines in such a way as to bring to the surface ethical implications that have been there all along but have been hidden because the right questions have not been asked. As a start in this direction, Weaver offers a brief account of "a historicized version of the *Christus Victor* motif"[100] as a narrative approach to Christology.

Clearly, what Weaver is trying to do is compatible with Yoder's project.[101] He and Thiessen Nation both think Yoder's thought is of significance for the future. Weaver is more concerned about developing a peace-church theology, while Thiessen Nation is more interested in Yoder's potential contribution to the wider church in a post-Christendom historical situation. I would suggest that perhaps Yoder's paradoxical understanding of social change would imply that Thiessen Nation's goal would best be achieved through Weaver's strategy.[102]

The "classically orthodox Mennonites" appear to critique Yoder not so much as a theologian *per se,* but as a *Mennonite* theologian. In other words, their concern seems to revolve primarily around what it would mean for the Mennonite community to embrace Yoder's theology, or rather what it would mean for Yoder's theology to be taken as representative of Mennonite theology in general and whether that would be good or bad. None of these scholars would want to repudiate Yoder's pacifism,

97. J. Denny Weaver, "Peace-Shaped Theology," *Faith and Freedom* 5 (June 1996): 22–28.

98. Ibid., 23.

99. Ibid., 24.

100. Ibid., 25–26.

101. Weaver makes this claim explicitly (ibid., 22).

102. See chapter 8 for a discussion of Yoder's understanding of how social change is usually effected by nonconforming minorities.

but all are interested in developing Mennonite theology in an ecumenical and orthodox direction. All see both good and bad in their Mennonite heritage and wish to retain what is good while rejecting that which prevents Mennonites from identifying with classical orthodoxy. In this section, we return to the views of Rodney Sawatsky, which were discussed earlier in the section on the recovery of the Anabaptist vision.[103]

Sawatsky outlines the dissolution of the normative Anabaptist vision in the relativizing historicism of modern scholarly study of sixteenth-century Anabaptism and then asks, "If the old norm has lost its validity, how are Mennonites to determine the essence of Mennonitism?"[104] We saw earlier that, in evaluating Yoder's claim that the Anabaptist vision can be used to judge contemporary Mennonite practice, Sawatsky asks the important question:

> How can one moment in history which is the product of the cultural relativities of agents and interpreters stand in judgment upon another moment in history similarly shaped? Must not such moments in history assume the category of revelation to become normative of history?[105]

Sawatsky is thinking of the sixteenth-century Anabaptists standing in judgment on the twentieth-century Mennonites. If that is the proposal, the accusation of "sectarian perfectionism," that is, of seeing oneself as being "free from the relativizing of history, or if you will, of sin"[106] is perfectly valid, in my opinion. But is that what Yoder is about?

Sawatsky suggests that three approaches are possible to the construction of a post-Anabaptist vision hermeneutic for the contemporary Mennonite community. One approach (which he labels "neosectarian") emphasizes history and tries to distance the vision from the "facts" of history so as to keep history from contradicting the vision. A second approach (which he labels "neoevangelical") is to emphasize theology and enter into ecumenical conversation with the wider church in order to fashion a Mennonite theology adequate for today. A third approach recognizes a dialectic or a tension between history and theology, out of which a normative vision is defined.

Turning to a discussion of Yoder, whom Sawatsky recognizes as the Mennonite theologian who has pursued this problem more vigorously than any other, he says that Yoder uses sixteenth-century Anabaptism as a norm to the extent that it embodies Scripture. Anabaptism, for Yoder, is "the recourse to Scripture as an authoritative guide for church re-

103. Reimer's important critique of Yoder will be discussed in chapter 4 when the charge that Yoder's theology is reductionistic is considered.
104. Sawatsky, "Quest," 9.
105. Ibid., 11.
106. Ibid., 12.

newal."[107] It is crucial to see that, for Yoder, Anabaptism can be used as a norm to judge contemporary Mennonite reality *only to the extent that* sixteenth-century Anabaptism embodied the norm of Jesus Christ as testified to in Scripture. Previously I noted that Yoder used biblical arguments to support the *Concern* movement's critique of modern, denominational, Mennonite reality and that he referred to the power of the Holy Spirit as "a working reality within history" as what was missing in Niebuhr's liberal theology. While Yoder does not hesitate to apply his historicist method to both the Bible and history, he nevertheless is confident that relativism is no danger so long as the normativeness of Jesus Christ is confessed in the doctrine of the incarnation:

> Jesus, the prophets before him, and the apostles after him, as a base for evaluating what has been done since in their name, are to be found fully within the researchable, debatable particularity which according to the New Testament witness is the meaning of Incarnation.[108]

For Yoder, the ultimate Anabaptist hermeneutic is not the sixteenth century, but the first century, precisely because in the incarnation a moment of history *has* assumed the category of revelation and become normative.

Sawatsky does not seem to realize the full implications of Yoder's position, however, because he goes on to ask how Yoder can justify choosing one sixteenth-century Anabaptist over another as the model for today.[109] Does this mean, he asks, that each Mennonite church should choose its own hero and declare him normative? The answer to this question is clear, at least as far as Yoder is concerned. The incarnation provides a basis for the evaluation of all norms and models, including Anabaptist and Mennonite ones. Yet, Sawatsky categorizes Yoder as retaining a "sectarian perfectionist vision."[110] By way of contrast, Sawatsky quotes Walter Klassen as wanting to ground Anabaptist identity in a shared Christian theology: "Trinitarian theology remains a very important tenet of Anabaptism that is relevant for today."[111] Sawatsky points to A. James Reimer as one who is systematically developing Klassen's "more theological, less historical quest for a post-Anabaptist vision hermeneutic."[112] Klassen and Rei-

107. John Howard Yoder, "Anabaptist Vision and Mennonite Reality," in *Consultation on Anabaptist-Mennonite Theology*, ed. A. J. Klassen (Fresno, Calif.: Council of Mennonite Seminaries, 1970), 5, quoted in Sawatsky, "Quest," 13.

108. John Howard Yoder, "Anabaptism and History," *The Priestly Kingdom: Social Ethics As Gospel* (Notre Dame, Ind.: University of Notre Dame Press, 1984), 128.

109. Sawatsky, "Quest," 14.

110. Ibid., 16.

111. Walter Klassen, "The Quest for Anabaptist Identity," in *Anabaptist-Mennonite Identities in Ferment*, ed. L. Driedger and L. Harder (Elkhart, Ind.: Institute of Mennonite Studies, 1990), 19, quoted in Sawatsky, "Quest," 18.

112. Sawatsky, "Quest," 18–19.

mer are seen by Sawatsky as shifting away from a sectarian perfectionism and as being more open to "outside influences," as was Harold Bender.[113] Sawatsky ends his article by saying:

> A Mennonite hermeneutic adequate for today thus is both/and rather than either/or. It learns from its Anabaptist past as it formulates a Mennonite theology in conversation with other Christian traditions in the common pursuit of faithfulness to Christ in the present and in the future.[114]

Thus Sawatsky is left with a conversational hermeneutic that has no readily specifiable norm.

Sawatsky's view of Yoder is understandable if one takes into account the fact that he speaks of Yoder primarily as a Mennonite to other Mennonites. Sawatsky wants to open a relatively closed community to the catholic truth of the wider church and to encourage dialogue and mutual enrichment. Yoder's thought would seem to be a hindrance to the achievement of this goal because Yoder insists on things the wider church is not perceived as wanting to hear, such as pacifism, congregationalism, and the social relevance of Jesus. Because of Yoder's use of terms such as "the believers' church," "radical reformation," "Anabaptist," and "free church" as descriptive of his position in ecumenical dialogue, Yoder can appear to non-Mennonites to be merely the representative of a small sect with some extreme views. Sometimes his arguments are not dealt with because it is too easy to dismiss him as the representative of a position in which "nobody" believes anyway.

On the other hand, part of the strength of Yoder's position is that he can point to the existence of disciplined communities in history that, at various times and places and to varying degrees, have lived out the ideals of pacifism that he speaks of as being biblical. If Yoder were saying that sixteenth-century Anabaptism was perfect or calling all Christians to become Mennonites, then it would be fair to write him off as a "sectarian perfectionist." But asking all Christians to take seriously their own confession of Jesus Christ as true God and true man is hardly sectarian. My concern, as a non-Mennonite who admires much of what Mennonites stand for, is that, if contemporary Mennonites decide to replace the relativizing historiography of the Anabaptist vision with the historic orthodoxy of the ecumenical church, they will need to reckon with the fact that the same relativizing process has been going on for centuries in the wider church with respect to orthodoxy as has been going on in Mennonite circles recently with respect to the Anabaptist vision. Unbridled historicism is as much a threat to creedal orthodoxy as it is to pacifism.

113. Reimer would resist Sawatsky's interpretation of his intentions at this point, in that he would see his appeal to the historic trinitarian and christological orthodoxy of the ecumenical creeds as the ontological foundation for ethics (personal correspondence, James Reimer to Craig Carter, December 14, 1998).

114. Sawatsky, "Quest," 20.

In a 1995 article, Alain Epp Weaver looks back on *The Politics of Jesus* nearly a quarter of a century after its publication and offers an interesting and ironical thesis: Just as Yoder is being claimed by the larger academic community, Mennonite theologians are becoming increasingly critical of his approach.[115] Epp Weaver mentions Mennonite theologians such as J. Lawrence Burkholder, A. James Reimer, and Gordon Kaufmann as examples of those who, from different perspectives and for different reasons, criticize Yoder for maintaining pacifism too absolutely, for not being orthodox enough, or for being too orthodox to be meaningful to modern people. Epp Weaver calls attention to wider trends such as liberation theology, which makes it easier today than twenty years ago to think of Jesus as political, and the postliberalism of Lindbeck and Hauerwas, which today echoes Yoder's forty-year-old warning about setting Jesus aside in favor of "other lights." He ends his article by raising, but not answering, the crucial question of whether the "the growing historicist consciousness" among Mennonite theologians will make it impossible to sustain a pacifist commitment such as Yoder's.

Epp Weaver has put his finger on the problem with which Sawatsky is left at the end of his article. What, in the end, acts as the Christian norm, given the "growing historical consciousness" that faces us today? Sawatsky and other Mennonites are, naturally, concerned about what functions as the norm for the Mennonite community. But with all due respect, I as a non-Mennonite am not very interested in that debate per se. Rather, non-Mennonites are interested in a norm for evaluating what constitutes *Christian* faithfulness today and to what extent Yoder might be helpful in answering that question in the coming century. Yoder's position is that there is no norm to judge the Christian community except "Jesus Christ as he is known through scripture."[116] Is that not the position of historic Christian orthodoxy? And is that not at least implied in Sawatsky's goal of "faithfulness to Christ in the present and in the future"?

Yoder's Critique of His Own Tradition

The extent to which Yoder is critical of his own tradition is not well enough known outside of Mennonite circles.[117] If it were better known, it would make it more difficult to dismiss Yoder as merely a spokesperson

---

115. Alain Epp Weaver, "Review Essay: *The Politics of Jesus*, 20 Years Later," *Mennonite Life* 50 (September 1995): 14–17.

116. Gayle Gerber Koontz, "Confessional Theology in a Pluralistic Context," 173.

117. For example, a recent dissertation by Won Ha Shin, "Two Models of Social Transformation: A Critical Analysis of the Theological Ethics of John H. Yoder and Richard J. Mouw," (unpublished Ph.D. diss., Boston University, 1997), shows no awareness of Yoder's critique of his own tradition. As a result, it concludes that "the danger of self-righteousness" exists with regard to Yoder's theology and that the way to overcome this danger "may lie in a more serious reflection on the import of social reality" (232). This criticism of Yoder simply misses the mark.

for a small, pacifist sect. Yoder's critique of his own tradition is also important because it shows us how radical he is in attempting to employ a christological norm to critique contemporary church life. Finally, Yoder's critique of his own tradition gives us some idea of what he thinks, concretely, faithfulness to Jesus Christ would look like today.[118]

While Yoder criticizes the Lutheran and Roman Catholic positions for advocating a sub-Christian standard of justice for the state, which is not derived from revelation, he also criticizes the "traditional Amish-Mennonite" positions for having "a distinct and definite level of normative sub-Christian justice," which they apply to the state.[119] Yoder also criticizes those in his own tradition who advocate nonresistance and reject pacifism for falling prey to an "unavowed and uncritical acquiescence in nationalism."[120]

Yoder also criticizes the Mennonite tradition for becoming Constantinian itself under the pressure of persecution.[121] The first step in this process for a particular group of Mennonites was accepting the deal of toleration under the protection of a local lord, often displacing the local serfs, in return for a promise not to proselytize. This kind of deal was often the basis of the group gaining an opportunity to emigrate and thus escape persecution. This decision led to the next step, which was the group losing its missionary fervor and ceasing to evangelize. The result of taking that step was that the community recreated itself through its progeny, some of whom were only superficially and grudgingly committed to the ideals of the community.[122] This meant that the world was now inside the church. The result of this development is that the church becomes a mini-Constantinian establishment. Ironically, that from which the founders withdrew ends up being recreated in the alternative community they founded.[123] Yoder summarizes his critique of his own tradition at its worst:

> The defensiveness and authoritarianism with which conservative mini-Constantinian establishments sometimes govern a rural colony or a church agency, the way in which immigrant farmers can without intending it be allied with authoritarian rulers against the interests of the previous less technically advanced subjects of those same rulers, and the readiness to buy into some el-

118. This type of attention to concrete, historical specificity is what one misses in the writings of Stanley Hauerwas and constitutes a significant difference between the two thinkers.

119. John Howard Yoder, *The Christian Witness to the State* (Newton, Kans.: Faith and Life, 1964), 71.

120. Yoder, *Nevertheless*, 141.

121. Yoder, *Christian Attitudes to War*, 198ff.

122. Yoder, *Nevertheless*, 104.

123. A similar irony is seen in the Puritan persecution of religious dissenters in New England after they themselves had fled England to escape religious persecution.

ements of the dominant culture while claiming to be clearly nonconformed on others, represent besetting temptations and at times direct moral failures in the Mennonite experience.[124]

The other side of Yoder's criticism of his own tradition is his ability to see the Spirit at work as the Anabaptist vision appears in settings other than those denominations traditionally associated with Anabaptism. For example, Yoder is quite positive about the development of ecclesial base communities in Latin America, which have made possible "community life, prayer, praise, moral solidarity, the training and recognition of leaders, and growing social awareness" even without the availability of enough priests. He notes the positive symbiotic relationship between these communities and the theology of liberation.[125] Yoder contends that sixteenth-century Anabaptism intended to be a corrective measure and never claimed to be any more than "the rest of the Reformation." Therefore, he says, "those who represent the Anabaptist vision should be open to welcome every possible occasion to feed their corrective witness back into the mainstream of Christian thought."[126] Yoder would agree with Dale Brown, who remarks: "Consistent with its message that the church needs to be reborn in each generation, the Anabaptist vision will continue to become flesh in places where it may be the least expected."[127]

Yoder identifies himself with the Anabaptist vision, not because he believes it gives him a position of superiority from which to judge everyone else, but because he believes that everyone must start where he or she is situated historically. It is an act of humility, not self-righteousness, to eschew Olympian heights of objectivity and to admit that one comes from a particular historical tradition that has strengths and weaknesses.[128] For Yoder, the important thing is to place all Christian theology and ethics, all faith and practice, under the norm of Jesus Christ. This is what it means to embrace both "radical reform" and "radical catholicity" at the same time. In the next chapter, I will probe more carefully into the question of what it means to do theology under the norm of Jesus Christ.

Yoder should be seen as a critical heir of the Anabaptist theological heritage, neither as an uncritical Mennonite partisan nor as a modernist subverter of the tradition. It seems clear that Yoder identified strongly with the ideals of the radical wing of the sixteenth-century Reformation as expressed in the Swiss Brethren congregations. He endorsed the "recovery of the Anabaptist vision" because he judged that it expressed the

124. Yoder, introduction to *Priestly Kingdom*, 4.

125. Yoder, "The Wider Setting of 'Liberation Theology,'" 286.

126. Yoder, "Recovery of the Anabaptist Vision," 22.

127. Dale Brown, "Communal Ecclesiology: The Power of the Anabaptist Vision," *Theology Today* 36 (1979): 29.

128. See Gayle Gerber Koontz's discussion of Yoder's epistemological humility ("Confessional Theology in a Pluralistic Context," 172).

true spirit of Jesus' teachings as no other movement before or since has done. He used "the Anabaptist vision" to critique not only non-Anabaptist forms of Christianity but also his own Mennonite denomination. Despite his historicism, Yoder took the incarnation of God in the person of Jesus Christ as the criterion by which all Christian speech and action needs to be evaluated. He asks rhetorically: "What becomes of the meaning of incarnation if Jesus is not normative man?"[129] How and why Yoder did this cannot easily be explained with reference to his own Mennonite theological tradition or even the evangelical and neoorthodox theology of midcentury North America. In order to understand Yoder at this point, it is necessary to turn to the thought of the theologian who probably influenced his thought more than any other, namely, Karl Barth.

---

129. John Howard Yoder, *The Politics of Jesus: Vicit Agnus Noster,* 2d ed. (Grand Rapids: Eerdmans, 1994), 10.

2

Yoder and the Theology of Karl Barth

The theology of Karl Barth has been misunderstood by many North Americans for most of this century. Those who read Brunner in the 1940s and assumed that Barth was saying essentially the same thing, those who read Barth's commentary on Romans and were so put off that they never bothered to open *Church Dogmatics,* and those who believed that neoorthodoxy was a useful label to apply to theologians as diverse as Tillich, Bultmann, and Barth all failed to grasp the radical implications of Barth's approach to doing theology after the end of the modern (or Enlightenment) era of Western culture. Yoder was one of the few North Americans not only to study with Barth but also to read him seriously and sympathetically during the 1950s, before the fourth volume of *Church Dogmatics* was translated into English. We know that Yoder's book on Barth's view of war, which was published in 1971, actually was written in the mid-1950s because Yoder tells that a "text substantially similar to the present one was read by Professor Barth in the summer of 1957." Although some changes were made to the text to guard against possible misunderstandings, we are informed that "at no point did the paper's argument rest upon a mistaken understanding of Professor Barth's position and intention."[1] Yoder has been a pioneer in

1. John Howard Yoder, *Karl Barth and the Problem of War* (Nashville: Abingdon, 1970), 17. Yoder also warns the reader that his description of Barth's position is based upon personal conversations with Barth and may appear to contradict the apparent sense of certain passages in Barth's writings.

making Barth's ethics, particularly the radical implications of his social ethics, known in North America.[2]

Yoder, however, did not merely understand Barth better than most North Americans of his generation; he also found himself in sympathy with Barth's theological method.[3] It is, of course, dangerous to speak of Barth's "method" without remembering that Barth would be the first to be horrified at the suggestion that he had a "method," in the nineteenth-century sense of the term, that determined his system of thought. Yet reason played a significant role in Barth's thought.[4] I would say that Barth had a highly rational[5] "faith seeking understanding" method that consisted of critical reflection upon the self-revelation of God in Jesus Christ. This method can be described as postliberal or postmodern. It is not premodern because it makes use of the historical-critical method to elucidate the meaning of the biblical text, though not to go behind the text to something more fundamental. It is postmodern, however, in that it rejects the modernist belief that whatever truth is not accessible to human reason is necessarily to be rejected. Barth's method is rational but not rationalistic; it is rationality without rationalism.

2. Philip Thorne says that "one of the signal contributions" that Yoder and the Wesleyan theologian Donald Dayton have made to American evangelicalism is to "introduce Barth as a model for 'radical' social ethics in the face of a visible absence of Reformed Evangelical discussion of Barth's ethics" (*Evangelicalism and Karl Barth: His Reception and Influence in North American Evangelical Theology* (Allison Park, Pa.: Pickwick Publications, 1995), 150. Outside of evangelicalism, only the work of George Hunsinger immediately comes to mind as doing something similar. See his *Karl Barth and Radical Politics* (Philadelphia: Fortress, 1976).

3. This fact is being recognized by practically all interpreters of Yoder today, but as with most generalizations, it is necessary to unpack in detail exactly how it is true before it will be of much use to those wishing to evaluate Yoder's social ethics. This section aims to contribute to this task.

4. Eberhard Busch notes Barth's complaint that the students in his discussion keep coming back "again and again to the question raised by some young know-alls . . . as to what the characteristic 'thought-form' of the *Dogmatics* is. They feel that if they knew that, they could then decide whether or not to get on to the train which is apparently travelling inexorably from its specific starting point to its destination" (*Karl Barth: His Life from Letters and Autobiographical Texts* [Philadelphia: Fortress, 1976], 403). Yoder cites this passage in the context of his essay rejecting "the search for first principles" ("Walk and Word: The Alternatives to Methodologism," in *Theology without Foundations: Religious Practice and the Future of Theological Truth,* ed. S. Hauerwas, N. Murphy, and M. Thiessen Nation [Nashville: Abingdon, 1994], 77 n. 1).

5. Barth's theology is rational without being rationalistic or falling into rationalism. Rationalism rejects all truth that is not accessible to unaided human reason. Barth's theology, however, is not irrational. He investigates the speech of the church about God and evaluates it by the criteria of Jesus Christ as he is testified to in Scripture. Concepts, ideas, or arguments that are not consistent with the confession of Jesus Christ must be revised or rejected, and it is in this sense that Barth's theology is rational.

Areas of Agreement and Similarity

The following eight key points of agreement between Yoder and Barth on method are not summarized nicely in any one place in the writings of either theologian.[6] It is very difficult to get a handle on the method of theologians such as Barth and Yoder without also speaking of issues of substance, because both writers minimize the space they devote to discussions of method as such and reject the call to justify their method in some rationalistic way prior to employing it in the exposition of Christian doctrines.[7] They both believe that the best way to convince someone of the truth of the faith is to display the inner logic and coherence of the content of the faith as fully and as clearly as possible. Therefore, in my inductive analysis of their methodological similarities, it will often be necessary to illumine methodological issues by referring to issues of substance.

1. Inspiration. Yoder, like Barth, reads the Bible as a narrative centering on Jesus Christ and rejects the scholastic doctrines of verbal inspiration and inerrancy.[8] Yoder expresses concern about how easily those who, like himself, seek to be "guided by the Scriptures in a more natural and intellectually responsible way, can be written off as 'fundamentalist' without being heard."[9] He calls his position "Biblical Realism"[10] and rejects both *scholasticism,* which he characterizes as "a dogmatic insistence on the au-

6. Thorne also notes not only the influence of Barth's thought on Yoder but also the "convergence he [i.e., Yoder] discerns between the Anabaptist position and certain developments in Barth's own thinking" (*Evangelicalism and Karl Barth,* 173).

7. It should be stressed before proceeding that the similarity of method being described here should not be taken to imply that the two theologians agreed on most issues of substance. Indeed, Yoder's Anabaptist-Mennonite heritage influenced the substance of his theology more than did the theology of Barth. Yet at the point of method, Barth's influence on Yoder reached its peak. In many cases, the use of a similar method did not lead to identical conclusions, such as on the issue of war. This disagreement on conclusions is normal in the development and growth of a theological tradition (not "school") and should not cause the methodological similarities to be overlooked or downplayed.

8. See Yoder, "Walk and Word," 88.

9. John Howard Yoder, "How to Be Read by the Bible" (A Shalom Desktop Publication, 1996), 26.

10. Ibid., 12–13. The term *Biblical Realism* originated in the Biblical Theology Movement that flourished in the 1950s. Yoder defines it carefully as meaning maximally (for Tresmontant and Cherbonnier) that there is a biblical worldview that, once discovered and exposited, will be seen to be true forever and as meaning minimally (for Minear, Piper, M. Barth) that, as a methodological presupposition, the biblical text is supposed to contain a coherent testimony that it is the reader's task to discern. Yoder's version of Biblical Realism is minimalist. He simply approaches the Bible with the assumption that, once the best critical tools have been employed to establish the original meaning of each text in its proper context, the texts will all fit together. He says that he learned from Paul Minear and Karl Barth "the great value of approaching a text with the assumption that it might have something to say, so that the hermeneutically most valuable suspicion is not doubting the text but doubting the adequacy of one's prior understanding of it" (ibid., 8)

thoritative dignity of the biblical texts, concurrent with a relative disinterest in studying them very closely, since we already know what they say,"[11] and *humanism,* which is inadequate because when the texts are read critically they "say things which the humanist cannot handle."[12] Yoder says that the essence of Biblical Realism is the attempt to read the texts with all the critical tools but without knowing ahead of time "where we want it to fit into a pre-existent larger systematic scheme."[13]

The Bible, for Yoder, exhibits a unity, but it is a unity of a narrative that "goes somewhere" as opposed to a flat unity in which every text in every part of the Bible is to be read in exactly the same way as every other text.[14] The radical Protestant, he says, will always have a "canon within the canon," namely, Jesus.[15] On the other hand, Yoder also claims that the free-church stance is the most ecumenical one possible because it "means a commitment to a constant recourse to the entire testimony of the New Testament, rejecting the concentration upon any one doctrine as a 'canon within the canon' and rejecting, as well, the choice of any one normative post-canonical development."[16] Is Yoder contradicting himself in these statements? No, the apparent contradiction disappears once one realizes that, for Yoder, there is only one *true* or *proper* "canon within the canon." There is only one true center of the Bible, and it is neither justification by faith nor predestination nor any other doctrine. It is nothing other than Jesus Christ himself. Like Barth, who taught that "revelation does not differ

11. John Howard Yoder, *Christian Attitudes to War, Peace and Revolution: A Companion to Bainton* (Elkhart, Ind.: distributed by Co-op Bookstore, 1983), 424.

12. Yoder, "How to Be Read by the Bible," 11–12.

13. Ibid., 13. He rejects as inappropriate "subjecting it [i.e., the Bible] to the superior authority of our own contemporary hermeneutical framework" (116). However, Yoder does not deny that there is a hermeneutical problem, as fundamentalism does. See his *The Fullness of Christ: Paul's Revolutionary Vision of Universal Ministry* (Elgin, Ill.: Brethren Press, 1987), 90. Yoder's "communal hermeneutic" is rooted in exegesis and makes use of all available critical tools. New Testament scholar Richard Hays credits Yoder's interpretation of texts with being informed by "detailed and sophisticated interaction with historical-critical scholarship" (*The Moral Vision of the New Testament: Community, Cross, New Creation: A Contemporary Introduction to New Testament Ethics* [San Francisco: HarperSanFrancisco, 1996], 245). See chapter 7 of this book for a discussion of communal hermeneutics.

14. Yoder writes, "One of the marks of the 'believers' church' heritage is that it sees movement within the canonical story, and therefore a difference between the Testaments. Instead of a timeless collection of parabolic anecdotes for allegorical application, or of propositional communications ready for deductive exposition, the Bible is a story of promise and fulfillment which must be read directionally" (introduction to *The Priestly Kingdom: Social Ethics As Gospel* [Notre Dame, Ind.: University of Notre Dame Press, 1984], 9).

15. Yoder, "The Hermeneutics of Peoplehood: A Protestant Perspective," *Priestly Kingdom,* 37.

16. John Howard Yoder, "The Free Church Ecumenical Style," *The Royal Priesthood: Essays Ecclesiological and Ecumenical,* ed. Michael Cartwright (Grand Rapids: Eerdmans, 1994), 238.

from the person of Jesus Christ" and that "revelation engenders the Scripture which attests it,"[17] Yoder views the Bible as cohering in Jesus and springing from Jesus.[18] Barth gives priority to the New Testament in terms of interpretation, in that the fulfillment of the Old Testament is taken into consideration in the interpretation of the Old Testament.[19] According to Nigel Biggar, Barth also interprets the whole Bible from its center, which is for him Jesus Christ, that is, "the salvific work of God in Jesus Christ as broadly conceived by classical orthodoxy."[20]

2. Christology. Yoder's Biblical Realism, like Barth's, leads him to adopt a "high" Christology and to reject liberal views of Jesus as less than divine.[21] Yoder looks at five New Testament texts (John 1, Philippians 2, Colossians 1, Hebrews 1–2, and Revelation 4:1–5:4) that all make a similar move in relating Jesus to the cosmology or worldview of the people they are addressing.[22] Each time the writer uses the language of the new linguistic world into which the gospel is being proclaimed, but instead of fitting Jesus into the slots the cosmic vision has ready for him, the writer places Jesus above the cosmos, in charge of it. In each case, suffering in human form is that which accredits Jesus for lordship. Instead of salvation consisting of our being integrated into a salvation system the cosmos has ready for us, we are called to enter into the path of the self-emptying, death, and resurrection of Jesus in order to find salvation. Behind the cosmic victory of Jesus, enabling it, is what later confession called preexistence, coessentiality with the Father, possession of the image of God, and the participation of the Son in creation and providence. Finally, the writer and the readers shared by faith in all that this victory means.[23] Christians are called to proclaim the lordship of Jesus Christ over the cosmos. The extent to which Yoder has a stake in maintaining a

17. *CD* I/1, 119, 115. The abbreviation "*CD*" hereafter will refer to Karl Barth, *Church Dogmatics*, 2d ed., 4 vol., ed. G. W. Bromiley and T. F. Torrance, trans. G. W. Bromiley, (Edinburgh: T. & T. Clark, 1975). Yoder's use of historical-critical scholarship is very similar to Mary Kathleen Cunningham's description of Barth's theological exegesis. See her *What Is Theological Exegesis? Interpretation and Use of Scripture in Barth's Doctrine of Election* (Valley Forge, Pa.: Trinity Press International, 1995).

18. Yoder says, "What God really wants, who God really is, is known ultimately and fully only in Jesus" (*Christian Attitudes to War*, 443).

19. *CD* I/2, 481–82.

20. Nigel Biggar, *The Hastening That Waits: The Ethics of Karl Barth* (Oxford: Oxford University Press, 1993), 122.

21. For a similar interpretation of Yoder on this point, see Joel Zimbleman, "Theological Ethics and Politics in the Thought of Juan Luis Segundo and John Howard Yoder" (unpublished Ph.D. diss., University of Virginia, 1986), 196–97. He says: "Biblical Realism establishes the normativeness of Scripture and its dependence for legitimacy on the Word of God" (196).

22. Yoder, "'But We Do See Jesus': The Particularity of Incarnation and the Universality of Truth," *Priestly Kingdom*, 50–52.

23. Ibid., 53.

high Christology is revealed when he says, "Only this evangelical Christology can found a truly transformationalist approach to culture."[24] The function of the high ontological claims made for Jesus is that they guarantee the truth of his teaching and make putting one's faith in him totally appropriate because his teaching is in conformity to the true nature of reality.[25]

In *The Politics of Jesus,* Yoder claims that his use of the human life of Jesus as the norm for Christian ethics is simply the logical reflex of the high Christology of classical orthodoxy. He asks:

> What becomes of the meaning of incarnation if Jesus is not normative man? If he is a man but somehow not normative, is this not the ancient ebionite heresy? If he be somehow authoritative but not in his humanness, is this not a new gnosticism?[26]

We must take Yoder's claims at face value unless we can show incoherence in his thought, and this issue will be addressed in chapter 4 when I consider the charge of reductionism explicitly. My point here is simply that Yoder explicitly *claims* to have a "high" Christology rooted in Nicene and Chalcedonian orthodoxy.[27]

This point is important because the term *Anabaptist* is sometimes assumed to refer to what George Williams called the "evangelical rationalists," the followers of Michael Servetus and other unitarians who denied

---

24. Ibid., 61.

25. Yoder has been accused of reductionism at this point and of not holding firmly enough to the ontological underpinnings of the Christian faith. The critics worry that Yoder is watering down traditional Christian claims about the reality of God and the deity of Jesus in favor of a view of Jesus as a great ethical teacher and example. In other words, Yoder is accused of being a liberal. We will examine this charge in the final section of chapter 4. For now, we can anticipate the argument there by making two points. First, claiming not to believe that one can *prove* something on the basis of neutral, universally accessible criteria is not the same as not believing it to be true. Second, Yoder's call to follow Jesus in the way of peace has no rationale if Jesus is merely a human teacher. In other words, the validity of his ethics *logically requires* a high Christology.

26. John Howard Yoder, *The Politics of Jesus: Vicit Agnus Noster,* 2d ed. (Grand Rapids: Eerdmans, 1994), 10. Yoder goes so far as to accuse those who reject Jesus' humanity as the norm for Christian social ethics as "seeing Jesus through ebionitic eyes, that is, limiting his relevance to that which one chooses to attribute to his human status as a radical rabbi (98). He also says: "When the later, more 'theological' New Testament writings formulated the claim to preexistence and cosmic preeminence for the divine Son or Word . . . the intent of this language was not to consecrate beside Jesus some other way of perceiving the eternal Word, through reason or history or nature, but rather to affirm the exclusivity of the revelation claim they were making for Jesus. The same must be said of the later development of the classic ideas of the Trinity and the Incarnation" (99). Yoder here challenges those who affirm classical orthodoxy to take his claims seriously as the logical implications of their own position.

27. See also Glen H. Stassen, D. M. Yeager, and John Howard Yoder, *Authentic Transformation: A New Vision of Christ and Culture* (Nashville: Abingdon, 1996), 73.

classical, orthodox Christology. For example, Nigel Biggar contrasts Barth's Christology as "Nicene and Chalcedonian" with that of Stanley Hauerwas, which he calls "Anabaptist." He then explicitly identifies Hauerwas as having a "low" Christology.[28] To paint all Anabaptists with the brush of christological unorthodoxy is neither historically accurate nor ecumenically responsible. One really needs to distinguish between "ecclesial Anabaptists" and "evangelical rationalists," because to fail to do so is to portray the entire Mennonite family of denominations as heretical, which is clearly unfair.[29] But the main question I am dealing with here is whether Yoder, who is clearly an Anabaptist, has a low Christology or not.

First, we must admit that Biggar's assessment of Hauerwas's Christology as not clearly orthodox in the classical sense and, therefore, to be contrasted sharply with that of Barth is at least debatable. Biggar is right to suggest that Hauerwas and Barth share some important common concerns, such as making the biblical narrative central in ethics and correcting the view of ethics that sees it as basically a conceptual and logical affair. According to Biggar, the difference between them, however, is that

> In contemporary Christian ethics the emphasis placed on the social formation of moral character is very marked indeed. As a corrective to an earlier, individualistic preoccupation with moral decision-making, that is certainly to be welcomed. But in much contemporary discussion this new emphasis is exaggerated to the point where the transcendent God and the individual's relationship to him disappears from view.[30]

This certainly sums up nicely the difference between Barth and much of what is going on in those streams of contemporary Christian ethics that have begun to emphasize the categories of narrative and community. The issue comes down to Barth's realism. He actually believes that the living God is more real than anything else and that the narrative of God's action in Scripture is authoritative because it describes the real world in terms of which we must understand ourselves. Hauerwas, on the other hand, is interested in narrative because of its sociological function in forming the identity of the Christian community and providing a rationale for the moral beliefs of that community.[31] But is the narrative true?

Hauerwas's rhetoric in *The Peaceable Kingdom* may not be representative of his considered position, but, as it stands, it is reminiscent of classic liberalism and quite different from that of Yoder as quoted above, insofar as Hauerwas appears to *contrast* christological orthodoxy with a concern for the ethical implications of the man Jesus:

28. Biggar, *The Hastening That Waits,* 143 n. 67.
29. See the discussion of Anabaptist historiography in chapter 1.
30. Biggar, *The Hastening That Waits,* 145.
31. Ibid., 118.

Christian ethics has tended to make "Christology" rather than Jesus its starting point. His relevance is seen in more substantive claims about the incarnation. Christian ethics then often begins with some broadly drawn theological claims about the significance of God becoming man, but the life of the man whom God made his representative is ignored or used selectively. . . . This emphasis on Jesus' ontological significance strikes many as absolutely essential . . . Christologies which emphasize the cosmic and ontological Christ tend to make Jesus' life almost incidental to what is assumed to be a more profound theological point.[32]

Michael Cartwright notes that one of the problems in the recent interpretation of Yoder's thought has been that too often he has been read through the lens of Hauerwas.[33] Cartwright also notes that Hauerwas has never gone so far as to adopt the tag of Biblical Realism and suggests that the reason may be that "Hauerwas would have a problem with the term 'realism' insofar as it seems to suggest that there is a 'correspondent reality' which exists apart from the narrative and its visible embodiment in a community."[34] Cartwright puts his finger on the same point as being the difference between Hauerwas and Yoder as Biggar identified as being the difference between Hauerwas and Barth.[35]

I do not think that the overall trajectory of Hauerwas's thought is toward such a reductive, functional, antiontological stance. Instead, I think Hauerwas

32. Stanley Hauerwas, *The Peaceable Kingdom: A Primer in Christian Ethics* (Notre Dame, Ind.: University of Notre Dame Press, 1983), 72–73. One needs to be careful about attributing to Hauerwas a total lack of appreciation for the ontological basis of Christology. He certainly distances himself from a liberal view of Jesus as exemplar, saying that "without the ontological change occasioned through Christ's resurrection, there would be no possibility of living as he did. . . . Our obedience to his life is only because of the Father's vindication of Jesus' obedience through the resurrection" (epilogue in Paul Ramsey, *Speak Up for Just War or Pacifism: A Critique of the Methodist Bishops' Letter "In Defense of Creation"* [University Park: Pennsylvania State University Press, 1988], 162).

33. Michael Cartwright, "Radical Reform, Radical Catholicity: John Howard Yoder's Vision of the Faithful Church," in *Royal Priesthood*, 15 n. 25. For example, we can point to the comments of Richard B. Miller, who says: "For authors like Stanley Hauerwas and John Howard Yoder, the truths of one's religion or culture serve as a beacon to other travelers. . . . Epistemologically, this approach is unabashedly relativistic: ethical beliefs are obligatory only within distinct webs of beliefs or cultural languages" (*Interpretations of Conflict: Ethics, Pacifism and the Just-War* [Chicago: University of Chicago Press, 1991], 6). This assessment may not even be fair to Hauerwas, and it certainly distorts Yoder's position.

34. Michael Cartwright, "Practices, Politics, and Performance: Toward a Communal Hermeneutic for Christian Ethics" (unpublished Ph.D. diss., Duke University, 1988), 140.

35. Hauerwas credits Yoder for converting him to pacifism and for giving him an ecclesiology. So many people who read Hauerwas assume, first, that Hauerwas is an "Anabaptist" and, second, that Yoder's theology is similar to that of Hauerwas (Hauerwas, *Peaceable Kingdom*, xxiv–xxv). But Hauerwas is a United Methodist whose ecclesiology is quite thin compared to that of Yoder, and they disagree on fundamental issues of style, substance, and emphasis. The contrast between these two thinkers will be developed throughout this book at appropriate points.

has been moving in the other direction and that he actually wants to embrace a Barthian type of nonfoundationalist realism because he realizes that only such a realism can adequately ground a nonviolent ethic based on Jesus' teaching and example. But I realize that there are probably more scholars who agree with Biggar and Cartwright than with me at the present time. In some ways, perception is more important than reality in this case! This book is about Yoder, not Hauerwas, and as far as Yoder interpretation is concerned, it is crucial that an antirealist reading of Hauerwas not be imposed on Yoder, whether or not it proves, in the end, to be accurate with respect to Hauerwas.

Yoder clearly distinguishes his position from that of those narrative theologians who employ narrative as a master concept into which the narratives of Scripture must fit. While he expresses appreciation for the emphasis on narrative as a corrective, two points need to be made. First, Yoder was employing narrative as a category in describing the biblical way of rendering the identity of Jesus Christ before the current fad of narrative theology got off the ground.[36] Second, Yoder's theological realism requires him to affirm the priority of the biblical story over all other narratives. He explains:

> Only from within the community of resurrection confession is the cruciformity of the cosmos a key rather than a scandal. Therefore the particular narrative is prior to the general idea of narrative. . . . One will welcome the creative imagination of structuralists who protect narration from reduction to "truths" and "concepts;" yet an equal vigilance is needed to defend the particularity of Abraham, Samuel, Jeremiah and Jesus from reduction to mere specimens of a new kind of universal, namely narrative forms lying deeper than the ordering events and sufficient to explain them.[37]

In Yoder's narrative theology, theological realism is carefully and specifically affirmed. Even he criticizes Hauerwas for not giving enough emphasis to "the objective reality of salvation history":

> One reason Hauerwas does not do text-based Bible study is that he is overawed by the notion of community-dependency and underawed by the objective reality of salvation history. Also underawed by the study of real (unsaved) history. He would rather read novels.[38]

36. See chapter 3, in which Yoder's view of narrative is discussed based on his lectures from the 1970s entitled "Preface to Christology."

37. Yoder, "The Hermeneutics of Peoplehood," 36. See Yoder's claims for realism in "Jesus: A Model of Radical Political Action," *Faith and Freedom* 1 (December 1992): 5. Yoder's approach to narrative is compatible with the approach described by Hans Frei in *The Eclipse of Biblical Narrative* (New Haven: Yale University Press, 1974) as the classical Christian position.

38. John Howard Yoder, "Absolute Philosophical Relativism Is an Oxymoron" (unpublished 1993 supplement to the paper, "Meaning after Babble: With Jeffrey Stout Beyond Relativism," *Journal of Religious Ethics* 24 [Spring 1996]: 125–39).

I do not think it was fair of Yoder to infer that the reason Hauerwas himself does not do text-based Bible study is due to Hauerwas's antirealism. But insofar as Hauerwas is understood as part of the North American, liberal, Protestant, social-ethical tradition, the criticism has merit. Hauerwas has spent his writing career trying desperately to break free of the grip of certain presuppositions deeply embedded in this tradition, and Yoder's work has helped him crucially in the process of doing so.

Barth's Christology is unfolded in paragraph 15 of *Church Dogmatics*, "The Mystery of Revelation."[39] There can be no question of whether or not Barth has a high Christology. The heart of his exposition is the phrase "very God and very man." He says: "The miracle of the incarnation, of the *unio hypostatica*, is seen . . . when we realize that the Word of God descended from the freedom, majesty and glory of His divinity, that without becoming unlike Himself He assumed His likeness to us."[40] Barth soundly rebukes Brunner for indifference to the sign of the divinity of Jesus Christ: the virgin birth.[41] It is possible that Barth would have found reason likewise to be concerned about the degree of Hauerwas's commitment to theological realism, but it is likely that he would have found Yoder's Biblical Realism to be quite compatible with his own approach.[42]

3. Natural Theology. Yoder's concentration on the particular narrative history of Jesus Christ as the starting point for all theological reflection, like Barth's, leads him to reject natural theology, apologetics, and systematic theology.[43] Yoder refers to his "post-modern acceptance of the particularity of the Christian story without subjecting it either to the claimed objectivity of general consensus or to that of some specific 'scientific method'"[44] and states his agreement with Barth's well-known rejection of the program of Schleiermacher to base theology on "Feeling."[45] For Yoder, the historical narrative centered on Jesus and the life of the community that witnesses to Jesus is prior to "all possible methodological distillations."[46]

In rejecting apologetics, Yoder suggests that the alternative is "confes-

39. *CD* I/2, 122.

40. Ibid., 165.

41. Ibid., 183–84.

42. See Yoder, *Christian Attitudes to War*, 437, for Yoder's affirmation of the bodily resurrection of Jesus as an event within history.

43. For a discussion of Yoder's rejection of natural theology, see ibid., 46–48, where he deals with Romans 2:14ff.

44. Yoder, introduction to *Priestly Kingdom*, 9. Gayle Gerber Koontz has a good discussion of Yoder's view of the narrative character of theology and the church as rooted in the particularity of Christian revelation ("Confessional Theology in a Pluralistic Context: A Study of the Theological Ethics of H. Richard Niebuhr and John H. Yoder" [unpublished Ph.D. diss., Boston University, 1985], 36–37).

45. Yoder, "How to Be Read by the Bible," 7.

46. Yoder, "Walk and Word," 82.

sion."[47] He also explicitly rejects natural theology as a source of moral knowl-edge.[48] Richard Hays rightly states that, for Barth, natural theology was a form of idolatry,[49] and Yoder sharpens this point when he states: "The worst form of idolatry is not the carving of an image; it is the presumption that one has—or that a society has, or a culture has—the right to set the terms under which God can be recognized."[50] He also rejects systematic theology in the sense of a sys-tem of thought, based on general first principles, from which timeless, univer-sal truth can be generated. The proper movement is from the particular to the general, not from the general to the particular, and this rule is given to us in the fact that God's revelation is historical. Commenting on the words of Less-ing—"The accidental truths of history can never become the necessary truths of reason. . . . that . . . is the ugly, broad ditch which I cannot get across"—Yoder says that we do not have to get across that ditch because, in the incarnation, "the truth has come to our side of the ditch."[51]

Is Yoder as radically christocentric as Barth? Several commentators see a difference between the two theologians at this point. Gerber Koontz claims that "it is necessary to carefully distinguish Barth's Christocentric theology from Yoder's. . . . Yoder does not claim that Jesus is the only source of human knowledge of God while Barth comes close to this position."[52] Gerber Koontz is not wrong to say that, for Yoder, Jesus is not the only source of truth, but her statement, taken by itself without clarification, could be misleading in two ways. First, for Yoder, although not all truth is found in Jesus or the Bible, the truth that is found in Jesus is "the truth that matters the most, which must therefore regulate our reception and recognition of other kinds and levels of truth rather than being set in parallel or subordinated thereto."[53] Second,

47. John Howard Yoder, "Firstfruits: The Paradigmatic Public Role of God's People," *For the Nations: Essays Public and Evangelical* (Grand Rapids: Eerdmans, 1997), 25. Ger-ber Koontz notes that Yoder shares with Barth the conviction that the best way to dia-logue about foundational issues and communicate the intelligibility of Christian faith is not to argue its foundational assumptions but to describe it as coherently as possible starting with those assumptions ("Confessional Theology in a Pluralistic Context," 281).
48. Yoder, *Christian Attitudes to War*, 46–48.
49. Hays, *Moral Vision of the New Testament*, 238.
50. Yoder, "Walk and Word," 89.
51. Yoder, "'But We Do See Jesus,'" 46, 62.
52. Gerber Koontz, "Confessional Theology in a Pluralistic Context," 261. See also Kent Reames, "Histories of Reason and Revelation: With Alasdair MacIntyre and John Howard Yoder into Historicist Theology and Ethics" (unpublished Ph.D. diss., University of Chicago, 1997), 271. Reames sees Yoder as moving Barthianism much closer to what he calls "reasonism" by finding ways to be confessionalist and at the same time deeply ratio-nal. The rationality of Barth's theology is consistently underestimated by North American theologians.
53. Yoder, "The Use of the Bible in Theology," in *The Use of the Bible in Theology: Evangelical Options*, ed. Robert K. Johnston (Atlanta: John Knox Press, 1985), 117. Yoder denies that Biblical Realism includes any disrespect for human rationality, but he acknowledges that "some Barthian rhetoric" may have played into the hands of this mis-interpretation (ibid., 116).

there is essentially no difference between Yoder and Barth on this point. Barth makes unsystematic use of philosophy and other human thought forms in his task of theological reflection. However, as George Hunsinger points out, there is always a move from the particular to the general.[54] As Mary Cunningham puts it: "Barth's logical insistence that Jesus as the logical subject governs the use of predicates descriptive of Him reflects his commitment to the priority of the particular over the general."[55]

Another related area of purported difference between Barth and Yoder has to do with the issue of the historical character of revelation. Hays claims that, while Yoder stands close to Barth in rejecting the normative claims of nonbiblical sources of authority for ethics, Yoder's position is more nuanced, insofar as Yoder "finds in history the hermeneutical point of contact with human reason that Barth steadfastly refused to acknowledge."[56] Bruce McCormack shows that this common, but mistaken, reading of Barth is not valid, at least not after May 1924. According to McCormack, it was at this point that Barth discovered the anhypostatic-enhypostatic christological dogma of the ancient church and saw in it "an understanding of the incarnate being of the Mediator which preserved that infinite qualitative distinction between God and humankind which had been at the forefront of his concerns."[57] This enabled Barth to give the incarnation "its due. No longer did Barth need to reduce the 'site' of revelation to a single 'mathematical point,' the event of the cross."[58] In fact, Barth was "able quite calmly to assert that 'Christian revelation and Christian faith are historical. . . . The hiddenness of God is a hiddenness in history."[59] With this discovery, Barth was now in a position to "affirm the presence in history of the second Person of the Trinity . . . without fear of historicizing revelation,"[60] and he was now able to "appeal to the incarnation as the ground and prototype of the *analogia fidei.*"[61]

The similarity of Yoder's position to that of Barth can be seen in a line of criticism of Yoder's hermeneutics developed by Michael Cartwright. As I noted in the last chapter, Yoder does not merely say that pacifism is *one possible way* to read the significance of Jesus for ethics. If he did, he

54. See his discussion of the motif of particularism in Barth's thought (George Hunsinger, *How to Read Karl Barth: The Shape of His Theology* [Oxford: Oxford University Press, 1991], 32–35).

55. Mary Cunningham, *What Is Theological Exegesis?* 70. See Hans Frei's discussion of the role of general human knowledge and Christian self-description in Barth's theology (in *Types of Christian Theology,* ed. G. Hunsinger and W. C. Placher [New Haven: Yale University Press, 1992], 19–27, 38–46).

56. Hays, *Moral Vision of the New Testament,* 250.

57. Bruce McCormack, *Karl Barth's Critically Realistic Dialectical Theology: Its Genesis and Development 1909–1936* (Oxford: Oxford University Press, 1995), 327.

58. Ibid., 328.

59. Ibid., 363.

60. Ibid., 366.

61. Ibid., 367.

would be able to accept Niebuhr's vocational pacifism and would not have to defend pacifism as the norm for all Christians. Pacifism could be right for Mennonites, and participation in war could not necessarily be wrong for Presbyterians. In that case, Yoder would not receive the kind of criticism Michael Cartwright offers concerning Yoder's hermeneutic. Cartwright criticizes Yoder for distinguishing between what a text meant and what it means, because this distinction presupposes a stable meaning of the biblical text. Cartwright thinks this concept of a stable meaning in the text stands in tension with Yoder's communal hermeneutic and his emphasis on a sociopolitical interpretation of the New Testament. Cartwright would like Yoder to implement his historicism and his communal hermeneutic consistently. Cartwright is unhappy with what he regards as Yoder's "privileging his own reading of Scripture by way of appeals to historical reconstruction of the first century context," forgetting that "such interpretations are political, and therefore subject to contested readings."[62] Cartwright is a sensitive and astute interpreter of Yoder, and here he puts his finger on a point with which those who would accuse Yoder of a totally relativizing historicism need to come to terms.

One of Yoder's greatest concerns is the way that many mainstream ethicists turn Scripture into a wax nose and use it to undergird ideologies of power. As the representative of a minority position, he is searching for ways to argue the case for peace persuasively in terms familiar to the majority. Yoder thinks that it is possible to appeal to Jesus as the norm that judges varying readings of Scripture in the support of various sociopolitical options. Why? This is possible only because Yoder views Jesus Christ as the incarnate Son of God in history. So Yoder cannot follow the proponents of deconstruction all the way. He makes good use of their hermeneutic of suspicion in his subversion of Constantinianism, but he is not really one of them, and this is the point at which his true colors show. Since the incarnation happened in history, it is necessary (and not merely a concession to modern biblical scholarship) to use all historical and critical means possible to establish the meaning of the biblical texts. But it is not necessary to go behind the texts to get at "what really happened" because it is the texts themselves, as the authors (or redactors) produced them, that "render" (as Frei would say) the identity of Jesus Christ. Since the texts witness to the incarnation, which is historical, what they *meant* cannot change.[63] Of course, what they *mean* may change as the situation of the reader changes. But there is a sense of stability at the base of the interpretive process that is rooted in the *historical*

62. Michael Cartwright, "Practices, Politics, and Performance," 386–87.

63. Of course, Yoder would be quick to point out that our appreciation and understanding of what they meant can and does change, sometimes for the better and sometimes for the worse. History is not the story of unalloyed progress from one degree of hermeneutical glory to another.

character of divine revelation. It is this rootedness in history that makes it possible (or rather, from Yoder's perspective, necessary) to stand firmly for nonviolence as the true meaning of discipleship.[64]

It is my contention that Yoder's historicism is thoroughgoing *except* at the crucial point of the incarnation and that this essentially Barthian methodological move is what often causes interpreters great confusion. They either want Yoder to renounce, or at least restrain at key points, his historicism in the interests of maintaining an "Anabaptist hermeneutic," or, alternatively, they accuse him of selling out to modernity in the form of complete moral relativism. Since Barth himself is not well-understood at this point, it is not easy for many interpreters to see how Yoder, following Barth, can calmly refuse to do either and remain consistent. For Yoder, everything except the reality of Jesus Christ is relative, yet because of Jesus Christ nothing is completely relative because everything is affected by the reality of God become flesh. The Anabaptist vision is not merely a statement of the ethical preferences of a small sect of farmers from Europe, but neither is it an absolute principle to be elevated above the Word of God.

Although Hays overstates the contrast between Barth and Yoder, he is not wrong to see some development between the thought of Barth and that of Yoder. Yoder's appreciation of the necessity of a continuing process of communal moral discernment leads him to flesh out the process by which Scripture is interpreted within the body of Christ. Hays recognizes what Yoder is about when he says:

> Thus Yoder develops a hermeneutic which acknowledges the necessary places of tradition, reason and experience in the interpretive process. At the same time, he insists that the New Testament's portrayal of Jesus must remain the fundamental norm for all Christian ethics.[65]

Saying that Jesus should remain the fundamental norm is one thing. Actually finding a way to do it, and maintaining one's concentration on the focal point of Jesus Christ all along the line, is much more difficult. I am not claiming that Yoder does it perfectly. What I am trying to point out (which I do not think has been adequately appreciated up to this point) is that Yoder's method of attempting to accomplish this goal is essentially Barthian.

4. Pacifism. Yoder's concentration on the particular narrative history of Jesus Christ leads him to an emphasis on pacifism as being of decisive importance for discipleship and ethics. This emphasis is a legitimate de-

64. See Kent Reames, "Histories of Reason and Revelation," 125–29, for a good discussion of Yoder's hermeneutics. Hays's summary is also insightful (*Moral Vision of the New Testament,* 239–53).

65. Hays, *Moral Vision of the New Testament,* 252.

velopment of certain trends in Barth's thought.[66] It is true that Barth did not take a completely pacifist stance, although he did come to advocate a practical pacifism in his later writings:

> According to the sense of the New Testament we cannot be pacifists in principle, only in practice. But we have to consider very closely whether, if we are called to discipleship, we can avoid being practical pacifists, or fail to do so.[67]

The point being made here, however, is that Yoder's way of arguing for pacifism on the basis of the incarnation is in harmony with Barth's theological method. Yoder says, "If Jesus Christ was not who historic Christianity confesses he was, *the revelation in the life of a real man of the character of God himself,* then this one argument for pacifism collapses."[68] My focus here is on *how* Yoder is arguing; I will develop the substance of his argument more fully in the next two chapters. For now, we simply need to note that Yoder is explicitly grounding his pacifism in the person of Jesus Christ.

Furthermore, I want to emphasize that Yoder is arguing that grounding pacifism in the person of Jesus Christ is a legitimate development of Barth's theology. As Philip Thorne puts it: "Yoder identifies a line or movement of thought in Barth that leads, if consistently pursued, to a pacifist and even Anabaptist ethic."[69] As Thorne points out, Yoder argues that even though Barth did not become a fully consistent pacifist, "Barth's radically Christological orientation, his emerging position on baptism, and his development of the doctrine of sanctification as obedient imitation of the life of Christ definitely tend in this direction."[70] Thorne correctly (in my opinion) interprets Yoder as meaning to argue that *The Politics of Jesus* is "an extension of the bib-

---

66. This is a controversial development of Barth's thought, one that many other Barth interpreters would see as illegitimate. However, the point under discussion here is primarily not, "Should a good Barthian be a pacifist?" but rather, "Does Barth's theology provide methodological resources for undergirding pacifism theologically?" Perhaps the difference is overly subtle, but it could be argued that Barth is honored more when his work is taken as helpful for another generation to use in constructing a theological position that enables faithfulness in that generation's situation than when self-styled "disciples" slavishly repeat his conclusions.

67. *CD* IV/2, 550. This passage is in Barth's section, "The Call to Discipleship," in his doctrine of sanctification.

68. Yoder, *Politics of Jesus,* 237 (emphasis added). See also Yoder's statement that his type of pacifism is the only type for which the person of Jesus is indispensable. Yoder says, "It is the only one of these positions which would lose its substance if Jesus were not Christ and would lose its foundation if Jesus Christ were not Lord" (*Nevertheless: The Varieties and Shortcomings of Religious Pacifism* [Scottdale, Pa.: Herald, 1992], 134).

69. Thorne, *Evangelicalism and Karl Barth,* 174. See also Yoder's "Karl Barth: How His Mind Kept Changing," in *How Karl Barth Changed My Mind,* ed. Donald McKim (Grand Rapids: Eerdmans, 1986), 166–71.

70. Thorne, *Evangelicalism and Karl Barth,* 174. The quote above from Barth, *Jesus Christ, Servant As Lord,* 550, shows how close Barth came to consistent pacifism.

lical realist revolution instituted by Karl Barth."[71] Richard Hays also sees Yoder's pacifism as growing out of his understanding of Barth's theology:

> Like his teacher Barth, Yoder affirms that Jesus reveals the true nature and vocation of human beings. This affirmation calls for a sweeping reformulation of our approach to theological ethics, for a christocentric ethic must take its bearing from the historical particularity of Jesus, who disclosed definitively that "God's will for God's man in this world is that he should renounce legitimate defence."[72]

Yoder interprets Barth as being well on the way to pacifism: "Our conclusion is therefore that between Barth and an integral Christian pacifism the only differences lie at points where Barth did not finish working out the implications of his originality."[73] Yoder points to the doctrine of sanctification in *Church Dogmatics* IV/2 as key evidence for this conclusion:

> The approach of "The Holy One and the Holy Ones" marked the maturing of a shift from a Christology where the Jesus of the chapters on Nicea and Chalcedon was little more than a cipher for the concept of revelation, to the human figure of the evangelical accounts. If discipleship is to be ethical rather than only pietistic, the One we follow must be known in his humanness.[74]

Once the significance of Jesus' humanness for Christian ethics is acknowledged, the way is paved for the kind of argument Yoder makes in *The Politics of Jesus* concerning the sociopolitical relevance of Jesus.[75]

Nigel Biggar's interpretation of Barth's ethics, however, raises a potentially fatal objection to this claim of a general similarity between the methods of Barth and Yoder. In the context of a discussion of the way in which Barth grounds ethics in the Bible, Biggar uses the concept of "correspondence" as an example of Barth's method:

> One of the most remarkable features of Barth's concept of correspondence with the action of God in Christ is its difference from either the Roman Catholic notion of the *imitatio Christi* or the Anabaptist notion of Christian discipleship.[76]

71. Thorne, *Evangelicalism and Karl Barth*, 174.

72. Hays, *Moral Vision of the New Testament*, 243.

73. Yoder, *Karl Barth and the Problem of War*, 118. Like Thorne and Hays, this essay argues that Yoder's use of Barth is not without warrant.

74. Yoder, "Karl Barth: How His Mind Kept Changing," 171.

75. As Hays notes, both Barth and Yoder eschew "the hermeneutical strategy of extracting moral principles from Scripture for the same reason: applying principles to situations leaves too much room for straying away from the truth revealed in Jesus" (*Moral Vision of the New Testament*, 249). Like Barth, Yoder is very concerned to let Jesus Christ himself be the source of Christian ethics.

76. Biggar, *The Hastening That Waits*, 108.

Biggar does not define what he means by "the Anabaptist notion of Christian discipleship" and does not mention Yoder in this regard. However, he gives a clue as to his meaning when he goes on to say that Barth rejected the idea that "correspondence to God Incarnate can be identified with the way of the cross . . . self-sacrifice is not the principle of the Christian life."[77] Biggar identifies Barth's concern at this point as being to head off all attempts simply to read a theological or ethical system out of the Bible. Biggar says: "Barth does not move from epitomical or characteristic acts of Jesus to moral prescriptions. Instead, he moves from the Bible directly to a general theological description of God's action in Christ . . . and it is from these that he draws moral conclusions."[78] According to Biggar,

> The methodological reason for the different moral conclusions at which Barth arrives is that, according to him, the normative "story" to which human conduct should correspond does not comprise an extract from Jesus' life or a refrain in it, but a theological summary of it.[79]

For Biggar, Barth's view of what is wrong with the Anabaptist notion of discipleship, then, is that it seizes on individual texts and reads them as immediately and literally binding for Christian disciples. Barth's method, on the other hand, involves coming to theological conclusions about the narrative of Jesus based on a reading of the narrative as a whole, from which moral propositions can be derived.

77. Ibid. Biggar's claim here is at least debatable. He is right to say that in the 1946 essay "Christian Ethics," where Barth develops the concept of correspondence, Barth does not refer to the call of Jesus to "take up your cross and come follow me." Biggar states that, although the concept of correspondence is not much mentioned in the special ethics sections of *Church Dogmatics*, it nevertheless is very much at work there (a claim that, in itself, is undoubtedly true). Biggar states this to support his claim that Barth's notion of discipleship does not focus on the call to cross-bearing. But paragraph 66 on sanctification in *CD* IV/2 is brought by Barth to its climax with section 6, "The Dignity of the Cross" (598–613), where Barth calls the cross the "indispensable element in any Christian doctrine of sanctification" (598) and says that "[t]he cross is the most concrete form of the fellowship between Christ and the Christian" (599). Barth specifically states that the cross means persecution (609) and so takes for granted that it means suffering that he takes the trouble to clarify at length the difference between the sufferings of Christ and those of Christians (604–5). Now, given that Biggar has stated that Barth's method is to derive his moral propositions from theological propositions, and given that Barth's doctrine of sanctification culminates in his section on the cross as the meaning of sanctification, can we accept Biggar's claim that Barth's notion of correspondence, which is supposed to govern his ethics, cannot be identified with the *centrality* of the cross in Christian discipleship? Barth not only makes suffering an important motif of the Christian life; it can be argued also that he makes it the central motif of the Christian life, at least with regard to how the Christian (and the Christian community) relates to the world, just as Yoder does.

78. Biggar, *The Hastening That Waits*, 109.

79. Ibid.

Biggar's interpretation of Barth's method at this point seems to me to be sound. I also have no problem admitting that the picture of Anabaptists simplemindedly reading isolated texts and taking them legalistically, while greatly overstated in the history of Protestant polemics against them, is nevertheless not without some historical foundation. The crucial question, however, is whether or not Yoder's method of coming to the conclusion that the moral action of Christians should correspond to God's character as revealed in the cross should be interpreted as falling under Barth's strictures at this point. In *The Politics of Jesus*, Yoder deliberately does not refer to the usual texts from the Sermon on the Mount that Anabaptists have traditionally emphasized as "prooftexts." Instead, he reads the Gospel of Luke as a whole and interprets the theological meaning of the narrative of Jesus and its implications for ethics, just as Barth does. He rejects the simplistic imitation of the incidentals of Jesus' life, such as deriving an injunction to be celibate from the fact that Jesus never married, which is just the sort of thing Barth wants to exclude.[80]

Yoder's method of arriving at the cross as the focal point of Christian discipleship is formally identical to the method Biggar describes Barth as using in the case of homosexuality. Biggar says that it would be a mistake to think that "the logic by which Barth arrives at his judgment about homosexuality from his theological concept of humanity proceeds without serious regard for the witness of the Bible" just because Barth only discusses one biblical passage (Romans 1:25–27) in the context of his treatment of this issue. Biggar points out that Barth's conclusion on homosexuality is derived from his theological anthropology, which in turn is derived from his exegesis of texts such as Genesis 1:27 and 1 Corinthians 11:11. It is not just a matter of plucking a likely-looking text out of the Bible to support an ethical conclusion; rather, it is a procedure of letting a particular text be interpreted by a theological anthropology that is built up and controlled by the canonical context as a whole. Yoder's choice of the cross as the central image in Christian discipleship is a theological decision based on a careful reading of the Gospel of Luke as a whole *and* the imitation-participation-correspondence language of the Epistles. The fact that the Epistles call for imitation of Jesus at the point of the cross only, and that they do so repeatedly, is the key to Yoder's interpretation: "Only at one point, only on one subject—but then consistently, universally—is Jesus our example: in his cross."[81] The fact that Barth and Yoder come to different conclusions on the very fine point of whether or not any possible exceptions to Christian pacifism can be imagined should not deter us from observing the essential similarity of their theological methods.

80. Yoder, *Politics of Jesus*, 95.
81. Ibid.

5. Doctrine and Ethics. Yoder's identification of doctrine and ethics as two sides of the same coin is simply the implementation of Barth's method. In *The Politics of Jesus*, Yoder argues for certain social-ethical implications of Christology on the basis of his reading of the text of the Gospel of Luke. However, he also says that

> the view of Jesus being proposed here is more radically Nicene and Chalcedonian than other views. I do not here advocate an unheard-of modern understanding of Jesus. I ask rather that the implications of what the church has always said about Jesus as Word of the Father, as true God and true Man, be taken more seriously, as relevant to our social problems, than ever before.[82]

In appealing to the classic doctrines of the Trinity and incarnation, Yoder is seeking to derive ethical implications from them. This has led some interpreters to assume that Yoder must be reducing doctrine to ethics. But there is another way to read Yoder at this point, namely, to see him doing the same thing as Barth does in *Church Dogmatics*.

For Barth, "dogmatics is ethics and ethics is also dogmatics";[83] they are not two things but two aspects of the one thing. Barth rejects all attempts to do theological ethics on the basis of "general human ethics" or "philosophical ethics."[84] Instead, he seeks to derive ethics from God's self-revelation in Jesus Christ: "In the one image of Jesus Christ we have both the Gospel which reconciles us with God . . . and the Law which . . . really binds and obligates us."[85] Theological ethics is grace, says Barth; "to become obedient, to act rightly, to realize the good, never means anything other than to become obedient to the revelation of the grace of God."[86] Since Jesus Christ is grace incarnate, for Barth, ethics is christological (in the sense of being a response to the grace incarnated in Jesus Christ) or else it is not Christian. Yoder makes the same point in rejecting natural theology as the basis for Christian ethics:

> If the meaning of Jesus is thus different from what he was understood by his Palestinian disciples and adversaries to mean, and if those ordinary meanings need to be filtered through a hermeneutical transposition and replaced by an ethic of social survival and responsibility, what then has become of the concept of revelation? Is there such a thing as a *Christian* ethic at all? If there be no specifically Christian ethic but only natural human ethics . . . does this thoroughgoing abandon of particular substance apply to ethical truth only? Why not to all other truth as well?[87]

82. Ibid., 102.
83. *CD* I/2, 793.
84. *CD* II/2, 543.
85. Ibid., 539.
86. Ibid.
87. Yoder, *Politics of Jesus*, 10.

For Yoder and for Barth, Christian ethics is the proper response of the Christian to the doctrine of God's grace as revealed in the incarnation.

6. Ethics As Obedience. Yoder's concept of ethics as obedience, rather than as the application of principles, also is like Barth's in many ways.[88] For Barth, "the good in human action consists in the fact that it is determined by the divine command."[89] John Webster makes the important point that the entire *Church Dogmatics* is an ethical dogmatics, a moral ontology in which "an extensive account of the situation in which human agents act" is given.[90] He also makes the point that Barth is "profoundly perturbed by modernity's primary image of the human person; that of the self as a centre of judgment, creating value by its acts of allegiance or choice, organising the moral world around its consciousness of itself as the ethical *fundamentum*."[91] In this context, it is illuminating to recall Barth's definition of most types of ethics as sin:

> in so far as this general conception of ethics seems to speak of an answer to the question which is to be worked out by man himself, it confirms also that man tries to escape the grace of God by which the question of the good is put, but by which it is also answered in advance. Strange as it may seem, that general conception of ethics coincides exactly with the conception of sin.[92]

Barth is convinced that "moral problems are resolvable by correct theological description of moral space," and, therefore, he gives low priority to both the issues of character and to the analysis of quandary situations.[93] For Barth, the command of God is definite and concrete. Likewise, Yoder does not spend much time on quandary situations or discussions of character. He focuses on theological description of Christ, history, and the church. Yoder implicitly rejects many forms of ethical deliberation (including all Niebuhrian ones) when he states, "the good action is measured by its conformity to the command and to the nature of God and not by its success in achieving specific results."[94] Michael

---

88. One could contrast the two by saying that, for Barth, ethics consists of obedience to the command of God, while, for Yoder, it consists of obedience to the teaching and example of Jesus. But that contrast obscures at least as much as it clarifies. To suggest that, for Barth, the command of God is heard more clearly when one's gaze has been moved from Jesus Christ would be to distort his whole approach, and to suggest that, for Yoder, the teaching and example of Jesus is any less than the command of God would be to misrepresent his approach.

89. Barth, *Election of God*, 547.

90. John Webster, *Barth's Ethics of Reconciliation* (Cambridge: Cambridge University Press, 1995), 1.

91. Ibid., 18.

92. *CD* II/2, 518.

93. Webster, *Barth's Ethics of Reconciliation*, 2.

94. John Howard Yoder, *The Christian Witness to the State* (Newton, Kans.: Faith and Life, 1964), 49.

Cartwright notes that "Yoder disagrees with the presumption that pre-scriptive use of Scripture is unthinkable" and goes so far as to say: "There is a strong sense in which everything that Yoder has written constitutes a challenge to this predisposition."[95]

Some of the charges leveled against Yoder, such as having a low doc-trine of sin, having a perfectionistic streak in his theology, and of lack-ing appreciation for moral ambiguity and the tragic dimension of life, could be explicable as misunderstandings of the fact that Yoder is work-ing with a concept of ethics as obedience to God's grace rather than as obedience to a law distinguishable from grace. In my opinion, to find Yoder guilty of these charges is unfair. Is it not more likely that Barth and Yoder share a concept of ethics as obedience to the gospel call, which is the experience of grace? In my view, Yoder's Barthian concept of ethics as obedience to the command of God, plus his Barthian un-derstanding of the command of God as being grace, are key to his whole approach to social ethics.

7. The Church and the World. Yoder's distinction between church and world as crucial for social ethics builds on and extends Barth's dis-tinction between the Christian community and the civil community. In his lecture "Why Ecclesiology Is Social Ethics," Yoder turns to a discus-sion of Barth's "The Order of the Community" in *Church Dogmatics* 4.2, where the notion of "True Church Law" is discussed. Yoder makes the point in this lecture that "Barth is affirming for the first time in main-stream Protestant theology since Constantine the theological legiti-macy of admitting about a set of social structures, that those who par-ticipate in them cannot be presumed to be addressable from the perspective of Christian confession."[96] In other words, Barth is saying that the contemporary European states, in which the European churches find themselves situated, are not Christian states. The distinc-tion between church and world is central to Barth's thought at this point. This means that Christian social ethics cannot consist of Chris-tian theologians and pastors calling on Christian political leaders to implement God's will. What, then, can Christian social ethics consist of in such a case?

One implication of the distinction between church and world is that Christian ethics is for Christians. When Christians address the world, there is an indirectness or a nuanced quality to that address that is not present in the command of God heard by the church. In his essay "The Christian Community and the Civil Community," Barth uses the con-cept of analogy as a possible way to facilitate Christian speech to the state. Yoder is of the opinion that a more carefully worked out, rigor-

95. Cartwright, "Practices, Politics, and Performance," 176.
96. Yoder, "Why Ecclesiology Is Social Ethics: Gospel Ethics versus the Wider Wis-dom," *Royal Priesthood*, 108.

ously applied use of analogy is the necessary basis for such speech.[97] But what is important to note here is the fact that both Barth and Yoder take the distinction between church and world as fundamental to their method of doing social ethics.

Another implication of the church-world distinction is that, for Yoder, good news is turned into bad news when it is forced upon people by coercive methods, whether they be crude physical methods of violence or sophisticated and refined epistemological theories. How can the proclamation of the gospel be experienced by its hearers as liberating, enabling, welcome news? It can be none of these things unless the method of proclamation respects the hearers' integrity as persons and offers them the opportunity to reject the message. The distinction between church and world respects the right of some people to refuse to believe the gospel. Yoder claims:

> the most important error of the Christendom vision is not first of all its acceptance of an ethic of power, violence, and the crusade; not first of all its transference of eschatology into the present providence with God working through Constantine and all his successors in civil government, not its appropriation of pagan religiosity that will lead to sacerdotalism and sacramentalism, not its modeling church hierarchy after Roman administration, nor any other specific vice derived from what changed about the nature of the church with the epoch of Constantine. Those were all mistakes, but they were derived from the misdefinition of the place of the people of God in the world. The fundamental wrongness of the vision of Christendom is its illegitimate takeover of the world; its ascription of a Christian loyalty or duty to those who have made no confession, and thereby, its denying to the non-confessing creation the freedom of unbelief that the nonresistance of God in creation gave to a rebellious humanity.[98]

Yoder claims that Barth's church-world distinction and his recognition that Christian ethics is telling the story of Jesus, and telling it in such a way that it is grace, gospel, and good news, makes him non-Constantinian. But Yoder goes much further than Barth ever did in unpacking the implications of the church-world distinction for social ethics.

8. The Mission of the Church. Yoder's view of the church's mission as being to witness to Jesus Christ is exactly the same as Barth's view. Yoder speaks frequently of not taking responsibility for making history come out right. Our call is to obey in a world that we do not control.[99] I will argue later in this book that this strong sense of God's sovereignty and the limited role of humankind is rooted in an eschatology that stresses the

97. Yoder discusses Barth's use of analogy in his unpublished paper, "The Basis of Barth's Social Ethics," 7. I analyze the use of analogy by Barth and Yoder in chapter 8.

98. Yoder, "Why Ecclesiology Is Social Ethics," 109.

99. Yoder, "Christ, the Hope of the World," *Royal Priesthood*, 204.

action of God in the world both now and in the future—action that calls humans to respond in faith by laying down their arms and standing by to watch the deliverance of Yahweh. Just as there is nothing we can do to extend or add to our salvation, there is nothing we can do to extend or add to the coming of the kingdom of God. The role of the church is that of witness. Yet, paradoxically, the witness offered by the church becomes the key to history, and "the ultimate meaning of history is to be found in the work of the church."[100]

In *Church Dogmatics* 4.3b, paragraph 72, "The Holy Spirit and the Sending of the Christian Community," Barth includes a section entitled "The Task of the Community," in which he stresses the point that the community is sent into the world and exists for the world.[101] The task of the church is quite definite: to bear witness to Jesus Christ by being itself. In the following section on "The Ministry of the Community," Barth makes it clear that the witness consists of both word and deed: "There is a work of the lips and also of the hands."[102]

Yoder's entire concept of social ethics is built on the premise that Jesus called the Christian community into being in order that it might be a continuing witness to him on earth and that, in order for that witness to be clear, it had to be a *community*. Why? It had to be a community because only in community can the love of God, which is displayed in his sending of his Son as the Savior of the world and which is rooted in his triune nature, be made manifest. This is the true work of the church, just as the establishment of the kingdom of God and the judgment of sin and evil is properly the work of God. In making this key distinction, I think that Barth and Yoder are not only in agreement with each other—I also think they are right.

Areas of Disagreement

There is really only one major area of methodological disagreement between Yoder and Barth: the problematic concept of the *Grenzfall*. In order to elucidate what is at stake in this disagreement, I want to examine, first, Barth's actual use of the concept, second, his account of why his ethical theory requires such a concept, and, third, Yoder's critique of Barth's ethics at this point. Finally, I will offer my evaluation of the outcome of this debate. In the third volume of his *Church Dogmatics*, Barth develops the concept of the "exceptional case" or *Grenzfall*.[103] Here Barth

100. "Peace without Eschatology," *Royal Priesthood*, 151.

101. *CD* IV/3:2, 795.

102. Ibid., 863.

103. *CD* III/4, 396. The subsection, "The Protection of Life" (397–470), comes after the first subsection ("Respect for Life") of paragraph 55, "Freedom for Life." The concept of the *Grenzfall* is employed most fully in Barth's ethics as a whole with regard to the issue of the taking of human life.

considers the issues of suicide, abortion, euthanasia, self-defense, capital punishment, and war. In each case, except for euthanasia, he outlines the circumstances surrounding a case in which he believes the command of God could be heard to take life.

With regard to suicide, he imagines a scenario in which a person in a horrible predicament might be commanded to take his or her own life. Who can say that the gracious God might not "help a man in affliction by telling him to take this way out" as, for example, in the case of a man being tortured and afraid of betraying his friends and cause and thus directly or indirectly deny his faith?[104] In the case of abortion, Barth comes close to enunciating a principle (!) for recognizing the exceptional case when he says that it could occur only if it is a matter of life for life, that is, a situation in which it is a choice between the life of the mother and the life of the child. Barth says that abortion is only possible when "it is a case of one life being balanced against another ... the sacrifice of one being unavoidable."[105] Given the elasticity with which the medical profession and ethicists have defined the "health" of the mother, however, it is hard to know what Barth means here. Does he mean that it is only possible in the case of the actual, physical life of the mother being in danger, such as in the case of a tubal pregnancy, or would he include threats to the mental health of the woman as well? If it is the former, then he could claim to derive the rationale for breaking the rule from the rule itself, that is, taking life only in order to preserve life. However, Barth does not seem to work with such a literal definition of the exceptional case. He considers euthanasia only briefly and comes to the conclusion that it cannot be justified as the command of God; here must be pronounced an unequivocal "No."[106] Barth's horror at the Nazi eugenics program probably influenced his conclusion on this issue. In his consideration of the question of self-defense, however, he appears to take a radical stance by arguing that, while it is a natural instinct, the New Testament declares it to be wrong.[107] However, Barth thinks that the instinct of self-defense can be "sanctified" and that "we may receive from the Lord orders which lead us beyond this line."[108] Barth then argues extensively against capital punishment as a social institution, except in two well-defined situations: high treason in the case of war and tyrannicide.[109]

104. Ibid., 410, 412.
105. Ibid., 421.
106. Ibid., 423, 427.
107. Ibid., 431.
108. Ibid., 434. Interestingly, Barth offers no specific examples here but mentions the upcoming case of capital punishment. It almost seems as though, although he cannot think of a legitimate exceptional case here, he cannot consistently deny its possibility in the case of the individual when he is on the verge of approving it in the case of the state.
109. Ibid., 448.

Finally, Barth turns to the question of killing in war. Here Barth begins by "demythologizing war."[110] He says that modern war is total war usually waged for the acquisition and protection of material interests with scientific objectivity and appalling effectiveness. War is characterized as "killing . . . with neither glory, dignity nor chivalry, with neither restraint nor consideration in any respect."[111] Barth says that if there can be any question of a just war, it can be only with "even stricter reserve and caution than have been necessary in relation to such things as suicide, abortion, capital punishment, and so on."[112] Barth's realism concerning war is stark:

> Does not war demand that almost everything that God has forbidden be done on a broad front? To kill effectively, and in connexion therewith, must not those who wage war steal, rob, commit arson, lie, deceive, slander, and unfortunately to a large extent fornicate, not to speak of the almost inevitable repression of all the finer and weightier forms of obedience? And how can they pray when at the climax of this whole world of dubious action it is a brutal matter of killing? . . . it is certainly not true that most people become better in war. The fact is that for most people war is a trial for which they are no match, and from the consequences of which they can never recover.[113]

In a discussion of the pacifism of the early church and the "elasticity with which the Church has countenanced war and war fever from the days of Constantine," Barth suggests that, of the two positions, that of the early church is superior. He goes so far as to assert that "the inflexible negative of pacifism has almost infinite arguments in its favor and is almost overpoweringly strong."[114] Nevertheless, he pulls back from the brink of consistent pacifism at the last moment.

Only in the case in which a nation's continued existence is at stake is the possibility of a divine command to wage war possible, and then only if there is bound up with the independent life of a nation "responsibility for the whole physical, intellectual and spiritual life of the people comprising it, and therefore their relationship to God."[115] Barth asserts that he would see this as the case if there were any attack on the independence, neutrality, and territorial integrity of the Swiss Confederation. Barth also gives approval to war in the case of a nation coming to the defense of a weaker state that finds itself in the above situation. Barth does not make explicit use of the traditional just-war criteria, probably because that would be a concession to casuistry.

110. Ibid., 458.
111. Ibid., 453.
112. Ibid., 454.
113. Ibid.
114. Ibid., 455.
115. Ibid., 462.

Why does Barth believe the concept of the "exceptional case" is necessary in Christian ethics? Several considerations enter into the picture. First, Barth is quite concerned not to have a system of casuistry that individuals can manipulate as a way of avoiding obedience, thus making themselves sovereign instead of God. Second, casuistry makes the command of God into an "empty form" instead of a concrete, definite, and personal address of the living God to the individual. Third, casuistry destroys the freedom of obedience by inserting something between the command of God and the human called to obey him.[116] Barth has been criticized for his portrayal of casuistry as "a closed, rationalistic ethical system which allows no room for the highly individual, vocational dimension of moral deliberation."[117] There is no doubt that Barth himself engaged in a form of casuistry in the passage described above, so his rejection of casuistry is, therefore, not entirely convincing.[118] But he would contend that he is not giving a complete casuistic system in advance, that his discussion of specifics is to give guidelines only, and that the real function of special ethics is "instructional preparation for the ethical event."[119] The line here between casuistry and noncasuistry is quite thin, though still perceptible.

Yoder criticizes Barth's concept of the *Grenzfall* in several different ways and from various angles. I will first examine Yoder's direct criticism as given in chapter 11 of his book on Barth and then examine a criticism that is implicit in many of Yoder's writings that applies to Barth on this issue.

Yoder points out that classical just-war theory was rooted deeply in natural theology, and this can be seen in two ways: (1) the self is a valid locus of ethical value and the source of duties, both for the individual and the nation, that are not subordinate to one's duties to God; and (2) the knowledge needed to make specific ethical choices is derived from "nature" rather than from revelation.[120] Yoder notes that, at both points, Barth's *Grenzfall* argument is weak. He observes that, although appeal is made to God's sovereignty, it is the individual who decides when to abort the fetus, go to war, or defend oneself. He says, "The only exceptions God

---

116. Ibid., 13.

117. Biggar, *The Hastening That Waits,* 163.

118. Perhaps it would be fair to say that Barth rejects a systematic casuistry while endorsing an *ad hoc* type. See Nigel Biggar's excellent discussion of Barth's use of a non-absolutist form of normative ethics that could, without doing violence to his concerns, be expanded into a nonabsolutist form of casuistry ("Hearing God's Command and Thinking about What's Right: With and beyond Barth," in *Reckoning with Barth: Essays in Commemoration of the Centenary of Karl Barth's Birth,* ed. N. Biggar [London: Mowbray, 1988], 113–18).

119. *CD* III/4, 18. In this regard, it is instructive that Yoder reports (*Karl Barth and the Problem of War,* 64) that in conversation Barth confirmed that his statement (*CD* III/4, 462) regarding an attack on Switzerland as being an example of a *Grenzfall* is misleading in that such an affirmation cannot be known theologically in advance.

120. Yoder, *Karl Barth and the Problem of War,* 70.

in His sovereignty seems likely to make happen to coincide with my or our righteous self-interest" and goes on to note that, while the imagery of the divine Word spoken vertically into the situation is retained, the substance of the choices made is derived from "common sense."[121] Yoder calls this a "concession" to natural theology. If the concept of the *Grenzfall* existed in Barth's thought simply as a reminder of the limit of human knowledge and the freedom of the commanding God, Yoder could agree with it fully.[122] However, it limits God just as much to affirm that God will ever command, or has ever commanded, killing as it does to say that one knows of no exceptions to the rule: "The finitude of human knowledge is in itself in no way a ground for assuming that God is going to command participation in war."[123] The concept of the *Grenzfall*, in and of itself, gives us no new knowledge of the war question. What, then, is Barth's basis for advocating killing in war on the basis of national defense in some cases? From what theological proposition or doctrine or interpretation of the story of Jesus is this position derived? Yoder says the basis is "common sense" or "natural theology." He concludes:

> The *Grenzfall* is not a formal concept with validity in the discipline of ethics. It is simply the label which Barth has seen fit to attach to the fact that, in some situations, he considers himself obliged to make a choice which runs against what all the formal concepts of his own ethics would seem to require.[124]

A second line of criticism of Barth's use of the *Grenzfall* runs through Yoder's writings in general and is also found in Barth's own theology, as discussed above. It is the rejection of the identification of church and state in the Christendom idea. The church-world distinction as basic to Christian ethics is common ground for Yoder and Barth, although it must be said that Barth only late in life came to make much theological use of the concept, whereas it was a major theme of Yoder's theology from his earliest writings all the way through. I will now attempt to summarize the main points of Yoder's criticism of Barth's position.

Throughout his discussion of the issue of war, Barth does not keep the church-world distinction rigorously in view. If he had, the results would have been very different. The most glaring example of the negative results of Barth's failure to keep this distinction in view is where Barth defines what would justify going to war to defend the national sovereignty of a given nation:

121. Ibid., 71.
122. Ibid., 72. That it does not can be seen in the fact that Barth does find it possible to say an unequivocal "No" to euthanasia. Apparently, no *Grenzfall* is needed here to protect God's sovereignty.
123. Ibid., 73.
124. Ibid.

Why do we have to allow the possibility that in the light of the divine command-ment this is a justifiable reason for war, so that a war waged for this reason must be described as a just war in spite of all the horrors which it will certainly entail? The obvious answer is that there may well be bound up with the independent life of a nation responsibility for the whole physical, intellectual and spiritual life of the people comprising it, and therefore their relationship to God.[125]

How could a nation-state be described this way without it having, in effect, become a church? Or has the nation, in this instance, assumed a divine character? It would seem that, at the least, the state has in this case assumed the eschatological role that properly belongs to the church. Just a few pages before, in a discussion of the "Fall of the Church," Barth argued that identifying the fall of the church with the Christian church's adoption of a positive attitude toward war was superficial and that:

If there is a fall of Christianity, then this is to be sought at a deeper level, and theologically we shall find it in the degeneration of ecclesiastical eschatology and the resultant overestimation and misinterpretation of the events and laws of the present world.[126]

It almost seems as though Barth has provided in advance the refutation of his own argument. If Barth had lived to work through the volume on redemption, if he had had a chance to rethink his eschatology in the light of the church-world distinction, if he had decided to abandon his advo-cacy of the possible rightness of war for Christians for purposes of national defense as leftover remnants of natural theology and Christen-dom thinking, and if he had reformulated his ethics of killing in the light of his writings on the "call to discipleship" and the "dignity of the cross," he would have been able to find within his own theology all the resources necessary for the development of a more consistent pacifism, and the result would have been greater internal coherence in his theology. Yoder's critique of Barth's use of the *Grenzfall* concept is entirely an internal cri-tique. The issue is how consistent Barth is with his own theology. On this basis, then, I conclude that Yoder's critique is justified and that Barth's ethics would be more consistent without this concept.

Anabaptism, Barth, and Yoder's Theological Method: A Summary

The purpose of this chapter and the previous one has been to place Yoder's thought in its historical context so that his theological method

125. *CD* III/4, 462.
126. Ibid., 455. In chapter 5 we shall investigate the important role Yoder's eschatol-ogy plays in his rejection of war.

could be discerned more clearly, as a preliminary step to the systematic exposition of his occasional and conversational writings. What has emerged is that Yoder has combined in a creative manner aspects of his Anabaptist theological heritage with the theological method of Karl Barth to construct an approach to social ethics that is clearly postliberal.

What Yoder does in developing his "pacifism of the messianic community"[127] is identical to, similar to, or a legitimate development of what Barth does in *Church Dogmatics* at the following key points: (1) the reading of the Bible as a narrative centering on Jesus Christ and the consequent rejection of the scholastic doctrine of inspiration; (2) a Biblical Realism that leads to a high Christology and the consequent rejection of liberal views of Jesus as less than fully divine; (3) concentration on the particular narrative history of Jesus Christ as the starting point for all theological reflection and the consequent rejection of natural theology, systematic theology, and apologetics; (4) concentration on the particular narrative history of Jesus Christ as leading to an emphasis on the pacifism of Jesus as being of decisive importance for discipleship and ethics; (5) the identification of dogmatics and ethics as two sides of the same coin; (6) the concept of ethics as obedience; (7) the distinction of church and world as the starting point for social-ethical reflection; and (8) the definition of the mission of the church as witness. Clearly, Thorne's insight that the influence of Barth "lies deep within the structure of Yoder's thought" is accurate.[128] It would be overstating the case, however, to say that Yoder simply took over Barth's methodology and applied it to social ethics, for Yoder's Anabaptist heritage and, in particular, his involvement in the Mennonite identity debate also shaped his theological method.

Which parts of his method, then, did Yoder get from Barth, and which did he get from his Anabaptist theological heritage? The themes of a biblically based, high Christology, pacifism, the concept of ethics as obedience, the church-world distinction, and the definition of the church's mission as witness are all found in Yoder's Anabaptist heritage. The narrative approach to Scripture, the rejection of natural theology, and the identification of ethics and dogmatics as two sides of the same coin appear to have come from Barth. Yoder's high Christology and his concept of ethics as obedience were reinforced and clarified by Barth. The church-world distinction and the concept of the church's mission as witness are found in Barth's thought, but Yoder develops and clarifies them. The emphasis on pacifism as rooted in the narrative history of Jesus Christ represents a definite development and extension, though not a contradiction, of the overall trajectory of Barth's thought. On one methodological point, the concept of the *Grenzfall,* Yoder is in clear disagree-

---

127. This is the phrase that Yoder uses to describe his own brand of pacifism in *Nevertheless,* 133–38.

128. Thorne, *Evangelicalism and Karl Barth,* 173.

ment with Barth, although Yoder mounts a strong case for regarding the concept of the *Grenzfall* as an alien concept that is not really consistent with the rest of Barth's thought. Yoder interprets Barth's methodology as leading to pacifism even though Barth himself did not work out the full implications of "his commitment to the free church vision."[129]

Whether or not one accepts Yoder's critique of Barth's use of the *Grenzfall* concept, it is nonetheless necessary to view Yoder as employing a method very much like that of Barth in the realm of social ethics. Moreover, one must also view "the pacifism of the messianic community" as a postliberal social ethic that depends in great measure upon Barth's theology, while going beyond it and building on it. The validity of this interpretation of Yoder's work, however, can only be assessed finally on the basis of an examination of Yoder's actual theology as a whole, because what a theologian says should be done and what is actually done are often two different things. Therefore, the rest of this book will expound the content of the theological basis of Yoder's social ethics systematically and, in so doing, provide a basis for coming to a conclusion about how consistently he worked out the theological methodology described in this chapter.

129. Yoder, "Karl Barth: How His Mind Kept Changing," 171.

Part II

Christology as the *Source* of Yoder's Social Ethics

That Christian pacifism which has a theological basis in the character of God and the work of Jesus Christ is one in which the calculating link between our obedience and ultimate efficacy has been broken, since the triumph of God comes through resurrection and not through effective sovereignty or assured survival.

John Howard Yoder
The Politics of Jesus, 1972

If we were to carry on that other, traditionally doctrinal kind of debate, I would seek simply to demonstrate that the view of Jesus being proposed here is more radically Nicene and Chalcedonian than other views. I do not here advocate an unheard-of modern understanding of Jesus. I ask rather that the implications of what the church has always said about Jesus as Word of the Father, as true God and true Man, be taken more seriously, as relevant to our social problems, than ever before.

John Howard Yoder
The Politics of Jesus, 1972

3

Yoder's Narrative, Postliberal Christology

The title of this chapter refers to Christology rather than simply to Jesus because I want to stress that Yoder's approach to social ethics is rooted in the classical, orthodox Christology that the ecumenical creeds affirm as the meaning of the Scriptures. In order to begin to turn this assertion into an argument, I need to examine the importance of Yoder's Christology for his social ethics.

The importance of Christology for Yoder's social ethics can be seen in the central claim set forth in *The Politics of Jesus* in particular and in Yoder's writings in general, namely, that the New Testament's rendering of Jesus Christ implies a certain shape for the moral life of the disciple. This claim can be broken down into three interrelated subclaims: (1) that the Jesus of the New Testament is both relevant to and normative for Christian ethics, (2) that a particular kind of pacifism is central to a Christian social ethic based upon Jesus, and (3) that the account of the significance of Jesus required by this approach to social ethics is more radically Nicene and Chalcedonian than the accounts found in mainstream Christianity since Constantine. I will unpack the first two subclaims in this chapter before addressing the third subclaim in chapter 4. At that point, I will be ready to discuss the charge of reductionism, which has been made against Yoder's theology.

First we need to examine Yoder's claim that the Jesus of the New Testament is both relevant to and normative for contemporary Christian social ethics. In order to do that, we turn to his exposition of the social ethic of Jesus in the first half of *The Politics of Jesus,* where Yoder offers his reading of the Gospel of Luke. The fact that Yoder's account of Christian ethics begins with a detailed reading of the Gospel narratives in the light of their historical context is a strength of Yoder's approach. Nigel Biggar, in the conclusion to his study of Karl Barth's ethics, refers to "the vague terms in which he [i.e., Barth] articulates Jesus' moral significance"[1] and argues that one respect in which contemporary ethics needs to go beyond Barth in determining the moral significance of Jesus Christ is "not only by way of an analysis of Christology, but also through close scrutiny of the particular political, social, religious and moral circumstances to which Jesus was responding."[2] That is precisely what Yoder does in *The Politics of Jesus.*

Yoder's Reading of the Gospel of Luke

Yoder does not comment on every pericope in Luke. Instead, he focuses on certain selected sections that illustrate the editorial stance of the Gospel author and that point to the overall message being conveyed. Yoder chooses Luke because it is generally agreed that one of Luke's editorial concerns is to show that Christianity is no threat to the Roman Empire. Thus, the bias, if any exists, would be in favor of downplaying the social radicality of Jesus.[3]

1. Nigel Biggar, *The Hastening That Waits: The Ethics of Karl Barth* (Oxford: Oxford University Press, 1993), 166.

2. Ibid., 167. Biggar's criticism of Barth on this point has some validity as far as ethics proper is concerned, and it is certainly true that Yoder does treat Jesus in his historical context more fully so far as social ethics is concerned. However, Biggar perhaps does not sufficiently take into account Barth's treatment of Jesus as "The Royal Man" in *CD* IV/2, 154–264, or his discussion of "The Holy One and the Holy Ones," 511–33. Barth's Christology is far from docetic; he pays serious and sustained attention to Jesus' humanity as portrayed in the Synoptic Gospels and lets that humanity become significant for his doctrine of sanctification. It also needs to be borne in mind that, for Barth, all of dogmatics is relevant to ethics and not just the material in the sections specifically labeled as ethics. Certainly Yoder makes good use of Barth's material for his purposes. If he goes beyond Barth, it is more like filling in the blank spaces than drawing new shapes. See Yoder's "The Basis of Barth's Social Ethics" (unpublished paper), 6–7.

3. John Howard Yoder, *The Politics of Jesus: Vicit Agnus Noster,* 2d ed. (Grand Rapids: Eerdmans, 1994), 11. Richard Hays notes that Yoder is referring to Hans Conzelmann's pioneering redaction-critical study of Luke (*The Moral Vision of the New Testament: Community, Cross, New Creation: A Contemporary Introduction to New Testament Ethics* [San Francisco: HarperSanFrancisco, 1996], 241 n. 107). In the second edition of *Politics of Jesus,* Yoder notes that new readings of Luke's intentions see Luke as especially attentive to the underdogs—women, tax collectors, soldiers, the poor, lepers, etc.—which would make his Gospel more likely to display Jesus' social concern. If the newer line of Gospel criticism is correct, then Yoder chose the Gospel that made his task the easiest,

In Yoder's reading of Luke, we see the emergence of the themes of eschatology and ecclesiology, which will be treated more extensively in chapters 5 through 8 of this book. It is important to understand how firmly Yoder's eschatology and ecclesiology are rooted in his Christology and that he rejects the violence of the imperial, Constantinian church, most fundamentally, for christological reasons. Yoder contends that Luke presents Jesus as the Messiah of Israel, as the founder of a new community of discipleship separate from the world around it, and as one who rejects violence both for himself and for his new community. Christology implies a specific type of discipleship, which implies a certain type of ecclesiology and which only makes sense within the context of a certain understanding of history, that is, within a certain eschatology.

We begin by noting that Yoder understands Luke as meaning to present Jesus as the Messiah of Israel.[4] The theme of messiahship is

---

not the hardest. He contends, however, that his reading of the significance of Jesus is the common witness of all the Gospels and thus not dependent upon any one of them. Yoder writes: "I have no stake in preferring one school of Gospel criticism to another" (*Politics of Jesus,* 54). Hays comments that Yoder may be going too far in saying that he has no stake in preferring some critical approaches to the Gospels to others. He points to the detached Cynic Jesus imagined by the historical critics of the Jesus Seminar as an example of Gospel criticism that would stand in fundamental tension with Yoder's view of Jesus (*Moral Vision of the New Testament,* 247 n. 141). However, the Cynic Jesus is a historical reconstruction of the phenomenon that is supposed to be the "reality" behind the text. Such a historical reconstruction is a shifting, ephemeral, and uncertain human construct, in contrast to the relatively more stable Jesus of the canonical texts. Like Barth, Yoder focuses on the canonical text of Scripture and has no stake in either the fundamentalist or the liberal focus on the "thing" behind the text, both of whose foci are essentially modern. Yoder's point that the interpretation of the canonical text is not decisively affected by changing fads in historical research would only be invalid if it could be proven somehow that Jesus never lived or if his bones were conclusively identified or some such thing. The more mundane, day-to-day changes in what used to be referred to as "the assured results of higher criticism" are hardly earth-shattering. Such research can be helpful in establishing the original meaning of the text, but it can never become a substitute for the text. Yoder contends that his Biblical Realism is only possible as a postcritical phenomenon ("How to Be Read by the Bible" [A Shalom Desktop Publication, 1996], 116). Hays himself notes that, like Barth, Yoder aims to take the entire New Testament canon into account and "succeeds to an impressive degree" (*Moral Vision of the New Testament,* 246).

4. Yoder's exegetical approach here is a canonical one in the sense that he, like Brevard S. Childs and Karl Barth, is interested in the meaning of the text in its final form, not in a reconstruction of supposed historical events behind the text, to which the text may or may not be a more or less faithful guide. While Yoder takes great pains to distance himself from scholastic and fundamentalist theories of verbal inspiration and inerrancy, the fact is that, as in the case of Barth, a doctrine of inspiration is at work here. Yoder seems to proceed on the assumptions that biblical narrative is true and that the narrative of Jesus' life, death, resurrection, and ascension is the center of the biblical narrative. Thus, the task of interpretation is to understand the text, relate that understanding to Jesus Christ, and then to apply it to our contemporary situation. See Hays, *Moral Vision of the New Testament,* 248–52, for an excellent discussion of Yoder's hermeneutics.

prominent in the Gospel texts, and much of the debate they present concerns what kind of messiah should be expected and what kind of messiah Jesus is. Yoder interprets the story of the feeding of the multitude (Luke 9) as a conflict between Jesus and the crowds over what kind of messiah he is. Yoder explains: "The cross and the crown are alternatives."[5] The estrangement of Jesus from both the crowds and the Jewish leaders begins at this point. Jesus has earned the contempt of the crowds for refusing insurrection and the animosity of some Jewish leaders for refusing quietism. But note that the issue at stake concerns the kind of messiahship, not messiahship or not. It is at this point that Jesus renews his messianic claims and begins his "march to Jerusalem."[6]

Yoder also interprets the account of Jesus' temptation in the wilderness just prior to the beginning of his public ministry as centering on the issue of what kind of messiah Jesus believed himself called to be. Yoder says that here we have to do with the "conferring of a mission in history ... this mission is then further defined by the testing into which Jesus moves immediately."[7] Yoder notes that "all the options laid before Jesus are ways of being king."[8]

Yoder thus interprets the temptations as essentially sociopolitical in nature. The first temptation is an economic one: feed the crowds and you will be king. Ironically, the image used of Jesus' second coming in Revelation 19 is the wedding supper of the Lamb. The problem with this temptation is not that the Messiah should be ethereal and otherworldly but rather with the timing. Satan is tempting Jesus to get to the crown directly and not by means of the cross. The second temptation, which is more obviously sociopolitical in nature, is interpreted as an offer of secular power. The offer is rejected, not simply because the offer comes from Satan, but because secular power is not suitable for the carrying out of Jesus' mission. Yoder asks, "Are we to imagine some sort of Satan cult?" He thinks not. Rather, Yoder believes that the concrete meaning of the temptation being put forward here is actually the idolatry of nationalism. Jesus is wrestling, not with the worship of Satan directly, but with the worship of the nation. The point of the story is that nationalism is described as being on the same moral level as Satan-worship. The third temptation, throwing himself down from the pinnacle of the temple and being miraculously saved, is interpreted as a temptation to make a claim for kingship. The punishment for blasphemy was to be hurled down from the pinnacle of the temple, so if Jesus were to be miraculously saved from this punishment, it would validate his messianic claims. Here we see Jesus "contemplating the role of religious reformer, heavenly messenger,

5. Yoder, *Politics of Jesus,* 35.
6. Ibid., 36.
7. Ibid., 24.
8. Ibid., 25.

appearing unheralded from above to set things right."[9] But this too is rejected by Jesus.

Exegesis of this passage has often centered on the personal temptation experienced by a hungry Jesus to make bread for himself to eat, to worship Satan, and to draw attention to himself in a proud and flamboyant manner. The social-economic-political nature of the temptations is often ignored because this passage challenges, in a fundamental manner, the legitimacy of the whole Constantinian ecclesiastical establishment. Wielding economic power over the masses, making use of nationalism and violence, and assuming a divine or semidivine character are the marks of Constantinianism. Yoder is not the first to interpret these temptations in this manner, but it has usually been novelists and other outsiders to the Constantinian establishment (i.e., sectarians) who have seen the issues most clearly.[10]

Jesus' response to growing tensions between his concept of messianity and that of the crowds, on the one hand, and the Jewish leaders, on the other, was to set up a new community, a renewed people of God (Luke 12). Yoder points out that this in itself was revolutionary: "in a society characterized by very stable, religiously undergirded family ties, Jesus is here calling into being a community of *voluntary* commitment."[11] Jesus specifies the way in which this new community is to be different by saying, "The kings of this earth lord it over their subjects; but it shall not be so among you. . . . For I am among you as one who serves" (Luke 22:25–27, Yoder's translation). This new social order is both of this world, in the sense that it is neither a monastery in the wilderness nor a strictly individualistic and private affair, but it is also not of this world, in the sense that it is a community in which servanthood replaces domination and violence is rejected. As Yoder puts it: "The alternative to how the kings of the earth rule is not 'spirituality' but servanthood."[12] Yoder points out that every pericope in Luke 19:47–22:2 reflects in some way the "confrontation of two social systems and Jesus' rejection of the status quo."[13]

---

9. Ibid., 27.

10. See, for example, Fyodor Dostoyevsky's great novel, *The Brothers Karamazov* (trans. A. R. MacAndrew [New York: Bantam Books, 1970]). This novel, first published in 1880, contains a passage (297–318) in which a poem called "The Grand Inquisitor" describes the church's acceptance of Satan's offer that is refused by Jesus in the temptation story. The offer is to make use of "miracle, mystery and authority" rather than simply heralding the truth and giving people the freedom to accept or reject it. The poem is a biting critique not only of the Constantinian church but also of the later communist tyranny, which Dostoyevsky foresaw. According to the Grand Inquisitor, what Satan saw more clearly than Jesus is that people need to be enslaved by promises of having their material needs met by a central authority that gives them a visible object of worship, i.e., the state. What is wrong with communism and Constantinianism is that both ideologies fail the test that Jesus passed when he rejected Satan's version of how to be a messiah.

11. Yoder, *Politics of Jesus*, 37 (emphasis in the original).

12. Ibid., 39.

13. Ibid., 44.

The voluntary nature of the community rules out coercion and makes freedom integral to the nature of the community. For Yoder, the distinction between the church and the world allows for the freedom of non-confession, which in turn allows for the freedom of confession. The kind of leadership to be exercised in this community must be different from that exercised in a community based on coercion, such as the state or the Constantinian church. Servant leadership and voluntary confession are the marks of the community founded by Jesus and are the distinguishing marks of the New Testament doctrine of the church. Only within this kind of community is fellowship based upon love actually possible.

The issue of eschatology is also implicit in Yoder's reading of Luke, along with ecclesiology, and the same issues of the existence of God and the freedom of humanity impinge upon it. Only if God exists and has the power to raise the dead is it possible to believe that accepting suffering to the point of death, rather than resisting violently, can be meaningful action. The point of the resurrection is that Jesus' life and teachings have been vindicated by God, and the point of faith in Jesus is the belief that love is greater than violence and domination because God is love. The fact that Jesus refused to take matters into his own hands is the basis of Yoder's rejection of coercion, violence, and taking matters into our hands as disciples. Jesus demonstrated that doing so is not necessary for the one who trusts in the sovereignty of God over history.

Yoder argues that the temptation for Jesus to take matters into his own hands continued right up to the very end. He thinks that the temptation Jesus wrestled with in the Garden was, once again, the temptation to assume leadership of an armed nationalistic and messianic violent uprising.[14] He notes that Matthew interprets the incident of Peter and the sword by having Jesus say, "Do you think I cannot call on my Father, and he will at once put at my disposal more than twelve legions of angels?" (Matthew 26:53). Yoder comments:

> I have little qualification for surmising what it would have looked like for twelve legions of angels—a Roman legion is said to have been 6,000 soldiers—to come into that garden. But what I can imagine is not very much to the point. Matthew's report is clear, and Matthew *could* imagine that this final encounter with Judas and the Jewish and perhaps Roman police would have been just the point at which God would unleash the apocalyptic holy war, where the miraculous power of the angelic hosts, Jesus' disciples as shock troops, and the crowds in Jerusalem with their long-brewing resentment would rise up in one mighty surge of sacred violence and finally drive the heathen from the land and restore to God's people (as Zechariah had predicted) the possibility to serve YHWH in freedom and without fear.[15]

14. Ibid., 46.
15. Ibid., 47.

Yoder notes that the assistance of warrior angels was a regular element of the Zealot hope. He asserts that just as Jesus was tempted to messianic violence at the very beginning of his ministry (in the desert) and at the turning point (the feeding of the multitude), so he is tempted here for the third time to use violence and coercion to set up the kingdom. The temptation is to disbelieve that God is actually in control of history and, therefore, to assume that one must take matters into one's own hands, using violence if necessary, rather than walk the path of suffering servanthood in obedience to the will of the Father.

In chapter 4 of *Politics,* Yoder explores the Old Testament theme of the holy war in which God fights for his people. The cross is interpreted by Yoder as Jesus' renunciation of violence as the means by which the social order is to be set right. Jesus rejected the Essenes' option of withdrawal, the Herodians' and Sadducees' option of compromise in the name of realism, the Pharisees' option of stressing personal holiness and compromising where necessary in politics, and the Zealots' Maccabean option of violent uprising. Yoder's contention is that Jesus fulfilled the Old Testament by rejecting all these options and choosing the way of the cross.[16]

Yoder contends that, after the exile, "it had become a part of the standard devotional ritual of Israel to look over the nation's history as one of miraculous preservation," which sometimes included the Israelites' military activity and sometimes not.[17] In this light, Yoder contends that it would have been "at least *possible* if not *normal* for those 'waiting for the consolation of Israel' to see in these miraculous deliverances of the Old Testament story a paradigm of the way God would save his people now."[18] This means that Jesus could have addressed concrete sociopolitical issues using the language of kingdom and liberation without endorsing violence (though, of course, such misunderstanding would always be possible), and, in doing so, he could have both understood himself and been understood by others as "updating the faith of Jehoshaphat and Hezekiah."[19]

Jesus was put to death as a threat to the established social order by the authorities, and this threat was real, according to Yoder.[20] The rejection of Jesus was the rejection of the new social option he first embodied and then built out of those who accepted his message. In the acceptance of his message by some, the rejection of it by others, and in the collision between his new messianic community and the power of the state, we see

---

16. These options are more fully developed by Yoder in his essay, "The Original Revolution," *The Original Revolution: Essays on Christian Pacifism* (Scottdale, Pa.: Herald, 1971), 19–20.

17. Yoder, *Politics of Jesus,* 83.

18. Ibid., 84.

19. Ibid.

20. Ibid., 50

the coming of the kingdom into the world. The eschatological tension between a kingdom that is both here and yet not entirely here is the basis of the dramatic tension that runs through the Gospel narratives.

One flaw in this book is that Yoder does not here, though he does in other writings, make as central as he could have the importance of the resurrection to the ability of the story to go on after the crucifixion. He appears to take for granted the fact that it is precisely the resurrection that allows the infant church to survive, develop, and reach out in a hostile environment. He also seems to take for granted that his readers already believe in the atoning death and resurrection of Jesus.[21] Instead of spending much time on the resurrection as such in his discussion of Luke's Gospel, Yoder assumes the resurrection in his discussion of the incarnation in chapter 6, "Trial Balance," where he argues that the function of the New Testament claims for the preexistence and cosmic preeminence of the Word is to "affirm the exclusivity of the revelation claim they were making for Jesus."[22] Thus, his affirmation of the reality of Jesus' resurrection is more implicit than explicit.

Nevertheless, Yoder's major achievement in *Politics* is to have seen that the Jesus of the Gospel narratives is an eschatological Jesus who calls into being an eschatological community that is in tension with the established social order of this world and to have seen, in that depiction of Jesus' person and work, the basis for a social ethic that is distinctively Christian. This reading of the Gospel narrative is one that challenges, and seeks to undermine, other long-established apolitical readings. It is therefore reasonable, before simply accepting it, to pause to reflect upon the hermeneutical principles being used to build up this new reading of Luke.

The profundity of what Yoder has done already in *Politics* should not be underestimated. He mentions in the preface that, on the deepest level, his work "represents an exercise in fundamental philosophical hermeneutics."[23] What does Yoder mean by this characterization of his work? He tells us that he is trying to apply the insights of Biblical Realism, which he says makes it "thinkable that there might be about the biblical vision of reality certain dimensions which refuse to be pushed into the

21. In a very real sense, for Yoder, the resurrection constitutes the new community. Yoder says: "Only from within the community of resurrection is the cruciformity of the cosmos a key rather than a scandal" ("The Hermeneutics of Peoplehood: A Protestant Perspective," *The Priestly Kingdom: Social Ethics As Gospel* [Notre Dame, Ind.: University of Notre Dame Press, 1984], 36). He also claims that it is the resurrection that makes the cross meaningful (*Christian Attitudes to War, Peace and Revolution: A Companion to Bainton* [Elkhart, Ind.: distributed by Co-op Bookstore, 1983], 437).

22. Yoder, *Politics of Jesus*, 99. The thought seems to be: Who would ever imagine a Jesus, of whom preexistence and cosmic preeminence could be predicated, who was not raised from the dead?

23. Ibid., x.

mold of any one contemporary worldview."[24] But this statement requires interpretation and elaboration. Is it possible to describe the hermeneutical moves made in *Politics* more precisely? We can reflect on Yoder's hermeneutics by comparing what he does in *Politics* to what another postliberal author does in another, very different, book on the Gospels.

A Comparison of the Hermeneutics of Yoder and Frei

Just three years after the publication of *The Politics of Jesus*, a quite formal, densely written book by Hans Frei appeared, *The Identity of Jesus Christ: The Hermeneutical Bases of Dogmatic Theology.*[25] A comparison of the books by Frei and Yoder reveals some interesting insights. On the surface the two works exhibit some significantly different attributes. *Politics* is written in a much more free-flowing and rhetorical style, while *Identity* is full of close reasoning and technical thought. Also, while *Identity* is a book on method that never really fleshes out any major constructive theological proposals, *Politics* is the application of a presupposed method to a problem and a statement of ethical conclusions. Furthermore, *Politics* engages the biblical text to a much greater degree than does *Identity*, which is unsurprising given the more methodological focus of *Identity*. Precisely because these two books are so different, a consideration of *Identity* can help illumine Yoder's method. Since *Politics* is so substance-oriented and Frei's book is so methodology-oriented, comparing the two can help bring to light the methodological features of Yoder's book. This is especially true because the two books, for all their differences, share some important similarities.

First, both Frei and Yoder reject what could be termed "systematic or philosophical hermeneutics" (of either an idealist or existentialist type) in favor of what Frei terms a lower-level understanding of hermeneutics as "the rules and principles governing exegesis."[26] Yoder, who later looked back on *Politics* and reflected on his use of Scripture in that book, stated that his concern was to try to let the Bible say what it means without "subjecting it to the superior authority of our own contemporary hermeneutic framework."[27] Both Frei and Yoder make use of historical criticism, but they see it as having limited value for theological exegesis.[28] George Hunsinger's description of the relevance of historical criti-

---

24. Ibid.
25. Hans Frei, *The Identity of Jesus Christ: The Hermeneutical Bases of Dogmatic Theology* (Philadelphia: Fortress, 1975).
26. Frei, *Identity*, xvi. Frei uses adjectives such as "old-fashioned," "low-keyed," and "narrow" to describe his view of hermeneutics.
27. Yoder, "How to Be Read by the Bible," 39.
28. See Yoder, *Politics of Jesus*, 12 n. 17, where Yoder states his openness to historical criticism while asserting its inadequacy as a substitute for engaging the canonical text for constructive Christian ethics.

cism for Frei applies also to Yoder. Hunsinger says that, for Frei, faith needs only two minimal assurances: that the resurrection has not been disconfirmed historically and that a man named Jesus of Nazareth did in fact live, did proclaim the kingdom of God, and was executed.[29] While historical criticism could, theoretically, disprove the resurrection, it never could prove it because the resurrection is an absolutely unique event.[30] Once the basic historicity of the Gospel narratives (in the sense described above) is established, and as long as it is not disconfirmed, theology is free to go on with its work using the narratives of the Gospels as identity descriptions but not as either historical sources or as myths. Yoder uses historical criticism in order to help establish the meaning of the text to a greater degree than Frei, but he has no interest in historical reconstructions of a reality behind the text.[31]

Second, both Frei and Yoder employ an Anselmic/Barthian "faith seeking understanding" method.[32] Frei writes: "I remain convinced that a sound basis for good dogmatic theology demands that a sharp distinction be observed between dogmatic theology and apologetics."[33] He begins, in chapter 1, with the question: "How shall we speak of Christ's presence?" and then says that he is not going to write a "rational defense of the possible or actual truth of the Christian faith."[34] Instead, he tells us, what he is going to write "constitutes a reflection within belief."[35] Yoder, in contrast, is as methodologically reticent in public as Frei is methodologically preoccupied. Most of Yoder's methodological reflections occur in unpublished papers or as clarifications of previously misunderstood writings. The result of this approach is that the reader of *Politics* has no way of knowing whether Yoder's approach in *Politics*, in which he assumes Jesus as authoritative and takes as his task to show

29. George Hunsinger, "What Can Evangelicals and Postliberals Learn from Each Other?" in *The Nature of Confession: Evangelicals and Postliberals in Conversation*, ed. T. R. Phillips and D. L. Okholm (Downers Grove, Ill.: InterVarsity Press, 1996), 143.

30. Frei, *Identity*, 151.

31. See above, n. 3. In this respect, both writers resemble Barth. See Mary K. Cunningham, *What Is Theological Exegesis? Interpretation and Use of Scripture in Barth's Doctrine of Election* (Valley Forge, Pa.: Trinity Press International, 1995).

32. For Barth's Anselmic method, see his *Anselm: Fides Quarens Intellectum: Anselm's Proof of the Existence of God in the Context of His Theological Scheme*, trans. I. W. Robertson (London: SCM, 1960; repr. Pickwick Publications, 1975) and also John Webster, *Barth's Ethics of Reconciliation* (Cambridge: Cambridge University Press, 1995), 218. It should be noted in passing that the "characteristic absence of crisis" that Barth noted in Anselm's theology, which Webster says also characterizes Barth's own theology, is also a feature of Yoder's writings. Mark Thiessen Nation says, "At least as revealed to others, Yoder certainly did not agonize much over issues. That is who he was" ("He Came Preaching Peace: The Ecumenical Peace Witness of John Howard Yoder," *Conrad Grebel Review* 16 [Spring 1998]: 72).

33. Frei, *Identity*, ix.

34. Ibid., 1.

35. Ibid., 4.

that loyalty to Jesus involves something radically different from what most people have thought it meant, is a principled or an incidental one. His other writings do make clear the answer, however. The title of one of his later essays, "Walk and Word: The Alternatives to Methodologism,"[36] expresses his view well. Yoder is not willing to engage in apologetics if that requires imposing a preunderstanding on the text, which limits what the text can say.

Third, both Frei and Yoder are concerned to assert the immediate presence of Jesus Christ to believers so that the Christian life can be one of obedient discipleship rather than autonomous or semiautonomous decision making.[37] In a later reflection on the method of *Politics,* Yoder stated that the particular challenge addressed in that book was "how, once we know what the text says, it has authority for us."[38] Yoder points out that both "orthodox" and "liberal" theologians of Christendom typically have said that the Scriptures undergird some "general anthropology of sin and grace" and "a general doctrine of the rightness of there being a civil order in the world" and then do ethics on the basis of something other than Scripture.[39] In *Politics,* Yoder attempts to reestablish the "immediate relevance of Jesus as liberator and Lord."[40] His basic conviction seems to be that, once we see clearly who Jesus is, we automatically know what it means to follow him and, therefore, what ethical action is fitting.

Frei is doing something similar in *Identity* when he argues, "The governing conviction in this essay is that in Jesus Christ identity and presence are so completely one that they are given to us together: We cannot know who he is without having him present,"[41] and "factual affirmation of him and commitment to him cannot be conceived apart either."[42] Charles L. Campbell draws attention to the "pattern of exchange" in *Identity,* in which Jesus forsakes the power to save himself in order to save others, and comments that Frei fails to note that the way in which Jesus' refusal to take the military option, his decision for powerlessness in the face of the hostile forces of history, is in fact his most profound challenge to those forces and the embodiment of God's reign.[43] He criti-

---

36. John Howard Yoder, "Walk and Word: The Alternatives to Methodologism," in *Theology without Foundations: Religious Practice and the Future of Theological Truth,* ed. S. Hauerwas, N. Murphy, and M. Thiessen Nation (Nashville: Abingdon, 1994), 77–90. See also Yoder, "How to Be Read by the Bible," 26–29.

37. In this respect, both thinkers echo the concerns of Karl Barth. See Webster, *Barth's Ethics of Reconciliation,* 18, and Biggar, *The Hastening That Waits,* 14–15, 120.

38. Yoder, "How to Be Read by the Bible," 17.

39. Ibid.

40. Ibid.

41. Frei, *Identity,* 4.

42. Ibid., 156.

43. Charles L. Campbell, *Preaching Jesus: New Directions for Homiletics in Hans Frei's Postliberal Theology* (Grand Rapids: Eerdmans, 1997), 214.

cizes Frei for not exploring the continuity between Jesus' ministry and his crucifixion-resurrection and the possible ethical implications that could be drawn from the connection. He argues that the connection consists of "Jesus' intentional enactment of the way of nonviolent resistance."[44] Although Frei does not take this step, Campbell contends that his work does at least suggest it. What Frei does formally, Yoder does materially by interpreting the cross in terms of the ministry of Jesus.

Campbell states that, for Frei, Jesus' identity was centered in a "moral decision," so now "the clue to our relationship to Jesus lies not in a 'profound self grasp,' but in moral obedience patterned after that of Jesus."[45] Campbell contends that at the center of that "moral obedience" is the church's nonviolent resistance to the powers of the world. Campbell's words here could easily have been written about Yoder's position. For both Frei and Yoder, it is "the identity of Jesus rendered in the Gospels, which provides the pattern for the life of discipleship."[46]

Fourth, both Frei and Yoder use an intention-action model to describe Jesus' identity.[47] Frei gives the definition of this model: "intention . . . is nothing in itself without enactment. Enactment does not merely illustrate, but constitutes, intention."[48] Who, then, is Jesus for Frei? "He was what he did, the man completely obedient to God in enacting the good of men on their behalf."[49] Frei notes that, in both the Gospel narratives and the apostolic writings that comment on these narratives, Jesus' obedience, rather than faith, is stressed.[50] Jesus' identity is centered on moral action in moving toward a certain goal rather than on his basic, unchanging self-understanding.[51] In the course of the Gospel narrative, the "individual, specific and unsubstitutable identity of Jesus" is more and more clearly set forth until a climax is reached in the resurrection. Frei says, "Indeed, in the Gospel story the human person of Jesus of Nazareth becomes most fully himself in the resurrection."[52] We have seen above how Yoder describes the identity of Jesus by recounting incidents from his life and how Yoder interpreted the narrative as movement toward a goal rather than merely as a series of illustrative stories. Yoder sums up the first half of his book with the words: "his deeds show a coherent, con-

---

44. Ibid., 215.
45. Ibid., 216.
46. Ibid., 212.
47. Both writers appear to be indebted to the narrative Christology of Barth in the fourth volume of *Church Dogmatics* so far as method is concerned. No claims are being made here for the material consistency of the three theologians, although that would be a worthwhile project to explore in and of itself.
48. Frei, *Identity*, 110.
49. Ibid., 111.
50. Ibid., 106.
51. Ibid., 108.
52. Ibid., 49.

scious social-political character and direction, and . . . his words are inseparable therefrom."[53]

These observations lead us to a contrast that needs to be drawn between Yoder and Frei, which highlights a major shortcoming in *Politics*. Despite Yoder's more in-depth and constructive engagement with the text of Scripture in general, at one point there is a glaring lacuna in his presentation, which I have already mentioned: his failure in *Politics* to give sustained attention to the meaning of the resurrection of Jesus for the identity of Jesus. Yoder's focus is on the cross to such an extent that some readers have been misled into thinking that the resurrection is of little importance to Yoder's social ethics. Nothing actually could be further from the truth, but Yoder himself is at least partially responsible for the misunderstanding, and this fact is never more obvious than when Frei's book is set alongside Yoder's.[54]

However, this criticism should not blind us to the fact that both Yoder and Frei are heavily indebted to the theological method of Karl Barth in these two books. Like Barth, both reject philosophical hermeneutics in favor of a low-level use of historical criticism as a way of illumining the meaning of the canonical text, which always remains central in theological reflection. Like Barth, both employ a rational, Anselmic, faith-seeking-understanding method that sets apologetics aside in order to explore the inner logic of belief. Also, like Barth, both attempt to let Jesus Christ himself become immediately present to the believer so that his lordship can be concrete and definite. Finally, like Barth, both employ an intention-action model to describe Jesus' identity, the description of which is their central preoccupation. Clearly, the influence of Barth's method on both of these postliberal theologians is important.

Yoder's goal in the first half of *Politics* was to demonstrate how the Gospel narratives can be read in such a way as to make Jesus relevant to social ethics. On the basis of this discussion of his book, it can now be concluded that he achieved that goal. He has depicted a Jesus who is firmly rooted in the biblical texts and who creates a new social order deliberately calculated to challenge the old one. Yoder has linked the themes of faith in God, the freedom of humanity, and love as the basis of true worship of God together in such a way as to make the cross meaningful as a way of life in a sinful world. Jesus offers a new way of living, but the implication of accepting his offer is a cross. All of this implies a

---

53. Yoder, *Politics of Jesus*, 112. Frei, typically, gives this move a name, insofar as he develops an understanding of Jesus' words as "performative utterances" (*Identity*, 97).

54. This is especially true when one considers that, for Frei, it is in the crucifixion-resurrection sequence that the identity of "the unsubstitutable Jesus of Nazareth who, as that one man, is the Christ and the presence of God" (*Identity*, 137) is most fully revealed. Yoder does not deny the importance of the resurrection, but he leaves himself open to being misconstrued because he treats the cross so explicitly and the resurrection so implicitly. Hence, Yoder is often interpreted as having a low Christology.

certain eschatology and a certain ecclesiology, and Yoder's understanding of these two doctrines will be expounded in chapters 5 through 8 of this book. But before we move on to those topics, we need to focus on the theme of discipleship as the implication of Yoder's view of Jesus' radical social ethic. If the nature of the Christian community is voluntary, and if the only way that the kind of life he calls people to embrace makes sense is on the basis of faith in God, then it stands to reason that personal discipleship precedes and enables entrance into the Christian community. This is the theme that Yoder takes up in the second half of his book.

The Implications of Yoder's Christology for Discipleship

In chapter 7 of *Politics,* Yoder turns from Luke's Gospel to the New Testament epistles to investigate the question of whether or not there is preserved in the various strands of apostolic writings any consciousness of a radical social ethic stemming from Jesus. If the thesis argued in the first half of *Politics* is assumed to have been substantiated and Jesus was, in fact, relevant to and normative for social ethics, then either an awareness of the need of the Christian believer to take seriously that aspect of the Christian life should be present in the apostolic tradition or else there is a major gap between the Gospels and the rest of the New Testament.

1. The New Testament Concept of Discipleship. Yoder directs our attention to a concept that is found throughout the New Testament, namely, that of the correspondence of the believer's behavior and attitude to that of the Lord. Correspondence or participation, in which the believer's behavior or attitude is said to "correspond to," "reflect," or "partake of" the same quality or nature as the Lord's, appears sometimes without any specific terminology. But usually it is expressed in two related verbal traditions: discipleship and imitation. The first tradition centers on the noun "disciple" and the verb meaning "to follow after" or "to learn." The image is of the Israelites "following after" the pillar of cloud. The other tradition focuses on "imitation" language. Its imagery is more structural or mystical in that it can refer both to conformity of behavior and similarity of inner intent or character of which that behavior is expressive. The core idea here is that of the appropriateness of the human being reflecting the nature of God, as in "Be holy, for I am holy" (Leviticus 19:2, Yoder's translation). Yoder concludes that the two concepts are similar enough to treat together.[55]

Yoder quotes the New Testament extensively as he marshals evidence for his contention that the theme of correspondence is pervasive in the apostolic writings. He notes that the language varies but that there is a consistency of thought in the call for the believer to share in the life of

55. Yoder, *Politics of Jesus,* 113–114.

God by being rooted in Christ, dying and rising with Christ, loving and serving as Christ did, and being subordinate as Christ was. Yoder also notes that there is a particular and heavy emphasis placed on the disciple suffering with Christ at the hands of the world instead of exercising dominion, and on doing so without complaint even though innocent. Yoder sums up the witness of the New Testament epistles regarding the meaning of discipleship by saying that the apostles appear to have preserved a "core memory" of their Lord's earthly ministry and centered their ethic on the cross as "a substantial, binding and sometimes costly social stance.[56]

Yoder points out that this body of material has, of course, not gone unnoticed by mainstream Christian ethics, but it has been interpreted differently. Rather than making the "exemplary quality of Jesus' social humanity" a model for our social ethics, the tradition has managed to "appropriate much of the New Testament idiom without catching its central historical thrust."[57] Yoder points to the way in which the phrase "bearing one's cross" is often taken in Protestant pastoral care to mean enduring sickness, accidents, loneliness, or defeat.[58] But, says Yoder, the cross was not an inexplicable or chance event that happened to strike Jesus. It was accepted by him as his destiny when he could have turned away from it. His disciples are warned to count the cost before consciously taking up their own cross (Luke 14:25–33). Another interpretation of the cross has been to make of it an inward experience of the self, as in Thomas Müntzer, Zinzendorf, revivalism, and Christian existentialism. Still another interpretation makes use of cross language to express subjective brokenness and the renunciation of pride and self-will, as in Dietrich Bonhoeffer and the Keswick renewal movements. Yet another interpretation is the concentration on and imitation of the outward form of Jesus' life (forsaking home and property, celibacy, manual labor, barefoot itinerancy) that is found in the "mendicant" tradition such as the Franciscans. But, says Yoder, in the New Testament there is no general concept of imitation.[59]

Yoder sets all these interpretations of the cross aside. While they may have value as emphases more or less warranted in the Christian life, they do not do justice to what the New Testament teaches in the passages cited by Yoder in chapter 7 of *Politics of Jesus.*

There is thus but one realm in which the concept of imitation holds—but there it holds in every strand of the New Testament literature and all the more

56. Ibid., 127.
57. Ibid., 128 n. 33. Yoder mentions the evangelical Carl F. H. Henry as a notable case in point.
58. For what follows, see ibid., 129–30.
59. Ibid., 130.

strikingly by virtue of the absence of parallels in other realms. This is at the point of the concrete social meaning of the cross in its relation to enmity and power. Servanthood replaces dominion, forgiveness absorbs hostility. Thus—and only thus—are we bound by the New Testament to "be like Jesus."[60]

Yoder contends that New Testament discipleship means being like Jesus, following Jesus, and taking up one's cross. What does this concept of discipleship mean for Christian ethics?

2. The New Testament Concept of Discipleship and Christian Ethics. In various ways, throughout his writings, Yoder reflects theologically on the meaning for social ethics of discipleship as the implication of New Testament Christology. He says:

> With regard to the logic of ethical thinking it [discipleship] means that Christian behaviour is Christological, drawing its guidance not from a set of general philosophical principles nor from a collection of codified precise obligations, but from the person and the teachings of Jesus.[61]

Yoder denies that this is an "interim ethic," the credibility of which depends on one's expectation of an imminent end to the world, as Albert Schweitzer contended. It is not derived from any such calculations, he says, "but simply from Christology."[62]

For Yoder, New Testament Christology contains the key to the ultimate meaning of the cosmos:

> By confessing that Messiah has been placed by God above and not within the cosmology and culture of the world they invade, the messianic Jewish witnesses also affirmed that under his lordship that cosmos would find its true coherence and meaning. . . . Even before the broken world can be made whole by the Second Coming, the witnesses to the first coming—through the very fact that they proclaim Christ above the powers, the Son above the angels—are enabled to go on proleptically in the redemption of creation. Only this evangelical Christology can found a truly transformationalist approach to culture.[63]

The Christian community knows that the cross reveals the ultimate meaning of reality and the true nature of God.[64] Therefore, it is enabled

60. Ibid., 131.

61. John Howard Yoder, "The Recovery of the Anabaptist Vision," *Concern* 18 (July 1971): 14.

62. John Howard Yoder, "A People in the World," *The Royal Priesthood: Essays Ecclesiological and Ecumenical,* ed. Michael Cartwright (Grand Rapids: Eerdmans, 1994), 95.

63. John Howard Yoder, "'But We Do See Jesus': The Particularity of Incarnation and the Universality of Truth," *Priestly Kingdom,* 60–61.

64. As Joel Zimbleman rightly sees, Yoder's starting point in ethics is a reflection on the divine nature ("Theological Ethics and Politics in the Thought of Juan Luis Segundo and John Howard Yoder" [unpublished Ph.D. diss., University of Virginia, 1986], 193).

to suffer patiently while bearing witness to this fact, consoled by the cheerful expectation that the truth revealed in the Lord Jesus Christ can be denied but never overcome.

Yoder believes that this understanding of Christian ethics as following Jesus was a source of the nonresistant convictions of the early Anabaptists. Unlike most mainstream Reformation historiography, which tends to paint all the Anabaptists with the same brush of legalism, Yoder argues that article 6 of the Schleitheim Confession links ethics and Christology in such a way as to ground the rejection of the sword, not in prooftexts, but in conformity to Christ.[65] This, and this alone, is the point at which the sixteenth-century Anabaptist vision is relevant to us today.[66]

This concept of discipleship enables martyrdom, which is an essential aspect of the witness to the kingdom of God in this present world. Although Yoder fails to give sufficient attention to the resurrection of Christ in *The Politics of Jesus,* he does make up the deficit in other contexts by stressing that the cross that is central in Christian ethics only makes sense in the post-Easter context. For example, Yoder says:

> As the cross becomes meaningful in the New Testament only in relation to the resurrection and to Pentecost, so in sectarian ethics is forgiving grace rightly understood only in the context of enabling grace. Interpreting justification by faith as a ratification for conscious compromise with the presence of sin is what Paul calls "sinning that grace may abound;" what Bonhoeffer called "cheap grace."[67]

The cross-resurrection of Jesus not only provides an example for, but also elicits a response from, the believer. It not only reveals the truth about the cosmos but also draws the disciple into behavior that corresponds to the divine action in Jesus Christ, specifically at the point of taking up one's cross.

In this way, the meaning of the cross for Yoder is not outside of history, as it is for Reinhold Niebuhr. As Ronald Stone comments in describing the thought of his mentor: "the crucifixion was the ultimate symbol of love's fate; the resurrection was a symbol of an ahistorical fulfillment of love."[68] But for Yoder, the behavior of the disciple can correspond *in his-*

---

65. Yoder, *Christian Attitudes to War,* 185.

66. See the discussion of this point above in chapter 1.

67. John Howard Yoder, "The Anabaptist Dissent: The Logic of the Place of the Disciple in Society," *Concern* 1 (June 1954): 60.

68. Ronald Stone, *Professor Reinhold Niebuhr: Mentor to the Twentieth Century* (Louisville: Westminster/John Knox, 1992), 107. Richard Hays asks if Niebuhr really thinks of Jesus as a historical human being, notes the influence of Paul Tillich on Niebuhr's theology, and offers this comment on Niebuhr's Christology: "It is difficult to see how Niebuhr's account of the ethic of Jesus avoids the pitfalls of docetism" (*Moral Vision of the New Testament,* 218). This is a "Yoderian" criticism of Niebuhr.

tory to the action of God in Christ, precisely because God acted in Christ *in history.* Gayle Gerber Koontz summarizes Yoder's concern at this point nicely:

> At the root of Yoder's ethical work is the assumption that in Christ humans see the kind of humanity that is pleasing to God. Such humanity both reveals and is derived from the nature of God and is defined fundamentally by agape, unconditional love of others. Therefore, the pattern or example of the historical Jesus has direct import for Christian ethics.[69]

The concept of correspondence, which Yoder sees as the core idea deployed in the New Testament teaching on discipleship and imitation, is important to Barth's theological ethics as well. Critics of Barth who accuse him of having a monism in which no room is allowed for meaningful human action fail to appreciate the radical challenge to modernity inherent in Barth's reconception of fully human action as action that is enabled and elicited by God's action and, more specifically, God's action in Jesus Christ. In a discussion of Barth's view of prayer, John Webster speaks of "a complex Christological statement, which both strongly affirms the vicarious character of Jesus' human action and yet does not suppress the reality of genuine human analogies to that which is accomplished outside the realm of our agency."[70] The language of correspondence, Webster points out,

> furnishes a way of affirming both the unique, incommunicable nature of God's action . . . and the reality of the human "venture of action." To embark on that venture is not to aspire to become co-regents with God, but rather to enter into and act out an order which, in its specificity and limitation, receives and testifies to the generative action of God in Christ. . . . That, in sum, is what it means to be creature and covenant partner of the God and Father of our Lord Jesus Christ.[71]

Yoder's concept of obedient discipleship as the implication of his narrative Christology is substantially the same as that of Barth. Both differ from most modern accounts of human action, which emphasize the autonomous, value-creating, choosing self as the prerequisite for genuinely moral action. The result is that both Barth and Yoder develop an approach to Christian ethics that stands in tension with most modern approaches to ethics, whether they are idealist or existentialist, Marxist or liberal.

69. Gayle Gerber Koontz "Confessional Theology in a Pluralistic Context: A Study of the Theological Ethics of H. Richard Niebuhr and John H. Yoder" (unpublished Ph.D. diss., Boston University, 1985), 81.
70. Webster, *Barth's Ethics of Reconciliation,* 78.
71. Ibid., 80.

L. Gregory Jones notes that Protestant theology has been nervous about language such as "imitation of Christ," "friendship with God," and "virtue" because it appears to "detach the moral life from the objective accomplishment of human righteousness in Christ."[72] The result of this reticence to talk about such issues is that "the subject as an ethical agent with duration through history is eliminated or at least paralyzed by the sole agency of Christ."[73] Jones calls for

> a way of speaking of the prior action of God, namely the saving life, death, and resurrection of Jesus Christ, which also calls forth an account of the shape human activity is to take in response. Such an emphasis is found by recovering the relationship between being *conformed* to Christ and being called to imitate—or, as I think is preferable language, *to pattern one's life in*—Christ.[74]

What Barth provides in his ethics is such a way of speaking, and Yoder has built upon this concept of ethics by exploring the social-ethical implications of it.

On the basis of this understanding of Yoder's ethics, it is clear that those who criticize Yoder for being arbitrary in his choice of the cross as the point at which we are to follow Jesus[75] and those who accuse him of selective prooftexting[76] have simply not analyzed his thought with sufficient care. Likewise, the criticism that Yoder should not make pacifism an absolute prescription when so many other Christian moral principles are not treated this way does not take account of Yoder's grounding of discipleship in New Testament Christology.[77] I conclude that Yoder has demonstrated that his concept of social ethics as discipleship—following Jesus in the way of peace—is rooted in the Christology of the New Testament. But can this interpretation of biblical Christology and its implications for discipleship be meshed with the classical christological orthodoxy of the ecumenical creeds of the ancient church? That is the question I seek to address in the next chapter.

---

72. L. Gregory Jones, *Transformed Judgment: Toward a Trinitarian Account of the Moral Life* (Notre Dame, Ind.: University of Notre Dame Press, 1990), 109.

73. Ibid., 110.

74. Ibid.

75. For example, Robert M. Parham, "An Ethical Analysis of the Christian Social Strategies in the Writings of John C. Bennett, Jacques Ellul and John Howard Yoder" (unpublished Ph.D. diss., Baylor University, 1984), 197.

76. Philip LeMasters, *The Import of Eschatology in John Howard Yoder's Critique of Constantinianism* (San Francisco: Mellen Research University Press, 1992), 54–55, 66–67.

77. It is puzzling that Zimbleman makes this criticism ("Theological Ethics and Politics," 310), since he apparently understands clearly that Yoder is not being arbitrary in picking and choosing his moral principles.

4

Classical Orthodoxy and Social Ethics

In the last chapter, I argued for a view of Yoder's social ethics as being rooted in a narrative, postliberal Christology that preserves theological realism and has, as its implication, a concept of ethics as discipleship. But the question that has yet to be addressed, and that inevitably arises with regard to Yoder's Christology, is the question of how compatible his understanding of Christology is with that of classical orthodoxy as expressed in the Nicene and Chalcedonian creeds. It is unfortunate that Yoder's class lectures *Preface to Theology: Christology and Theological Method* were only informally published and, therefore, are not more widely known. It is in this work that Yoder directly addresses the development of christological orthodoxy in the first five centuries of the Christian era. We first need to examine Yoder's reading of this development in order to provide the basis for an accurate response to this question in the final section of this chapter, where the charge of reductionism will be examined.

Yoder's Affirmation of the Creeds

In chapter 1, I sketched out an account of Yoder's historicism, which described it as being thoroughgoing except at the key point of the incarnation. Even there, Yoder is quite concerned to say that the event was historical. But what we mean by the incarnation is that we believe that that one, particular, historical event, in all of its historical particularity, is actually revelatory of the Creator God. Since Yoder accepts this doctrine, he is not a theological or ethical relativist.

Not everyone is convinced of this assessment, however. James Reimer interprets Yoder as conforming to modern historicism:

> In an anti-metaphysical and anti-ontological age like ours, which has, it appears almost totally lost a concept of radical transcendence—a belief in the first article of the creed—to emphasize the historical-political essence of the kerygma is in fact not a radical critique of the fundamental assumptions of the modern world (as Yoder intends it to be) but a tacit acknowledgement of modern historicist assumptions.[1]

This evaluation of Yoder would be accurate if the doctrine of the incarnation were not central to Yoder's theology. Then Yoder would logically have no way to prevent his historicism from leading to an absolute relativism, since he does reject the possibility of finding a universal method that can establish truth for everyone. However, given the nature of the gospel, Yoder says:

> we must not abandon the claim that the validity of what we believe is founded on grounds more solid than whim, flipping a coin, accident, or provincial bias. Instead of seeking to escape particular identity, what we need, then, is a better way to restate the meaning of a truth claim from within particular identity.[2]

Yoder affirms the ontological truth of the gospel and the necessity of proclaiming it as true for all who hear it because the gospel is the message of the incarnation.

In *Preface to Theology,* Yoder discusses the development of the Apostles' Creed from the simple New Testament statement "Jesus is Lord" into a baptism formula that outlines the essentials of the Christian faith.[3] The second article is the longest and the only one of the three that retains any sign of the original narrative character of the Gospels.[4] Yoder says that

---

1. A. James Reimer, "The Nature and Possibility of a Mennonite Theology," *Conrad Grebel Review* 8 (Spring 1990): 41.

2. John Howard Yoder, "On Not Being Ashamed of the Gospel: Particularity, Pluralism, and Validation," *Faith and Philosophy* 9 (1992): 290.

3. John Howard Yoder, *Preface to Theology: Christology and Theological Method* (Elkhart, Ind.: distributed by Co-op Bookstore, 1981), 103.

4. Ibid., 103–4. Yoder notes that the second article is made up of participles describing Christ, while the first and third articles have no verbs except the "I believe," which introduces each article. The text of the second article is as follows: "[I believe] in Jesus Christ, His only Son, our Lord, Who was conceived by the Holy Spirit, born of the Virgin Mary, suffered under Pontius Pilate, was crucified, dead and buried. He descended to hell, on the third day rose again from the dead, ascended to heaven, sits at the right hand of God the Father almighty, thence He will come to judge the living and the dead" (*Creeds of the Churches: A Reader in Christian Doctrine from the Bible to the Present,* ed. John H. Leith, rev. ed. [Atlanta: John Knox, 1973], 24).

the centrality of Christology is still clear here, although, unlike the New Testament kerygma, there is no call to repentance and the "fullness of time" theme is missing.[5]

Yoder follows the thread of doctrinal development through the first four centuries to Nicea. He treats creedal development historically and considers intellectual, political, and linguistic factors that fed into the process. He describes the various heretical positions, such as Ebionitism, Docetism, Modalism, and Arianism. The basic problem with which the church wrestled during this process was how to preserve the New Testament concept that "Jesus, the Word in Jesus, is genuinely of the character of deity and genuinely human, and that his work is the work of God and yet the work of a man"[6] as it moved from the still-Hebraic context of Hellenistic Judaism, out of which the New Testament documents emerged, to the Greek philosophical context of the wider Greco-Roman world. The church wanted to affirm both the deity of Jesus and monotheism.

Yoder says that the Nicene solution (which grew out of Tertullian's terminological distinction between person and substance), in which *person* (Latin *persona,* Greek *hypostasis*) refers to the threeness of God and *substance* (Latin *substantia,* Greek *ousia*) refers to the oneness of God, was the solution to a verbal formality, but it was a verbal formality that met a real need because it "safeguards the New Testament content . . . in a different thought world."[7] The *homoousios* of Jesus and the Father preserves the core of New Testament teaching,[8] insofar as it allows the church to affirm Jesus' deity without abandoning monotheism. All this sounds very affirming of the creeds.

James Reimer, however, calls into question Yoder's commitment to creedal orthodoxy. He rightly points out that Yoder is engaged in a polemic against individualistic, existentialist, and spiritualistic interpretations of Christianity and further contends that Yoder, therefore, emphasizes the historical-eschatological character of the faith at the expense of the metaphysical and the ontological.[9] The problem with Reimer's assessment of Yoder's position is that he fails to make a crucial distinction between Yoder's epistemology and his ontology. He assumes that, because Yoder rejects a foundationalist epistemology, he must not really mean (or is being inconsistent in asserting) that the gospel is ontologically true. Reimer observes that Yoder treats the Logos doctrine of Christ and the trinitarian and christological creedal formulations with "remarkable sympathy."[10] But why should it be remarkable that Yoder would do

5. Yoder, *Preface to Theology,* 104.
6. Ibid., 138.
7. Ibid.
8. Ibid., 135.
9. Reimer, "The Nature and Possibility of a Mennonite Theology," 43.
10. Ibid.

this? Reimer is convinced that Yoder's emphasis on the historical-eschatological character of Christian faith has to be *at the expense of* the metaphysical-ontological character of the faith. But this is certain only if we assume a necessary connection between the existence of ontological truth and the existence of a rational method by which anyone can access that truth; thus, if one does not have a universal method for getting to truth, one cannot claim to know truth. Yoder would say: Why not, if your claim is that, instead of you getting to the truth, the Truth has instead come to you?[11]

Reimer has argued in a series of articles that Yoder's position is incompatible with the trinitarian and christological affirmations of the ecumenical creeds, which (ironically, since Reimer himself is a Mennonite) is just what many Roman Catholic and Protestant theologians assume must be the case with any Anabaptist writer.[12] Reimer says: "The ancient ecumenical creeds, particularly in their Trinitarian affirmations, represented a coming together of Athens and Jerusalem that I believe to be important for Christian theology and ethics."[13] He finds this perspective lacking in Yoder and other nonfoundationalists. Reimer goes on to say that, although the theological orthodoxy of the first five centuries "stands in fundamental continuity with the Scriptures, it went beyond the Scriptures in formulating a uniquely Christian doctrine of God."[14] He also criticizes Yoder for underestimating the discontinuity between Judaism and Christianity, then asks, "Is one not finally faced with some radically new developments in the Christian understanding of God that include the move toward Nicea and Chalcedon, incorporating both Judaism and Hellenism in a new third way?"[15] Reimer laments the "tragic nature of the historic split between Judaism and Christianity, and the consequent anti-Semitism,"[16] but he asserts that "to claim that in the first 500 years following the death of Christ a new 'religion' with a distinctive 'doctrine of God' evolved surely does not necessarily entail supercessionism and anti-Semitism."[17]

11. John Howard Yoder, "'But We Do See Jesus': The Particularity of Incarnation and the Universality of Truth," *The Priestly Kingdom: Social Ethics As Gospel* (Notre Dame, Ind.: University of Notre Dame Press, 1984), 62.

12. See especially Reimer, "The Nature and Possibility of a Mennonite Theology"; idem, "Trinitarian Orthodoxy, Constantinianism and Theology from a Radical Protestant Perspective," in *Faith to Creed: Ecumenical Perspectives on the Affirmation of the Apostolic Faith in the Fourth Century*, ed. S. Mark Heim (Grand Rapids: Eerdmans, 1991), 127–61; and idem, "Theological Orthodoxy and Jewish Christianity: A Personal Tribute to John Howard Yoder," in *The Wisdom of the Cross: Essays in Honor of John Howard Yoder*, ed. Stanley Hauerwas et al. (Grand Rapids: Eerdmans, 1999), 430–48.

13. Reimer, "Theological Orthodoxy and Jewish Christianity," 436.

14. Ibid., 437.

15. Ibid., 448.

16. Ibid., 447.

17. Ibid., 448.

It is difficult to know just how to interpret what Reimer means at this point. How seriously should we take his statements about the Christian doctrine of God being distinct from the Jewish-Christian one? Does Reimer actually mean to say that Christianity as expressed in the ecumenical creeds is a synthesis of Judaism and Hellenism, as opposed to being a restatement of biblical teaching in Hellenistic thought forms? Reimer's claim that the "the central theological affirmations found in classical orthodoxy are needed to undergird the very moral and ethical claims that Yoder witnesses to so singularly"[18] is surely correct. I agree that a high Christology is essential to Yoder's entire system. Why, then, does Reimer persist in questioning Yoder's commitment to orthodoxy? One reason has already been mentioned—Reimer's assumption that epistemological nonfoundationalism necessarily entails ontological relativism—but there may be a deeper reason.

We can get at this issue by asking what Reimer and Yoder respectively mean by *God*. Yoder clearly affirms that the God of the New Testament, the Father of Jesus Christ, is the same God as the Old Testament Creator and the God of the Apostles' and Nicene creeds. For Yoder, the Old and New Testaments and the creeds all speak of the same God. What the creeds do, as far as Yoder is concerned, is to reject all statements about God that are not compatible with the biblical narrative centered on Jesus Christ as the incarnation of God.

Is this the case for Reimer? Probably it is, although some of the unguarded statements quoted above might lead one to conclude that Reimer sees the distinctively Christian doctrine of God as deriving some of its substance from Greek philosophy and some of its substance from the Bible. Or one could interpret him as saying that the creeds identify Aristotle's "Unmoved Mover" with the biblical God. Since the Middle Ages, Christian theology has often made this move. A Greek concept of God is fused with the biblical concept of God, with the result that the biblical proclamation gains "credibility" by being identified with the highest and best insights of the wider pagan world. The incorporation of natural theology into Christian theology is totally rejected by Barth and also by Yoder. This rejection can be seen in Yoder's account of the rejection of Arianism by the church at Nicea.

The conflict between the views of Arius and Athanasius lasted over a century. Yoder is fully aware of the political factors that entered into the decision at the Council of Nicea in 325 and of the long struggle over the next fifty years, during which imperial politics, popular opinion, and theological debate were all part of the mix leading to the Council of Constantinople in 381. He notes further that the "Nicene Creed" was not really recognized until 431. Yoder says that most of the emperors and court officials during this period favored Arianism, while Athanasius enjoyed

18. Ibid.

117

more popular support. Arianism was a more fitting imperial ideology, claims Yoder, because

> if you lower your concept of who Christ was, then you raise your vision of the emperor, because the logos was in both Jesus and the emperor. We saw, way back in Proverbs that it is by the wisdom of God that the kings reign. Well if Jesus is a little smaller, the king will be a little higher, and that is just what Constantine and his advisors wanted.[19]

Yoder says that it was also the case that the masses, who were moving into the church after it became the official religion of the empire, found Arianism more appealing because "it is respectable, it is popular, it is intelligent, it is an edifying and high religion." They did not want to "be bothered too much about Jesus in particular, or about the Jewish-Hebrew strain of Christian thought."[20] In addition, the Athanasian position was becoming identified with popularization, the ignorance of the common people, and the asceticism of the monastic movement, which was seen as anticulture and anti-intellectual. Yoder concludes: "Arius had a lot on his side. But Athanasius finally won out."[21] Reasons for this outcome include the support of Athanasius by the churches in the West, the staying power and moral character of Athanasius, and the efforts over time of Athanasius's friends (the Cappadocians), who worked out the logic and language of his position so that it became more compelling.

Is the doctrine of the Trinity valid for all cultures and all times? Yoder's answer to this question is two-sided. On the one hand, this doctrine is not itself biblical revelation. Yoder points to the medieval scholastic distinction between truths that can be known by natural reason and truths that can be known only by revelation. Which is the doctrine of the Trinity? It certainly is not known by natural reason, but it was not given by revelation either. It is not found in the New Testament. Rather, it is "something the Cappadocians figured out in the fourth century." But, on the other hand, it is "the solution of an intellectual difficulty which arises if we accept the statements of the Bible." Yoder says:

> The doctrine of the Trinity is a test of whether your commitment to Jesus and to God are biblical enough that you will have the problem which the doctrine of the Trinity solves. It may be that there will be other solutions, other words, other phrasings, or ways to avoid tripping over the problem the way the Greek fathers did. But we will have to do it with the same commitment to the man Jesus, and the same commitment to the unique God which those Fathers had, or else we have left the Christian family.[22]

19. Yoder, *Preface to Theology*, 136.
20. Ibid.
21. Ibid.
22. Ibid., 140.

In short, the Trinity guards and expresses biblical truth that is essential to the Christian faith.

Yoder's thought here is similar to George Lindbeck's rule theory of doctrine. For Lindbeck, the doctrine of the Trinity expresses three regulative principles: (1) "there is only one God, the God of Abraham, Isaac, Jacob and Jesus," (2) "the stories of Jesus refer to a genuine human being who was born, lived and died in a particular time and place," and (3) "every possible importance is to be ascribed to Jesus that is not inconsistent with the first two rules."[23] Yoder states: "Any doctrine, but especially a doctrine of this kind, is basically a set of assumptions about how we are going to use words and rules about what certain words ought to be used to mean and ought not."[24] For both Lindbeck and Yoder, this is a theory about how doctrines, as second-order language, regulate the first-order language of Christian worship and proclamation.[25] The rule-theory of doctrine as such does not necessarily entail theological realism, but it is compatible with a realist understanding of first-order Christian language. While there has been considerable debate about the interpretation of Lindbeck and Frei's postliberalism, namely, whether or not they affirm realism,[26] there can be little doubt of Yoder's Biblical Realism.

Yoder takes the position that the Athanasian view is the biblical one, while the Arian view is the one that fits best with Constantinianism, even though the Athanasian position prevailed to become the creedal orthodoxy of the imperial church. Reimer, however, says that it not clear whether Yoder views Nicene orthodoxy and Constantinianism to be part of the same movement. His evidence for this suspicion is that Yoder interprets the Council of Nicea in a sociopolitical framework, and this makes him suspicious of its formulations.[27] But Yoder's refusal to assume in advance the infallibility of the creeds is a function of his view of the authority of the canon of Scripture and its christological center. It does not, in the end, lead Yoder to deny the validity of the Nicene Creed.

Reimer notes Yoder's claim that the fall of the church occurred not in the fourth century, but in the second century when the apologists began

23. George Lindbeck, *The Nature of Doctrine: Religion and Theology in a Postliberal Age* (Philadelphia: Westminster/John Knox, 1984), 94.

24. Yoder, *Preface to Theology*, 136.

25. Michael Cartwright also notes that Yoder treats the doctrine of the Trinity as a second-order doctrine ("Practices, Politics, and Performance: Toward a Communal Hermeneutic for Christian Ethics" [unpublished Ph.D. diss., Duke University, 1988], 425).

26. See, for example, the doubts expressed by Alister McGrath ("An Evangelical Evaluation of Postliberalism," in *The Nature of Confession: Evangelicals and Postliberals in Conversation*, ed. T. R. Phillips and D. L. Okholm (Downers Grove, Ill.: InterVarsity Press, 1996), 35ff. My view, however, is that Jeffrey Hensley's argument that Lindbeck is an antifoundationalist thinker who is in principle open to metaphysical realism is convincing ("Are Postliberals Necessarily Antirealists? Reexamining the Metaphysics of Lindbeck's Postliberal Theology," in *The Nature of Confession*, 69–80).

27. Reimer, "Trinitarian Orthodoxy, Constantinianism and Theology," 136–37.

to downplay Jewish particularity.[28] But Yoder does not simplistically assume that Constantinianism happened overnight, and he does not see the "fall" as an all-or-nothing proposition. His portrayal of the church's fall is that of a gradual process. He affirms that biblical orthodoxy was still too strong simply to be set aside at this early point in church history. So the imperial power and the church entered into an alliance, rather than the church being completely taken over all at once. In this context, biblical orthodoxy (in the form of the Athanasian *homoousios*) remained within the bosom of the Constantinian church—its radical, social-ethical implications latent but not purged. This means that when Yoder speaks of the "fall of the church," as all branches of the Reformation did in the sixteenth century, he does not mean the total destruction of the church. Yoder thus in this regard is a reformer, not a restitutionist.

What Yoder is referring to, in pushing the beginning of the church's fall back to the second century, is the incipient Arianism that can be seen in the apologists. On this point he is supported by Aloys Grillmeier, who says: "The coming Arian struggles are no more than the consequences of the error which was introduced at the time of the Apologists. The error lay in the fact that the Stoic Logos was essentially monistic."[29] Reimer also recognizes that "It was the Arians who (influenced by middle Platonist cosmology) Hellenized the Gospel and tended to see Christ as a 'demigod' philosophically understood."[30] Reimer goes on to say that the trinitarian faith of Nicea was much truer to the biblical Christ than the theological positions of most theologians from the second century on. Yoder and Reimer are in agreement on this point.

Yoder continues his survey of the development of Christology up to Chalcedon by pointing out that the church, having affirmed the unity of Jesus and the Father, now had the problem of how to relate the Son of God to the man Jesus.[31] Again he surveys the various schools and heretical positions. If, in the fourth century, the influence of imperial politics on theological debate was strong, though not necessarily decisive, by the fifth century the balance was shifting toward more influence for politics than theology. Yoder notes the irony that Nestorius as a person was condemned as a heretic, while the substance of the Nestorian position was largely affirmed as orthodoxy.[32] After Chalcedon, many churches left the orthodox fellowship. Around the Eastern end of the empire various churches, which adhered to the monophysite position, broke off as national units. The Nestorian churches of Syria and beyond were pushed

28. Reimer, "Theological Orthodoxy and Jewish Christianity," 447.

29. Aloys Grillmeier, *From the Apostolic Age to Chalcedon*, 2d rev. ed., trans. John Bowden, vol. 1 of *Christ in Christian Tradition* (Atlanta: Westminster/John Knox, 1975), 110.

30. Reimer, "Trinitarian Orthodoxy, Constantinianism and Theology," 153.

31. Yoder, *Preface to Theology*, 148.

32. Ibid., 153.

out. Imperial unity gradually gained ascendancy over ecclesiastical unity. Despite the fact that the monophysite churches led by Alexandria left, the day-to-day life of the orthodox church remained monophysite, and the deity of Jesus tended to swallow up the humanity.

In evaluating the formula of Chalcedon, Yoder states that the controversy was a test of the seriousness of Nicea. If one takes seriously the statements that Jesus is divine and one with the Father, one must answer the question of how the divinity and humanity of Jesus go together.[33] Yoder notes that all the Eastern churches (both inside and outside the empire) tended to emphasize Jesus' deity at the expense of his humanity and continue to do so today. The birth of Jesus matters most: "We could say that this is a doctrine of salvation by birth."[34] The Roman Catholic tradition exalts Jesus as Lord and coming Judge: "Revelation is not in him, not in the book either. It is in the Church which he has mandated to work in the world."[35] For Protestantism (and, Yoder suggests, for the New Testament), Jesus' humanity matters more because it is the necessary prerequisite for what God wants to do with humankind: "The center, then, for Protestant thought, is neither on Incarnation nor on the authority given to the church to administer grace, but on what Jesus did as a man, giving himself."[36]

Yoder consistently emphasizes the humanity of Jesus, not because he does not accept Jesus' deity, but because he judges that the greatest danger in the church has been that of denying the humanity, rather than the deity, of Jesus. Those who came to theological maturity in the twentieth century, after nineteenth-century liberalism had caused a sensation by denying Jesus' deity, have been brought up in an atypical period of church history. In most periods, the problem has been that the humanity of Jesus has not been taken seriously enough, and that is still the problem in most of the more vitally alive parts of the church today. Yoder wants to remind the church that both the deity *and the humanity* of Jesus Christ are part of christological orthodoxy and that the denial of *either one* is the denial of orthodoxy. Hence, Yoder starts with the biblical teachings that the doctrines of the Trinity and the two natures were designed to affirm and stresses the humanity, the historical particularity, and the historicity of Jesus, and what that half of christological orthodoxy means for social ethics. A rule-theory of doctrine emerges once again as Yoder summarizes his own position on the creeds:

> The Creeds are helpful as fences, but affirming, believing, debating for, fighting for the Creeds, is probably something which a radical Anabaptist kind of

33. Ibid.
34. Ibid., 155.
35. Ibid.
36. Ibid.

faith would not concentrate on doing. Yet that gives us even less reason to join with Bishop Pike and Bishop Robinson in fighting against the Creeds. They are part of the only history we have. It is a fallible history and a confused history. A lot of dirty politics was involved in getting them defined, in explaining their meaning, and still more in applying their authority. But this is the history to which God has chosen to lead his confused people toward perhaps at least a degree of understanding of certain dangers, certain things not to say if we are to remain faithful.[37]

Yoder does not place the exact wording of the ecumenical creeds on the same level as the apostolic witness of the New Testament, but he affirms the New Testament teaching that they were concerned to protect from distortion. His historicism leads him to be suspicious of attributing absolute truth to any proposition just because it is enshrined within a historic creed. But Yoder's historicism, qualified as it is at the point of the New Testament proclamation of "God with us," does not lead him to doctrinal relativism either.

At this point, we need to draw together the threads of the argument of this section on Yoder's reading of the history of Christology. Three main points need to be emphasized. First, Yoder's historicism is qualified at the crucial point of the incarnation, which allows him to affirm wholeheartedly the biblical proclamation that God has become human in the man Jesus. Second, Yoder's nonfoundationalist epistemology should not be seen as calling in question his affirmation of the incarnation, since he affirms the incarnation on the basis of revelation, not reason. He believes that it is perfectly possible to believe (and herald) what one cannot prove by means of some sort of "neutral" or "scientific" method. Third, Yoder sees the Nicene and Chalcedonian creeds as protecting the biblical proclamation about Jesus, expressed mostly in narrative form in Scripture, by means of Greek thought forms. The content of biblical monotheism and the deity of Jesus are protected from a pagan form of monotheism that is incompatible with the incarnation and deity of Jesus Christ. For Yoder, the doctrine of the *homoousios* of the Father and the Son is not the result of the synthesis of a pagan concept of God with the biblical concept of God. Rather, it is foolishness to the Greeks and the confession of the mystery with which the church is left when she confesses both that Jesus is God and that God is one.

The Debate with H. R. Niebuhr over the Doctrine of the Trinity

Having examined Yoder's reading of the development of orthodox Christology, we are almost ready to move to the final section of this chap-

37. Ibid., 157–58.

ter, a consideration of the charge of reductionism. Before doing so, however, I want to examine Yoder's critique of H. R. Niebuhr's use of the doctrine of the Trinity because the contrast between the two theologians will
clarify Yoder's position. Yoder's use of the doctrine of the Trinity in constructive theological work is just as important, if not more so, to an evaluation of his true position on christological orthodoxy as is his historical
treatment of the creeds. Mainline liberal critiques of the type of position
represented by Yoder sometimes use, as H. R. Niebuhr did, the doctrine
of the Trinity in such a way as to imply that the Yoderian position does
not take account of the full-orbed doctrine of the Trinity. I want to turn
this argument around, however, and put forward the view that Yoder's
doctrine of the Trinity is in substantial continuity with Nicene orthodoxy,
while Niebuhr's is not.

Yoder notes that, in *Christ and Culture*,[38] Niebuhr uses the doctrine of
the Trinity to critique the radical "Christ against culture" position.[39] Niebuhr charges the radicals (of whom he gives as examples the author of
1 John, Tertullian, "certain sectarians," and Leo Tolstoy) with failing to
grasp adequately the meaning of the Christian doctrine of the Trinity. They
fail to grasp that the confession of orthodox Christian faith means that the
revelation in Jesus Christ needs to be kept in balance with the revelation of
the Father in nature and culture and that of the Spirit in the church and
history. Niebuhr asserts that "radical Christians . . . regard the development of Trinitarian theology to be a result of the introduction of a cultural
philosophy into the Christian faith, rather than a consequence of believers' efforts to understand what they believe."[40] Yoder also points to Niebuhr's famous article, "The Doctrine of the Trinity and the Unity of the
Church,"[41] which was published just three years before he gave the lectures which were later published as *Christ and Culture*, in which Niebuhr
criticizes certain segments of the church for a "Unitarianism of the Son."[42]

What is going on in Niebuhr's article? In order to understand why Yoder
does not feel that Niebuhr's critique has force against the "sectarian" or
"radical" position, it is important to answer this question as carefully as
possible. Niebuhr tells us that he wants to restate the doctrine of the Trinity for the modern age so that it has ecumenical significance. It appears
that, for Niebuhr, an ecumenical doctrine is one that sanctions theological
pluralism under the tent of Christianity. Niebuhr says that his restated

38. H. R. Niebuhr, *Christ and Culture* (New York: Harper & Row, 1951).

39. John Howard Yoder, "How H. Richard Niebuhr Reasons: A Critique of *Christ and
Culture*," Glen H. Stassen, D. M. Yeager, and John Howard Yoder in *Authentic Transforma-
tion: A New Vision of Christ and Culture*, (Nashville: Abingdon, 1996), 35. See Niebuhr,
Christ and Culture, 80–82.

40. Niebuhr, *Christ and Culture*, 114.

41. H. R. Niebuhr, "The Doctrine of the Trinity and the Unity of the Church," *Theology
Today* 3 (1946): 371–84.

42. Ibid., 374–75.

doctrine of the Trinity "will be an ecumenical doctrine providing not for the exclusion of heretics but for their inclusion in the body on which they are actually dependent."[43] In his article, he brands almost everyone in church history as being a unitarian of one sort or another. There are unitarians of the Creator, unitarians of the Son, and unitarians of the Spirit, none of whom can logically remain independent of each other, but all of whom are in reaction to the one-sidedness of the others. To do justice to the faith of the whole church, therefore, one must accept the Arians and liberals along with the Swedenborgians and pietists and no less than the mystics and metaphysical idealists. All are heretical in and of themselves, yet all are essential to the whole faith of the whole church.

Now, this modern restatement of the doctrine of the Trinity is quite the opposite of the doctrine of the ancient, ecumenical church. There the purpose was to define limits to orthodoxy and to exclude heretical statements of the faith. While Niebuhr accepts ongoing dialectical tensions as the price of polite, ecumenical pluralism, the ancient church faced logical contradictions and sought to prevent biblical affirmations from being turned on their heads so that later reformulations did not come actually to mean the opposite of the assertions found in the apostolic witness of the canonical Scriptures.

The difference between the ancient doctrine and the modern one is rooted in a doctrinal development that only gradually gained ground in the ancient church and did not flower until the high-Middle Ages but that is taken for granted by Niebuhr as a given, namely, natural theology. Niebuhr presumes no need to argue for the identification of the "God of nature" with the God and Father of our Lord Jesus Christ or for the validity of the project of natural theology. He says: "That God reveals his nature and his power in Jesus Christ *and not simply* in creation . . . is always implicit in the Unitarianism which asserts that the one God is the Father."[44] Again: "Having *begun* with the rational knowledge of a first principle of nature, but having *interpreted* that first principle in terms of revelation . . . this Unitarianism is either required to find in Jesus Christ a reconciler to the Creator or to ask whether the Christlike God has any existence."[45] Note that the source of the tension between the "unitarianisms" for Niebuhr is that the religion of nature and reason must somehow be made compatible with the revelation of God in Jesus Christ. Hans Frei quotes Niebuhr as stating: "When we say revelation we point to something in the historical event more fundamental and more certain than Jesus or than self. Revelation means God."[46] Frei also notes that, for

43. Ibid., 384.
44. Ibid., 380 (emphasis added).
45. Ibid., 381 (emphasis added).
46. H. R. Niebuhr, *The Meaning of Revelation* (New York: Macmillan, 1941), 151–52, quoted by Hans Frei, "The Theology of H. Richard Niebuhr," in *Faith and Ethics: The Theology of H. Richard Niebuhr,* ed. Paul Ramsey (New York: Harper & Row, 1957), 83.

Niebuhr, "when we speak of God, we must not speak of human personality, not even of the person of Jesus of Nazareth."[47] Niebuhr, in his doctrine of the Trinity, strives to hold together God and Jesus by means of a dialectical tension.

Niebuhr's restatement of the doctrine of the Trinity can be contrasted with the massive restatement of the same doctrine that fills the thick volumes of Barth's *Church Dogmatics*. Barth is not guilty of having a unitarianism of the Son, in Niebuhr's terms, because he simply refuses to play by the rules by which Niebuhr assumes we have to play. Barth's doctrine of the Trinity is christocentric, meaning that his doctrine of God the Father is developed not out of natural theology, but out of the biblical witness as it is interpreted christologically. Barth rejects the entire natural-theology project, including the analogy of being, apologetics, and reason and history as sources, independent of revelation, of the knowledge of God. For this reason, the doctrine of the Trinity is located in *Church Dogmatics,* not in the doctrine of God after the existence of "nature's God" has already been proven, but in the Prolegomena[48] as the presupposition of all dogmatic theology. For Barth, the Christian God is the God of Abraham, Isaac, Jacob, and Jesus; the God of the Bible, not Aristotle's Unmoved Mover; the God of the philosophers. So we know the Christian God (as opposed to the God of the Deists, the Muslim God, and the God of idealistic metaphysics) through God's own self-revelation in Jesus Christ. Any other God is simply an idol for Barth. Rather than a balance of unitarianisms in tension, Barth offers a christocentric trinitarianism that is distinctively Christian.

Niebuhr's account of trinitarianism is inherently open to syncretism, to the blending of pagan and Christian notions into a culture religion. It was against trends perceived by Barth to hold the potential for this kind of deformation of the Christian faith, which Barth regarded as more serious than anything faced by the church in many centuries, that he uttered his famous "Nein!" The Confessing Church claimed in the Barmen Declaration that it was, in fact, the German Christian movement that was sectarian and heretical. Against syncretism it declared that "Jesus Christ, as he is testified to us in the Holy Scripture, is the one Word of God whom we are to hear, whom we are to trust and obey in life and in death."[49]

Yoder's christocentric trinitarianism is Barthian in its rejection of natural theology. Although Niebuhr portrays the "Christ against culture" po-

---

47. Frei, "The Theology of H. Richard Niebuhr," 83.

48. *CD* I/1, 295–490.

49. The Barmen Declaration, article 1, quoted in Donald Durnbaugh, *The Believers' Church: The History and Character of Radical Protestantism* (New York: Macmillan, 1968), 184.

sition as both sectarian and narrow, Yoder's position is not thereby threatened, for his position is both as ecumenical and as wide as Jesus Christ, the Lord of the church and the Lord of the cosmos. Yoder sees no disjunction between the God of the Old Testament and the God of the New because he sees both Testaments as one story that climaxes in Jesus Christ. Yoder does theology with what could be called a "practical trinitarianism," that is, by means of assertions that depend for their coherence on the truth of the doctrine of the Trinity. To do this is to be in continuity with the ancient church that formulated the doctrine of the Trinity as a way of doing justice both to Jesus' deity and to monotheism. In the end, justice can be done to both only by asserting that the one God is revealed decisively in Jesus, and in this conviction Yoder, Barth, and classical orthodoxy are one.

The Charge of Reductionism: An Evaluation

James Reimer raises the question of whether Yoder's Christology is orthodox and whether, in the end, he does not reduce theology to ethics and spirituality to politics. Reimer recognizes that Yoder consciously and deliberately wrote and spoke as a corrective to other tendencies and distortions, seeking to call the church to balanced faithfulness:

> The existential dimension (one's individual stance before God) is subordinated to the "political" message—"political" interpreted not in any narrow sense but as a whole new way of living with others in the world. To confess Jesus as Lord is to commit oneself to the way of the cross in human relations. This is the gist of Yoder's best known work, *The Politics of Jesus*. The question is whether this is an adequate Christology. In his effective corrective to the evangelical tendency to interiorize the Gospel and that of the mainline churches to sacramentalize it, Yoder offers a powerful political reading of the New Testament which unfortunately devalues the existential-sacramental power of Jesus' message—that part having to do with divine grace, the personal forgiveness of sin, the inner renewal of the spirit, and the individual's stance before God.[50]

What Reimer is raising here is the very important question of reductionism. Did Yoder reduce theology to ethics? Did he reduce personal faith to political action? Did he reduce the meaning of Jesus Christ from cosmic Lord and Savior to moral teacher/example?

To begin, we can agree with Reimer's assessment in four ways. First, Yoder does underplay what Reimer terms the "existential" aspect of personal faith and the nonethical meaning of the sacraments. Second, it is true that Yoder's work is essentially a corrective to the evangelical and

---

50. A. James Reimer, "Mennonites, Christ, and Culture: The Yoder Legacy," *Conrad Grebel Review* 16 (Spring 1998): 8.

mainstream traditions at this point. Third, there can be no doubt that Yoder's interpretation of "the way of the cross" should be construed as "political" in the sense in which Reimer construes it. Fourth, this charge is clearly an important issue, and the long-term evaluation of the importance of Yoder's thought for the church will depend on how this issue of interpretation is resolved. A theologian guilty of the kind of reductionism that is in view here would not seem to have much to teach the ecumenical church. Does this mean, then, that Reimer's conclusion should be adopted and that Yoder should be assessed as reducing doctrine to ethics and spirituality to politics? No, the argument that Yoder's Christology should be considered inadequate is not compelling. It is an understandable mistake, but in the end still a mistake, to see Yoder as reductionistic. Yoder's is a project of retrieval, not reduction. Several points need to be made in support of this position.

1. Yoder's Conversational Style of Writing. First, we need to take into consideration the conversational nature of Yoder's writings and his conception of how theology is supposed to work. Reading his essays is a bit like listening to one end of a telephone conversation. We know that Yoder preferred the essay format and eschewed the writing of a systematic book of any kind, and he made it clear that this decision was rooted in his rejection of philosophical foundationalism and his consequent rejection of what he called "methodologism."[51] He did not believe in starting from "scratch" because he believed that there was no such thing as "scratch." Almost all of Yoder's scholarly output was written because some institute, editor, conference organizer, or panel discussion chair asked him to speak on a particular issue or topic at a particular time and place.[52] Yoder did not regret this fact; he thought it was natural and appropriate because he believed that theology should be a practical discipline serving

---

51. See the introduction to *For the Nations: Essays Public and Evangelical* (Grand Rapids: Eerdmans, 1997), 9–10, for Yoder's rejection of calls for him to write a "basic introduction" in social ethics. See also his "Walk and Word: The Alternatives to Methodologism," in *Theology without Foundations: Religious Practice and the Future of Theological Truth*, ed. S. Hauerwas, N. Murphy, and M. Thiessen Nation (Nashville: Abingdon, 1994), 77–90, where he explains in more detail his rejection of "methodologism." In the introduction to *Priestly Kingdom*, Yoder says that his articulation of the pacifist witness "has been predominantly dialogical, addressing issues in the terms in which they are put by others rather than explicating my own views or those of the historic peace churches" (1). He explicitly rejects the necessity of grounding theological ethics in "metaethics" or "fundamental moral theology" and substitutes for it the grounding of ethics in historical community (7). He argues that Judaism and Christianity, "by the nature of things," cannot but be grounded in particular historical communities (8).

52. Even *Politics of Jesus* was written on assignment, with the practical goal of producing a peace witness that Mennonites could recognize as their own but that would not be based on a denominational identity appeal and could make its way with a nondenominational publisher (John Howard Yoder, "The Politics of Jesus Revisited," [unpublished lecture given at the Toronto School of Theology, March 13, 1997], 1).

the needs of the church.[53] He believed that theology is inherently dialogical and that fraternal correction is an essential aspect of the theological process, not only within the local congregation but within the guild of theologians as well.[54]

To criticize Yoder for leaving himself open to misinterpretation by not saying everything that needs to be said at any one time would not be fair, given the type of writing he did. Of course, that is not what Reimer is doing. He is not saying that Yoder had to pay attention to the existential dimension of faith in every one of his writings or that he had constantly to be referring to the ontological truth status of the claims of Nicea and Chalcedon in every exposition of the ethical implications of Jesus Christ. But why did Yoder never, in forty years of writing, get around to emphasizing these themes? That is a fair question, one that requires further discussion.

A partial response is to extend the point made above about the conversational nature of Yoder's writings. Those with whom he was in conversation were already making those points forcefully and frequently, so there was no need for him to reiterate them. Evangelicals did not invite him to preach at evangelistic crusades or at deeper-life conferences; they asked him to make a contribution to the articulation of a biblically based social ethic in scholarly or social activist settings.[55] Mainline groups did not often ask him for his opinions on Nicea; they usually invited him to speak on how to have a viable peace witness in the modern world.[56] In

53. Stanley Hauerwas, in calling attention to Yoder's insistence that no theology is to be done in the abstract but must be done as part of a conversation for the purpose of building up particular Christian communities, comments that Yoder's writings remind him "more of the Patristic writings than the kind of systematic theology developed over the past two centuries" ("Reading Yoder Down Under," *Faith and Freedom* 5 [June 1996]: 39–40).

54. Yoder discusses what is termed "the Rule of Christ" (Matthew 18:15–16) and what is termed "the Rule of Paul" (1 Corinthians 14) in several places in his writings. He discusses the former practice in his essay, "Sacrament As Social Process: Christ the Transformer of Culture," *Theology Today* 48 (1991): 33–44. He discusses the latter practice in his essay, "The Hermeneutics of Peoplehood: A Protestant Perspective" (*Priestly Kingdom*, 15–45), where he unfolds a vision of "practical moral reasoning" in which there is liberty for all believers to speak and then for the body to deliberate and accredit that which is approved by all after thorough discussion. Both practices are discussed at greater length in *Body Politics: Five Practices of the Christian Community before the Watching World* (Nashville: Discipleship Resources, 1992), 61–80. See chapter 7 of this book for further discussion of Yoder's understanding of the process of ethical decision making within the church.

55. For example, Yoder was a keynote speaker at the founding meeting of Evangelicals for Social Action in Chicago in 1973.

56. For example, Yoder was invited to contribute a paper, "The Historic Peace Churches: Heirs to the Radical Reformation," to the Theological Committee of the Caribbean and North American Area Council of the World Alliance of Reformed Churches, in response to the World Council of Churches meeting in Vancouver (1983) around the theme of "Peace, Justice and the Integrity of Creation." This essay was published in *Peace, War and God's Justice*, ed. T. D. Parker and B. J. Fraser (Toronto: United Church Publishing House, 1989), 105–24.

the Biblical Theology and ecumenical circles in which Yoder moved during his years in Europe (which were heavily influenced by Barthian theology), in the Mennonite and free-church circles in which he moved for all of his career (which were very pietistic), and in the North American evangelical circles in which he moved during much of his career (in which personal piety was emphasized nearly to the exclusion of social witness), what was being denied in each case was neither orthodox Christology nor the gospel message of repentance and faith. And, of course, sacramental theology would not exactly be the neglected theme in need of emphasis with his Roman Catholic colleagues at Notre Dame. Rather, what was not being said in all of these contexts, and needed to be said, was that the life of discipleship means following Jesus rather than merely living up to the best moral wisdom of the pagan world.

2. Yoder's Own Claims Not to Be Intentionally Reductionistic. The proposal being defended here is that we take Yoder's word at face value when he says that his intention was not to reduce Christology to ethics but to speak a word of correction for his time. It is important to hear Yoder's own words at this point, so, begging the reader's indulgence, I will quote Yoder fairly extensively. In the first edition of *The Politics of Jesus*, at the end of his chapter on justification by faith, Yoder emphasizes the social character of justification in Paul's theology:

> Our presentation, in order to correct for the one-sided social ethic which has been dominant in the past, emphasizes what was denied before: Jesus as teacher and example, not only as sacrifice; God as the shaker of the foundations, not only as guarantor of the orders of creation; faith as discipleship, not only as subjectivity. The element of debate in the presentation may make it seem that the "other" or "traditional" element in each case—Jesus as sacrifice, God as creator, faith as subjectivity—is being rejected. It should therefore be restated that—as perusal of the structure of our presentation will confirm— *such a disjunction is not intended.* We are rather defending the New Testament against the exclusion of the "messianic" element. *The disjunction must be laid to the account of the traditional view, not of ours.* It is those other views that say that because Jesus is seen as sacrifice he may not be seen as King, or because he is seen as Word made flesh he cannot be seen as normative man.[57]

It is significant that in the second edition, written twenty years later, Yoder refers to this paragraph and says:

57. John Howard Yoder, *The Politics of Jesus: Vicit Agnus Noster* (Grand Rapids: Eerdmans, 1972), 232; unchanged in 2d ed. (1994), 226 (emphasis added). Yoder clarifies his criticism of the reductionism of both liberal and evangelical Protestantism when he says: "The canonical critical thrust is narrowed (though not necessarily betrayed) when, as we have done it in the West from Augustine through Luther and Pietism to Kierkegaard, Bultmann and Billy Graham, its focus is upon a righteousness which is *coram deo*, in 'the heart,' and not 'merely' civil" ("How to Be Read by the Bible" [A Shalom Desktop Publication, 1996], 51). Note that the narrowing is not necessarily a betrayal because the inward

The last paragraph of the above text should perhaps have been placed at a more prominent place in the book. Some readers, who missed that paragraph or did not believe it, have described *The Politics of Jesus* as reductionistic or materialistic, some intending that description as praise, but more of them as blame.

In an apologetic or missionary perspective, I am not sure that I should be sorry, if it were to turn out to be the case that my retrieval of the straightforward gospel message should be found understandable or interesting to my contemporaries not at home in classical Christian understandings of transcendence or inwardness. Yet such a potential apologetic value was, as the reader of my first chapters know, not the point of my exercise.[58]

So Yoder claims not to be reductionistic in his intent, both in 1972 and in 1994. He reiterates the same point in his final book, *For the Nations*, published in 1997. In his essay, "The Power Equation, Jesus and the Politics of King," Yoder speaks of the vision of the lordship of Christ over the powers and then says:

This is then the immediate political pertinence, in a situation of frustration, of confessing with the Creed that it is Jesus who for us and who for our liberation was made human. This is the New Testament refutation of the definition of Jesus as apolitical. Gustavo Gutierrez says this by denouncing the "distinction of planes." I said it simply by calling Jesus "political."[59]

Then, in a footnote to the last sentence, Yoder refers the reader to the discussion in *The Politics of Jesus* and states: "The use of the adjective did not mean a reduction; it rather sought to *safeguard the wholeness of the classical Christology.*"[60] In *For the Nations*, Yoder is attempting to defend his thought against the charge of sectarianism, and it is interesting to note that, in setting the record straight, he felt it important to affirm his commitment to classical Christology. Upon reflection, however, perhaps it is not so strange after all, since the charge of sectarianism, so far as

---

emphasis is valid in itself. Betrayal only occurs when the inward focus is allowed to crowd out the public implications of the gospel. Yoder goes on to say in this same passage: "That narrowing is however potentially, if not necessarily, a betrayal. When systematized, it sets up as a screen between us and the text the neoplatonic scheme according to which the opposite of the City of God is the earthly city, i.e. God is located in the other world" (ibid.). Note that Yoder exhibits hostility toward the "systematizing" of inward spiritual experience into a metaphysic, not toward the biblical emphasis on personal, inward spiritual experience itself.

58. Yoder, *Politics of Jesus*, 227.

59. John Howard Yoder, "The Power Equation, the Place of Jesus, and the Politics of King," *For the Nations*, 138.

60. Ibid., n. 26 (emphasis added). For Yoder, the denial of Jesus' humanity is just as much a denial of orthodox Christology as the denial of his deity—and more common.

pacifism is concerned, is logically rooted in and dependent upon the charge of reductionism in Christology.

3. Yoder's Criticism of Reductionism in Others. Furthermore, we need to note that on occasion Yoder could criticize the theology of others for not being sufficiently orthodox. How likely is it that as logical a thinker as Yoder would have indulged in such a blatant inconsistency as to hold up the substance of his own teaching as evidence of the weakness of others? For example, he criticizes Reinhold Niebuhr for not having a biblical doctrine of the resurrection of Jesus. Yoder says:

> Although the New Testament understands the cross only in the light of the res-
> urrection, Niebuhr speaks of the cross repeatedly, of the resurrection of Christ
> not at all, and of the resurrection of the body only as a mythological symbol
> for the fact that the superhistorical triumph of the good must also somehow
> involve history.[61]

He also criticizes Niebuhr for ethical pessimism resulting from not taking the effect of personal conversion seriously enough:

> The Bible teaches that there is a significant difference between the saint and
> the unbeliever by virtue of a change of motives so basic as to be called a new
> birth. Niebuhr has no place for the doctrine of regeneration since the saint is
> for him still a sinner, even though he may be a less offensive one.[62]

Here we see Yoder affirming by implication the doctrines of the resurrection of Jesus Christ and the new birth of the believer (and their connection: "the Bible speaks of our resurrection with Christ"[63]) in a very clear way. It could be argued that Yoder believed in these things in the 1950s and 1960s but later abandoned the transcendent in favor of more immanent theology, but it would be difficult to prove that any such gigantic shift in theology ever occurred from his writings.[64] One theme that he constantly reiterates in many different ways is that Christian ethics is for Christians only[65] and that how Christians are to behave is rooted in what

---

61. John Howard Yoder, "Reinhold Niebuhr and Christian Pacifism," *Mennonite Quarterly Review* 29 (April, 1955): 121.

62. Ibid., 21.

63. Ibid., 20.

64. See the quotations above from the second edition of *Politics of Jesus* and *For the Nations*, both of which were written in the 1990s.

65. See, for example, Yoder's "Response to Scott Paradise Paper: Vision of a Good Society," *Anglican Theological Review* 61 (1979): 118–26. Some sample quotes are: "Another element of the biblical vision is to say that the believing people of God, rather than the total empirical social order, is the primordial body of which we need to speak first in asking about the good society" (124), and "The question is not how we want the whole world to be or how we want our society to be but rather how we are to behave in a society that for the time being wants nothing of us of our faith or our Lord" (121).

they believe.[66] Why would it not be legitimate to suppose that one reason why, for Yoder, Christian ethics is for Christians is that Christian believers are the ones in whom the Spirit of Christ dwells?[67]

4. The Logic of Yoder's Position. We also need to bear in mind that the whole basis for Yoder's particular brand of pacifism, the pacifism of the messianic community,[68] collapses if Jesus is not divine. The logic of his position depends upon a high Christology. In *The Politics of Jesus*, Yoder explicitly states in several different ways that his intention was to display the inner logic of orthodoxy. In referring to the "War of the Lamb" narrated in Revelation, he says, for example, "If Jesus Christ was not who historic Christianity confesses he was, the revelation in the life of a real man of the character of God himself, then this one argument for pacifism collapses."[69] His point here is that his reason for pacifism is dependent on the truth of historic Christianity, unlike many other forms of pacifism that could still be held even if the historic orthodox doctrines of the deity of Jesus Christ and the incarnation were not true.[70]

Yoder appeals in this book to the concepts of revelation and incarnation as the basis for his reading of Christology. He asks:

> What becomes of the meaning of incarnation if Jesus is not normative man? If he is a man but not normative, is this not the ancient ebionitic heresy? If he be somehow authoritative but not in his humanness, is this not a new gnosticism?[71]

66. For example, in "Radical Reformation Ethics in Ecumenical Perspective," Yoder says that the distinctive ethic of the radical reformation involves a different doctrine of humanity or Christology or nature (*Journal of Ecumenical Studies* 15 [1978]: 650).

67. Yoder alludes to this point in one of his earliest writings, "The Anabaptist Dissent: The Logic of the Place of the Disciple in Society," when he says that "the sectarian believes that with the Holy Spirit's help the congregation can deduce from the New Testament a set of instructions, commands, and prohibitions, which are objectively valid" (*Concern* 1 [June 1954]: 61). Yoder still makes the same point about the indispensability of the Holy Spirit in Christian ethics in 1992 in *Body Politics*, where, in discussing why his view of ethical decision making will not lead to anarchy, he says, "because Jesus Christ is always and everywhere the same, any procedure that yields sovereignty to his spirit will have ultimately to create unity" (70).

68. See *Nevertheless: The Varieties and Shortcomings of Religious Pacifism* (Scottdale, Pa.: Herald, 1992), 133–38, for Yoder's own pacifist position as contrasted to other kinds of pacifism.

69. Yoder, *Politics of Jesus*, 237.

70. Yoder goes to great lengths to make a similar point in *Nevertheless*. There he speaks of the underlying axiom of his own position, "The Pacifism of the Messianic Community," as follows: "although all of the positions reviewed above are held by Christians, this is the only position for which the person of Jesus is indispensable. It is the only one of these positions which would lose its substance if Jesus were not Christ and if Jesus Christ were not Lord" (134). It is important to note that one of the positions to which Yoder is referring here is the imitation of Jesus position held by Tolstoy and others. This seems to imply that orthodox Christology, and not merely the human figure of Jesus, is seen by Yoder as necessary to his particular kind of pacifism.

71. Yoder, *Politics of Jesus*, 10.

Later Yoder argues that his view of Jesus is not reductionistic, but just the opposite, insofar as it seeks to develop the ethical truth latent in the Christology of the creeds. He says:

> If we were to carry on that other, traditionally doctrinal kind of debate, I would seek simply to demonstrate that the view of Jesus being proposed here is more radically Nicene and Chalcedonian than other views. I do not here advocate an unheard-of modern understanding of Jesus. I ask rather that the implications of what the church has always said about Jesus as Word of the Father, as true God and true Man, be taken more seriously as relevant to our social problems, than ever before.[72]

Furthermore, Yoder explicitly rejects the notion that we must choose, as much of the recent systematic tradition says we must, between the Jesus of history and the Jesus of dogma. Yoder says: "If we confess Jesus as Messiah we must refuse this choice," and "The Jesus of history is the Christ of faith."[73]

5. Yoder's View of the Authority of Scripture. One reason Yoder sometimes sounds less than fully accepting of the creeds (Apostles', Nicene, and Chalcedonian) is that, for him, the authority of the creeds can never supersede the authority of the biblical texts themselves. The creeds are guides to reading Scripture and have a useful, though limited, function. If one takes the position that the ecumenical creeds are on the same level as Scripture or are essential to salvation or are absolute definitions of true Christian faith, then Yoder certainly can be said to be noncreedal in those senses.[74]

However, to subordinate the authority of the creeds to that of Scripture is not necessarily to think that the creeds are wrong. In fact, as we saw above, Yoder claims that the Nicene Creed is trying to say the same thing about Jesus as the New Testament, but in a nonnarrative form, in ontological, philosophical language.[75] He explains the doctrine of Trinity as arising from the New Testament concept that "Jesus, the Word in Jesus, is genuinely of the character of deity and genuinely human, and that his work is the work of God and yet the work of a man"[76] and then calls the doctrine of the Trinity "a test of whether your commitment to Jesus and to God are biblical enough that you have the problem which the doctrine of the Trinity solves."[77] Yoder states that the Nicene Creed is valid, not because it is itself supernatural, revealed truth, but because it "reflects the

---

72. Ibid., 102.
73. Ibid., 103.
74. See, for example, John Howard Yoder and David Shank, "Biblicism and the Church," *Concern* 2 (1955): 38.
75. Yoder, *Preface to Theology*, 138. See chapter 3 of this book.
76. Ibid.
77. Ibid., 140.

serious struggle of men, within their language and their culture, with their commitment to an absolute God and to a normative Jesus."[78] The authority of the creeds is not equal to that of Scripture, but the creeds express truth precisely because they are biblical.

6. Yoder's Barthian Christocentrism. One reason why Yoder did not feel it necessary to emphasize or even be all that explicit about his orthodox Christology is that he was not primarily a systematic theologian working on the problem of Christology; rather, he was applying Barth's theology to social ethics.[79] Rather than reading Yoder as having a "monotheism of the Son," this essay proposes reading Yoder as working out of a Barthian christocentric trinitarianism. Having adopted Barth's christocentric approach to theology as his starting point, Yoder may well have been puzzled by interpreters who accused him of having a low Christology when his whole theological method was so obviously christocentric. I can easily imagine him asking his critics: "Why on earth would I make such a big deal out of a christological social ethic if I did not believe that Christ was God incarnate?"

If it is true that Yoder built on the theological foundation laid by Barth in *Church Dogmatics* in developing a christological approach to social ethics, then the issue that needs to be addressed is the adequacy of the Barthian approach itself. Of course, those of Barth's critics who accuse him of Christomonism will not likely shrink from making similar accusations against Yoder as well, but that is at least to get the real issues out on the table. If Yoder and Barth are guilty of anything, it is having too high a Christology, not too low a Christology.

How conscious Yoder was about using a Barthian methodology is not always clear because he deliberately tried not to focus too much on methodology in his writings. In a paper presented to the Karl Barth Society of North America in 1995, however, Yoder expresses his appreciation for Barth as a post-Christendom theologian and, near the end of that paper, makes a revealing comment about the extent and duration of the influence of Barth's theology on his own thought. Referring to one of his early articles, Yoder says: "The words were my own, but I think the position expressed was the Barthian one I have been describing here, when a lifetime ago I read in a lecture at Drew Seminary the words that have recently been reprinted in my *Royal Priesthood*."[80]

---

78. Ibid., 141.

79. See the discussion of the influence of Barth's theology on Yoder in chapter 2 of this book.

80. John Howard Yoder, "Karl Barth, Post-Christendom Theologian" (unpublished paper presented to the Karl Barth Society, Elmhurst, Ill., June 8, 1995), 7. See idem, "The Otherness of the Church," *The Royal Priesthood: Essays Ecclesiological and Ecumenical*, ed. Michael Cartwright (Grand Rapids: Eerdmans, 1994), 153–64.

7. Yoder's Radical "Catholicity." Catholics may miss what they consider to be a "normal" emphasis on the sacraments and spirituality in Yoder's writings, and evangelical Protestants may miss what they would consider to be the necessary slogans, such as "born again" and "saved by the blood." But these omissions can partially be explained when one pauses to reflect that Yoder embodies the truth of Walter Klassen's description of Anabaptism as neither Protestant nor Catholic.[81] To a great extent, Yoder does not fit preexisting categories. He did not have a personal felt need to be accepted as a "card-carrying evangelical" or "mainline ecumenist." He was, in the words of Michael Cartwright, a "radically catholic"[82] theologian, and he did not seem to fit snugly into either Roman Catholic or Protestant (either evangelical or liberal) categories for the very good reason that his thought cannot be reduced without remainder to either tradition. Reimer is correct in asserting that Yoder did not have a balanced enough approach to the existential and political dimensions of the faith and that he did not emphasize orthodox Christology (or the work of the Holy Spirit or the resurrection of Christ) enough in his best-known writings. But that does not mean that his ideas are not wholly compatible with a balanced approach to all of these things. The issue is balance and emphasis, not logical incompatibility. And if one's stated mission in life is to participate in the theological conversation going on in the church in one's generation and to contribute what one believes to be distinctive and helpful, how can one be faulted for beating the drum one feels is not being heard loudly enough at that particular time?

There are two logically distinct issues here. One is the interpretation of Yoder's own thought, which is an important issue of historical theology in and of itself. The other is the issue of the logical validity of this argument that the orthodox Christology of the New Testament, as expressed in the ancient ecumenical creeds, can be construed as the foundation for a view of a politically relevant Jesus whose humanity is normative for his disciples. The second issue is much more significant for the future of constructive Christian theological ethics. However, this section has, hopefully, clarified the fact that there is solid textual evidence in Yoder's writings for interpreting Yoder himself as holding to a solidly orthodox Christology as well.

In this chapter and the previous one, I have attempted to expound Yoder's Christology as the *source* of his social ethics. I have attempted to

81. Walter Klassen, *Anabaptism: Neither Catholic nor Protestant* (Waterloo, Ont.: Conrad, 1973).

82. Michael Cartwright, "Radical Reform, Radical Catholicity: John Howard Yoder's Vision of the Faithful Church," in *Royal Priesthood*, 41. Yoder explicitly accepted the label "radically catholic" as used by Cartwright as an appropriate description of his stance (*For the Nations*, 8 n. 19).

show that his concept of discipleship grows out of his narrative Christology, which has much in common with the postliberal Christology of Hans Frei, and is in continuity with the ecumenical creeds of the ancient church. I have also attempted to demonstrate that the concept of discipleship as correspondence is central to Yoder's ethics. Like Barth, Yoder understands the human action of the disciple to correspond to the divine action in Jesus Christ in the sense that the model of the human Jesus enables and elicits a response from the disciple. But we cannot fully grasp *why* the human action, which corresponds to the divine action in Christ, can and must take the form of pacifism until we understand the eschatological context in which Yoder's Christology functions. And we cannot fully grasp *how* this enabling and eliciting occurs until we understand the ecclesiological shape of Yoder's social ethics. Only in the context of the sovereignty of God in history and the work of the Holy Spirit in the Christian community is it possible to see how Yoder's christological ethics actually work. We turn, then, to a description of Yoder's eschatology in chapters 5 and 6 as the next step in the exposition of Yoder's thought.

Part III
Eschatology as the *Context* of Yoder's Social Ethics

This is what we mean by eschatology: a hope that, defying present frustration, defines a present position in terms of the yet unseen goal that gives it meaning.

John Howard Yoder
"Peace Without Eschatology," 1954

What the church accepted in the Constantinian shift is what Jesus had rejected, seizing godlikeness.

John Howard Yoder
The Priestly Kingdom: Social Ethics as Gospel, 1984

5

Yoder's Partially-Realized Eschatology

In chapter 3, I tried to show how Yoder's narrative, postliberal Christology is rooted in his reading of the canonical Gospels. In this chapter, I will continue my examination of the biblical roots of Yoder's social ethics as I turn to Yoder's eschatology. He develops his social ethics on the basis of an eschatological concept of Jesus, which, he contends, is relevant to the church conceived of as an eschatological community. As the founder of a new social reality, which is both of this world and not of this world, Jesus introduced an eschatological tension of "already–not yet" that is embodied in an eschatological community of disciples who both reject violence and live in tension with the old social order, just as Jesus did. I hope to make it clear that Yoder's rejection of the violence of the imperial church is thus done fundamentally for christological reasons.

In this chapter, I will discuss the way in which mainstream Christian ethics at mid-century worked with the view of the historical Jesus as a product of late Jewish apocalyptic, a view that was first put forward by Albert Schweitzer and that was highly influential in New Testament scholarship during the first half of the twentieth century. Reinhold Niebuhr, to take one leading representative of mainstream Christian ethics in this era, could no more imagine how such a Jesus could be relevant to contemporary Christian ethics than could Schweitzer. So Christian Realism, and mainstream Christian ethics in general, in the first half of the twentieth century, attempted to formulate an approach to ethics that legitimately could be called Christian, even though it differed in substance from the ethics of Jesus. Yoder's original contribution to Christian ethics in *The Politics of Jesus* was to approach the problem from the other end. Instead of setting Jesus aside in order to do ethics in the context of a modern understanding of history, Yoder suggested setting aside contemporary understandings of history and trying to do Christian ethics in the context of the eschatological-apocalyptic worldview of the Jesus of the Gospels.

In the process of beginning with the Jesus of the Gospels, Yoder discovered that a distinctive and coherent picture of eschatology emerges from the New Testament, one that has important implications both for how one reads the Old Testament and for how one reads the history of Western Christendom. Yoder developed a christocentric eschatology using his Barthian method of relating all doctrinal statements to their true center—Jesus Christ as he is attested in Scripture—and the result was the clarification of the true status and character of Constantinianism as an eschatological heresy. I wish to argue that Yoder developed an eschatology that is integrally related to, and internally consistent with, his Christology. Since that Christology, as we saw in the last two chapters, is both biblical in its origin and consistent with classical orthodoxy, it must, therefore, be the case that, if Yoder's eschatology can be seen as arising out of his Christology, it must also be part of the orthodox, ecumenical Christian faith and, therefore, anything but sectarian.

The purpose of this chapter, then, is to expound Yoder's eschatology as the context for his social ethics. In doing so, I will lay the foundation for the next chapter, in which I will show that Yoder's understanding of Constantinianism as an eschatological heresy is the basis for the refutation of the charge of sectarianism, which is so often made against the type of radical position represented by Yoder.

The Problem of the Eschatological Jesus

One of the major strengths of Yoder's thought is his serious interaction both with biblical studies, on the one hand, and with systematic theology and ethics, on the other. Yoder's eschatology needs to be understood within the context of the debate in New Testament studies that occurred between Schweitzer's *coup de grâce* to the original quest of the historical Jesus and the beginning of the second quest by members of Bultmann's school in the 1950s.

Twentieth-century christological thought has been shaped significantly by the conclusions of the revolutionary book by Albert Schweitzer, first published in 1906, *The Quest of the Historical Jesus*.[1] Schweitzer's

---

1. Albert Schweitzer, *The Quest of the Historical Jesus: A Critical Study of Its Progress from Reimarus to Wrede,* 3d ed., trans. W. Montgomery (London: Adam & Charles Black, 1954).

nineteenth-century survey of the life of Jesus historical-critical scholarship came to two main conclusions: that there is no intellectually honest way to get rid of the eschatological Jesus[2] and that the spiritual interpretation of Jesus, which has come to form the essence of Christianity, developed in the church after Jesus rather than springing from Jesus' own self-understanding.[3] Schweitzer contended that the fact that the world did not end, as Jesus had predicted it would, forced the early church to turn away from eschatology (or what we would today call "apocalyptic") and to fuse "the historical Jesus" and "the supra-mundane Christ" into "a single personality at once historical and raised above time."[4] This orthodox Christology buried the eschatological Jesus beneath mountains of dogma, and it had to be shattered in the Enlightenment before the quest of the historical Jesus could even begin. According to Schweitzer, the quest now has ended with a Jesus who is a product of late-Jewish eschatology, an eschatology that, it goes without saying, we moderns cannot accept. As a result of his history of the "lives of Jesus," Schweitzer concluded that it is evident that each epoch found its reflection in Jesus and each individual created him in accordance with his or her own character. "Lives of Jesus" tell us more about their authors than they tell us about Jesus.[5]

Like everyone else, Schweitzer had his own views of the spiritual significance of Jesus. But it was not his constructive views that exerted a great influence on New Testament scholarship, theology, and ethics in the following decades. It was his elimination of the option of what might be termed the domestication of Jesus that created a problem for theology after him.[6] Schweitzer's work exerted an enormous influence on Christian ethics during the first half of the twentieth century by forcing Christian ethicists to find ways to deal with the challenge of an eschatological

2. In the preface to the third edition (1954) Schweitzer writes: "The decision in favour of eschatology is hardly likely to be questioned again. It provides the only trustworthy clue to the text of Matthew and Mark, allowing words to remain as they stand, with their ordinary meaning. Otherwise meanings have to be read into the text, and the sincere student must entertain far-reaching doubts as to its trustworthiness" (*Quest of the Historical Jesus*, xiv).

3. Again, Schweitzer writes: "The Gospel of the Kingdom of God came into the world in its late-Jewish form, which it could not retain. . . . It may come as a stumbling-block to our faith to find that it was not Jesus himself who gave its perfect spiritual form to the truth which he himself brought into the world, but that it received this in the course of time through the working of the Spirit. But this is something we have to overcome" (ibid., xv–xvi).

4. Ibid., 3.

5. Ibid., 4.

6. See Stephen Neill and Tom Wright, *The Interpretation of the New Testament 1861–1986*, 2d ed. (Oxford: Oxford University Press, 1988), 205–15. Neill sums up the enduring significance of Schweitzer's work: "We can never go back behind the recognition of apocalyptic as the context, and at least part of the content, of the Gospel proclamation. We cannot be content with a picture of Jesus as a rather civilized man of the nineteenth or twentieth century" (215).

Jesus in whom we moderns cannot believe, while at the same time remaining adherents of the religion that bears his name. Somehow ethics must be "Christian," but not simply the ethics of Jesus, and the explanation for how this can be so must have some plausibility.

In *The Politics of Jesus,* Yoder offers a list of ways in which mainstream Christian ethics have attempted to deal with this problem. In the first edition he lists six approaches to this problem; in the second edition he adds five more.[7] First, some theologians have thought of Jesus' ethic as an "interim ethic," one that was meant to apply to the very short time period before the passing away of this world.[8] Second, some would agree with the Franciscan and Tolstoyan imitators of Jesus that he was a simple, rustic figure whose ethic can only apply in face-to-face situations of the small village. Third, some point out that Jesus and his earliest followers lived in a situation in which they had virtually no control over the larger social forces of history and that his ethic, therefore, cannot apply in the very different situation that prevailed after Constantine.[9] Fourth, the message of Jesus is one of an ahistorical self-understanding, not one of social change.[10] Fifth, Jesus was a radical monotheist who pointed people away from finite values to the sovereignty of the only one worthy

7. John Howard Yoder, *The Politics of Jesus: Vicit Agnus Noster* (Grand Rapids: Eerdmans, 1972), 15–19; 2d ed. (1994), 4–8.

8. This is obviously Schweitzer's position, although Yoder does not mention him here. Instead he names Reinhold Niebuhr and Paul Ramsey as examples of ethicists influenced by this position (Yoder, *Politics of Jesus,* 5 n. 9). Yoder later names Schweitzer as the father of the "interim ethic" position (103–4) and specifically defines his own view of Jesus as an attempt to take seriously the eschatological character of Jesus' message without having to set Jesus aside as irrelevant.

9. This position is taken by Paul Ramsey in *Basic Christian Ethics* (New York: Charles Scribner's Sons, 1950), 167ff.

10. This is the Bultmannian position. See his *Theology of the New Testament,* trans. K. Grobel, 2 vols. (New York: Charles Scribner's Sons, 1951, 1955), in which he begins with the acknowledgment of the eschatological nature of Jesus' message: "The dominant concept of Jesus' message is the Reign of God. . . . With such a message, Jesus stands in the historical context of Jewish expectations about the end of the world and God's new future" (1:4). For Bultmann, this naturally raises the question of whether we have to dismiss the entire message of Jesus as based upon an illusion (1:22). He avoids this conclusion by using existentialist philosophy to reinterpret the message of Jesus: "The essential thing about the eschatological message is the idea of God that operates in it and the idea of human existence that it contains—not the belief that the end of the world is just ahead" (1:23). This "idea of human existence" becomes the proclamation of the early church: "He who formerly had been the bearer of the message was drawn into it and became its essential content" (1:33). The Jesus who had been "the proclaimer of the radical demand of God" became the kernel of the church's proclamation, and gradually the Jewish, eschatological husk was allowed to fall by the wayside (34). By the time we get to the Fourth Gospel we have a "historically completely different picture from that depicted by the synoptics" (2:4). But this does not matter because salvation is a matter of the decision of faith in response to the "demand for faith" in the gospel proclamation of Jesus as the one in whom God is encountering the world (2:75). The life of faith is "eschatological

of worship.[11] Sixth, some would see the point of the incarnation as being only to enable Jesus to die for the sins of the world; thus, the kind of life he led is ethically immaterial.[12] Seventh, the radical historical skepticism of the "third quest of the historical Jesus" contends that we cannot be sure enough of anything the text says to build any sort of ethic on it.[13] Eighth, another critical objection to the reading of the Gospel texts as being ethically relevant is that the traditions behind the texts cannot be said to have any sort of consistency.[14] Ninth, there is the "general theological bias" against the "historical/particular quality of the narrative" in favor of "Wisdom, that is, in favor of moral insights less tied to time and place."[15] Tenth, there is the argument of H. Richard Niebuhr in his famous article on the doctrine of the Trinity that "one should not make Jesus too important for ethics, . . . since God the Father would call for a different (perhaps more institutionally conservative) social ethic, based on an understanding of creation or providence."[16] Eleventh, some would

---

existence . . . [a] turning away from the world . . . the willingness to live by the strength of the invisible and uncontrollable. . . . It means accepting the life that Jesus gives and is . . . a life that to the world's point of view cannot even be proved to exist" (2:75). When Bultmann comes to treat the New Testament ethical material, he presents it as a falling away from the message of Paul and John and a "sinking back into legalism" (2:204). The result is an ahistorical message of faith that contains or implies no specific ethical content. Theology and ethics are sundered completely.

11. This, of course, is the position of H. R. Niebuhr. Yoder cites Niebuhr's *Christ and Culture* (New York: Harper & Row, 1951) as well as *Radical Monotheism and Western Culture* (New York: Harper & Row, 1960) and *The Responsible Self* (New York: Harper & Row, 1963).

12. This position can be held by Roman Catholics and high Anglicans and Lutherans who emphasize the sacraments as the means of grace, or it can be held by Protestants who see salvation as a matter of a changed self-understanding in response to the proclaimed Word. Although they are about as far apart as possible on the liberal-conservative spectrum, Yoder sees Rudolf Bultmann and Billy Graham as similar in that they hold to a nonethical message of individual salvation that fits this perspective. See Yoder's "How to Be Read by the Bible" (A Shalom Desktop Publication, 1996), 51.

13. Yoder cites the survey of third-quest scholarship by Marcus Borg and N. Thomas Wright, "Portraits of Jesus in Contemporary American Scholarship," *Harvard Theological Review* 84 (1991): 1–22. Yoder notes that the trends in contemporary scholarship generally support the sociopolitical impact of Jesus (Yoder, *Politics of Jesus*, 13 n. 19 and 14 n. 21).

14. Yoder says that such an objection would be damaging to a fundamentalist or scholastic understanding of the Bible but not to his own postcritical or narrative understanding, in which the "witness of a text consists in the direction in which it pointed, along the trajectory from earlier tradition to present challenge" (ibid., 16).

15. Yoder interprets this as a mere swing of the pendulum in reaction to the "God Who Acts" emphasis of G. Ernest Wright and others in the 1950s (ibid.).

16. Ibid., 17. Yoder claims that this approach is derived from a modern epistemology alien to the New Testament. See chapter 4 above for a discussion of Yoder's critique of Niebuhr's doctrine of the Trinity.

argue that Jesus did not come to teach a way of life because his sole purpose was to achieve salvation. The purpose of the law is entirely negative.[17]

Obviously, most of these positions are either attempts to deal with the problem defined by Schweitzer at the turn of the century or the result of pietistic interpretations of the gospel that focus on an individualized and apolitical view of salvation. Yoder came to maturity as a scholar in an evangelical Mennonite community with strong leanings in the latter direction and a broader Protestant culture in which the Christian Realism of Reinhold Niebuhr was the dominant way of responding to Schweitzer.

It is important to note that, even though Reinhold Niebuhr came to believe that the eschatological, unconditional love of Jesus was impossible to implement in society because of the reality of original sin, he nevertheless continued to believe that it is only honest to admit that Jesus taught love of enemies and rejection of violence. Yoder specifically refers to Schweitzer later in his book as the one who set up the problematic of the eschatological Jesus, who is relevant to ethics but unacceptable to modernity, versus the Christ of faith, who is irrelevant to ethics. He writes: "As we look closer at the Jesus whom Albert Schweitzer rediscovered, in all his eschatological realism, we find an utterly precise and practicable ethical instruction, practicable because in him the Kingdom of YHWH has become human history."[18] Yoder is able to take the Schweitzer-Niebuhr view of Jesus and argue that it is a correct view but that Schweitzer is wrong to assume that eschatology is unthinkable for moderns and that Niebuhr is thus wrong to deny the relevance of Jesus for social ethics. How is he able to do this? Basically, he does it by using the thought of Oscar Cullmann to correct the eschatology of both Schweitzer and Niebuhr.[19]

17. Yoder notes that the classical Lutheran tradition comes close to this position and views the purpose of the law as being merely to drive us to grace (ibid., 18).

18. Ibid., 104.

19. Of course, Yoder also made use of the work of other scholars working along similar lines in the 1950s, such as H. Berkhof, G. B. Caird, and Gordon Rupp. Caird, in *The Language and Imagery of the Bible* (Philadelphia: Westminster, 1980), led the way in challenging Schweitzer's assumption that late Jewish apocalyptic (especially 4 Ezra and 2 Baruch) necessarily have an imminent end of the world in view. Caird argued that the language of apocalyptic was designed to denote events within the space-time universe and interpret them theologically. Neill and Wright cite T. F. Glasson's article, "Schweitzer's Influence: Blessing or Bane?" *Journal of New Testament Studies* 28 (1977): 289–302, as arguing this case as well (Neill and Wright, *Interpretation of the New Testament*, 378). As usual, Yoder's use of the New Testament is not eccentric or contrarian. Of course, no ethicist can use all the conflicting interpretations the various New Testament scholars argue over, but that is not something blameworthy in principle. The interesting debate begins when ethicists argue over which exegetical results should be employed for what purposes and why. Yoder has not been engaged often enough on this level because, for various reasons, most Christian ethicists are not involved enough in New Testament studies.

Cullmann was a professor at Basel when Yoder studied there, and his influence can be detected in the theology of Barth. As a leading member of the salvation-history school of thought, Cullmann, along with others, proposed a way of doing justice to Schweitzer's eschatological Jesus without having to reject Jesus as being wrong about the imminence of the kingdom and also without denying the reality or radical nature of the kingdom. In *The Christian Witness to the State,* Yoder summarizes his understanding of New Testament eschatology and acknowledges his indebtedness to Cullmann.[20]

Yoder's Understanding of New Testament Eschatology

Unlike many others, Yoder believes that it is possible to develop a viable and coherent eschatology on the basis of the exegesis of New Testament materials. The following interpretation of Yoder's eschatology is based on an analysis of how key biblical concepts are used in his various writings. The following eight concepts, considered in their interrelationship, may be taken as constituting a biblically based view of history, according to Yoder.

1. The Lordship of Christ. Yoder says: "the triumphant affirmation of the New Testament is that Jesus Christ, by His cross, resurrection, ascension and the pouring out of His Spirit, has triumphed over the Powers."[21] This is the concrete meaning of the term *Lord* that is used so often of Jesus in the New Testament. The meaning of Jesus Christ's ascension to the right hand of the Father is that he is now exercising dominion over the world.[22] He has attained this place of rule and authority by virtue of having been raised from the dead by the Father. He will reign until he has put all enemies under his feet (1 Corinthians 15:25).

2. The Two Ages. The present age, which lasts from Pentecost to the *parousia,* is one in which the new redemptive reality ushered in by Jesus Christ overlaps with the old eon that existed before his first coming. The old age is characterized by sin and rebellion against God. The new age, however, is characterized by the reign of Christ. The image suggested by Cullmann to describe the present age is the period of World War II between D-Day and V-E Day. After successfully landing on the beaches of

20. John Howard Yoder, *The Christian Witness to the State* (Newton, Kans.: Faith and Life, 1964), 9. See the discussion of the influence of Cullmann on Yoder's eschatology in David M. Hughes, "The Ethical Use of Power: A Discussion with the Christian Perspectives of Reinhold Niebuhr, John Howard Yoder, and Richard J. Barnet" (unpublished Ph.D. diss., Southern Baptist Theological Seminary, 1984), 125–26; and Kenneth Hallahan, "The Social Ethics of Nonresistance: The Writings of John Howard Yoder Analyzed from a Roman Catholic Perspective" (unpublished Ph.D. diss., Catholic University of America, 1997), 43–53.

21. Yoder, *Christian Witness,* 9.

22. Ibid., 8.

Normandy, the Allied forces steadily moved toward the heart of Germany. The issue of final victory was no longer in doubt, but the war was not over yet. Soldiers still died, and individual battles could be won or lost. This is the situation in which the world finds itself now, between Pentecost and the *parousia*. The final victory of Jesus Christ is now assured because of the resurrection, but the war is not over yet.

3. The Powers. The "powers" are angelic and demonic entities referred to as thrones, principalities and powers, archangels, and dominions in the New Testament. They correspond roughly to what we call "structures" in modern sociological language.[23] They are not under the control of human beings, but they exercise great influence over human affairs. In his last, unpublished section of his *Church Dogmatics,* Barth used the term "The Lordless Powers" to describe them.[24]

The powers are not entirely or originally evil. Even the demonic powers were once good and can never be totally evil. Yoder states that "Paul contends that the power structures of our world are not devils but creatures, intended for the well-being of humankind, yet 'fallen' and therefore oppressive."[25] Jesus disobeys, disarms, and saves them from enslavement by dying at their hands. He thereby "tames" them and makes them useable for his purposes.

Yoder proposes that the doctrine of the powers could function as a substitute for natural theology: "It would not be too much to claim that the Pauline cosmology of the powers represents an alternative to the dominant ('Thomist') vision of 'natural law' as a more biblical way systematically to relate Christ and creation."[26] One problem with implementing this suggestion is that most of those who have talked in terms of the "powers" so far have tended to be overwhelmingly negative, and to critics it all sounds like a denial of the fundamental goodness of creation. But if the analysis of the powers were to explain both the good and bad aspects of the powers, it might help us get a more balanced view of a good but fallen world.[27]

The present age is characterized by the defeat of the powers by Jesus Christ by means of his resurrection and by his rule over them. However,

---

23. Ibid. See also Yoder, *Politics of Jesus,* 136–37.

24. *CD* IV/4, 213–33. Charles Campbell points out that Hans Frei's understanding of the "forces of history" is compatible with Yoder's understanding of the powers (*Preaching Jesus: New Directions for Homiletics in Hans Frei's Postliberal Theology* [Grand Rapids: Eerdmans, 1997], 213 n. 75).

25. John Howard Yoder, "Jesus: A Model of Radical Political Action," *Faith and Freedom* 1 (December 1992): 8.

26. Yoder, *Politics of Jesus,* 159.

27. Barth's discussion of "The Lordless Powers" in *Christian Life* (213–33) is a good start in this direction, especially in his contention that the powers are forced to testify to God's power and Christ's lordship even in their rebellion.

"the present, paradoxical state of the world" is seen in 1 Corinthians 15:20–28, which says that, although Christ is now reigning, not all of his enemies have yet been subjected to him.[28] So, although they have been defeated, the powers still have great destructive capability and run rampant in the world. One day, every knee will bow "in heaven and on earth and under the earth, and every tongue confess that Jesus Christ is Lord, to the glory of God the Father" (Philippians 2:10–11). D-Day has occurred but V-E Day is still future.

4. The Kingdom of God. The phrase "kingdom of God" can be misleading unless it is understood in terms of the above overlapping of the ages. Jesus came proclaiming the imminence of the kingdom, as Schweitzer recognized. But Schweitzer failed to grasp that the kingdom actually did come in one sense, as well as being delayed in another sense. The New Testament language that makes this differentiation is the "kingdom of the Son" and the "kingdom of the Father." The reign of the Son is now going on, as we have seen above, but the rule of the Father is still future. In the words of Paul: "Then the end will come, when he hands over the kingdom to God the Father after he has destroyed all dominion, authority and power. For he must reign until he has put all his enemies under his feet" (1 Corinthians 15:24–25). The message of the church is that the kingdoms of this world *have become* the kingdoms of Christ *and are destined to become* the kingdom of God.[29]

5. The Church. The purpose of God in this present age is to create a new society, the church or the body of Christ, in which Jews and Gentiles are made one as an eschatological sign of the future kingdom of God.[30] Jesus made it clear that the Jewish nationalism of his day, which wanted a resumption of the Maccabean struggle on a grander scale, was mistaken. Jesus was a prophet in the line of Jeremiah, who, after the monarchy had been given an opportunity to work and had failed miserably, had called the people to a nonnational witness to monotheism in the dispersion.[31] The church is not to be identified with any one national, ethnic, or local solidarity but is "an aftertaste of God's loving triumph on the cross and foretaste of His ultimate loving triumph in His Kingdom."[32] The church is

28. Yoder, *Christian Witness*, 9.

29. Ibid.

30. See the chapter "Justification by Grace through Faith" in Yoder, *Politics of Jesus*, 212–27.

31. For an elaboration of this idea, see Yoder's essay, "See How They Go with Their Face to the Sun," For *the Nations: Essays Public and Evangelical* (Grand Rapids: Eerdmans, 1997), 51–78. After the failure of the Zealot revolt of A.D. 70 and the Bar Kokhba revolt of A.D. 135, Judaism was reconstituted by the rabbis along these lines. The rabbis reasoned that God had said "no" three times to nationalistic uprisings and concluded that God's will was the maintenance of the witness to monotheism among the nations by a scattered, powerless people whose dependence on God would be obvious.

32. Yoder, *Christian Witness*, 10.

made up of those who hear the gospel and consciously choose to become followers of Jesus Christ. The church is not the kingdom, but it is the effect of the coming of the kingdom in Jesus Christ, and it bears witness to the coming kingdom of the Father.

As in Barth's ecclesiology, for Yoder, the church is visible because it is distinct from the world.[33] For Yoder, the church is identified by "baptism, discipline, morality and martyrdom."[34] The church is not simply the result of the gospel and not simply the bearer of the message. Rather, explains Michael Cartwright, for Yoder, "That men and women are called together to a new social wholeness is itself the work of God that gives meaning to history from which both personal conversion . . . and missionary instrumentality are derived."[35] The church is the meaning of history because it is "the new world on the way."[36]

6. The World. If the church consists of those who hear Christ's call to discipleship and respond to his lordship by identifying themselves with his body, the world consists of those who do not follow Jesus Christ. There is thus a clear distinction between the church and the world, a distinction of confession.[37] Yoder makes the point that, if there is not a clear distinction between church and world, there can be no evangelistic call to a person to enter a new body of persons distinct from other societies.[38] If the call cannot be the invitation to join a new society, then the gospel inevitably becomes interiorized and individualized. The distinction is not between the sinful and the perfect or between those who are evil and those who are good; rather, it is between the sinful people who confess Jesus Christ as Lord and who live in the community that confesses him and strives to follow him and the sinful people who do not confess him as Lord and who, therefore, live outside that community in the world.

It should be stressed that the world, for Yoder, is not completely evil. According to the New Testament, the world (*aion houtos* in Paul, *kosmos* in John) "is not creation or nature or the universe, but rather, the fallen state of the same, no longer conformed to the creative intent."[39] It is

---

33. *CD* IV/3:2, 653, for his rejection of "ecclesiological docetism."

34. John Howard Yoder, "The Otherness of the Church," *The Royal Priesthood: Essays Ecclesiological and Ecumenical*, ed. Michael Cartwright (Grand Rapids: Eerdmans, 1994), 56. Barth would emphasize only confession and not morality or baptism, because of the dangers of moralism and sacramentalism (*CD* IV/3:2, 696). But he would be open to martyrdom, given his contention that "none can be a Christian without falling into affliction" because "the ministry of witness unavoidably brings the Christian into affliction" (618).

35. Michael Cartwright, "Radical Reform, Radical Catholicity: John Howard Yoder's Vision of the Faithful Church," in *Royal Priesthood*, 27.

36. Yoder, "Why Ecclesiology Is Social Ethics: Gospel Ethics versus the Wider Wisdom," *Royal Priesthood*, 126.

37. See David M. Hughes's discussion of this point in "The Ethical Use of Power," 123.

38. Yoder, "A People in the World," *Royal Priesthood*, 75.

39. Yoder, "Otherness of the Church," 55.

"structured unbelief."[40] The world is "a blend of order and revolt"[41] in which the good creation is distorted. Yoder does not deny the goodness of the created order, but he has a strong doctrine of its fallenness. It is the lordship of Christ that prevents the world from descending into chaos.[42]

7. The Meaning of History. The purpose of history is the evangelization of the world by the church so that there will be some from every tribe and nation to praise God around the throne. The role of the church is to bear costly witness to the lordship of Jesus Christ in word (the preaching of the gospel) and in deed (in loving service and acts of reconciliation).[43] The witness is costly because the powers, which have not yet submitted to Christ's lordship, are still dangerous and hostile.

The gospel says that the cycle of violence, in which each new act of vengeance elicits a new act of vengeance in return, has been broken in the cross. Jesus absorbed all the violence and hatred the world could hurl at him and bore it without retaliation or bitterness. He died forgiving those who tortured him. To bear witness to Jesus, the church proclaims the end of the cycle of violence through forgiving love, and it does so in word and deed. This is why the church must be pacifist. Logically there is no other way for it to fulfill its mission of witnessing to the cross and resurrection except to be "participants in the loving nature of God as revealed in Christ."[44] To preach that forgiveness is stronger than hatred and that God's love is freely given to all people in Jesus Christ and then to turn around and engage in acts of violent revenge, punishing the guilty according to what they deserve, would be to contradict in one's deeds the message one preaches in words. So martyrdom will often be the result of confronting the powers with a reminder of their defeat by Jesus in his cross and resurrection. Yet, martyrdom too is a form of witness, explains Yoder: "the kind of faithfulness that is willing to accept evident defeat rather than complicity with evil is, by virtue of its conformity with what happens to God when he works among us, aligned with the ultimate triumph of the lamb."[45] The ultimate meaning of history is the cross, and the church is to bear costly testimony to this truth in word and deed.

8. The State. If the church must be pacifist in order to bear witness to the Lamb who was slain, what plan, then, does God have to ensure the necessary social order for that witness to be made visible? The state plays a role in the current age insofar as it is the instrument of God's provi-

40. Ibid., 62.
41. Ibid., 56.
42. Ibid., 57.
43. See the final chapter of *Politics of Jesus*, "The War of the Lamb," for Yoder's reflections on the meaning of history.
44. Ibid., 240.
45. Ibid., 238.

dence. Since the state belongs to the old age of sin, it is characterized by "the appeal to force as ultimate authority."[46] Romans 13:1–7 and 1 Peter 2:13–14, however, teach that God, in his providence, uses the state to maintain order in society. Since the meaning of history is found in the church and its work of proclaiming the gospel, the state functions as a means ordained or ordered by God to provide the peace and social order necessary for the work of the church to go on. In this sense, the state is indirectly part of God's plan for the evangelization of the world.[47] But it is also true that the state, as part of the old order, is destined to wither away. God's new society will emerge from the church, his new creation. The state is not a means by which God brings his kingdom into history. However, the lordship of Jesus over the powers, of which the state is one, means that it is possible for the church to speak to the state in God's name, "not only in evangelism, but in ethical judgment as well."[48]

Yoder's eschatology can be said to be characterized by a theological realism that undergirds a view of Christ's lordship as having visible consequences in history. But his eschatology is only partially realized. The kingdom of God has come in the person of Jesus, but it has not yet come in its fullness. Yoder understands the present age, between Pentecost and the *parousia,* to be a period of eschatological tension in which the powers, including the state, still struggle against the church and often appear, at least temporarily, to triumph over God and his cause. The struggles, ambiguities, and tensions of this age will continue until a future decisive intervention by God, which will consummate the new age, the age of the final victory of the Lamb. Until then, the disciple and the Christian community as a whole must live by faith, be ready to accept suffering, and continue to bear witness to the Lord Jesus Christ. In Yoder's eschatology there is no shallow, liberal optimism, no doctrine of historical progress, no assurance that the social order is gradually being Christianized. But, on the other hand, there also is no reason to despair, for even Caesar is subject to the lordship of Jesus Christ, and the God who raised Jesus from the dead still rules sovereignly over history.

The Old Testament Roots of Yoder's Eschatology

Yoder's understanding of New Testament eschatology is rooted in his understanding of the specific way in which the new covenant is a fulfill-

---

46. Yoder, *Christian Witness,* 12. Yoder has no doctrine of the state. He simply observes the empirical fact that entities that establish order by the appeal to force do exist.

47. Ibid., 13. Yoder does not mean by this statement that the state is Christian.

48. Yoder, "Otherness of the Church," 56. The implications of this statement will be explored in chapter 8, when the charges that Yoder's ethics promote the irrelevance and withdrawal of the church are explored.

ment of the old covenant. Yoder looks back to the call of Abraham as the beginning of a pattern of divine activity in which a distinct people is called out to witness to the saving grace of God that is for all the nations.[49] In Abraham, Moses, Gideon, and Samuel, "He gathered His people around His word and His will."[50] Yoder believes that a certain continuity of divine purpose can be seen in God's historical drive to create a people for himself. Israel was called to be a light to the nations (election for service, not privilege), and the gentile mission of the New Testament is an extension of the mission of Israel.[51]

1. The Relation of the Testaments. Yoder rejects several standard ways of relating the old and new covenants.[52] First, he rejects the view of dispensationalism because it entails God acting in contradictory ways in different periods of history and, thus, not always acting in harmony with his own perfect character. Second, he rejects the idea that, in the Old Testament, God was permissive as a concession to the unreadiness of people to accept his perfect will. The problem with this view is that some of what we find problematic in the Old Testament, like the holy wars of Israel, were not merely permitted but rather commanded by God. Third, Yoder rejects the concept of a pedagogical concession as too similar to the liberal evolutionist perspective that tends to be patronizing toward the Old Testament. Fourth, he rejects the division of levels or realms approach in which the Old Testament deals with outward, social reality, while the New Testament deals with inner, personal reality. In Yoder's opinion, the lines simply cannot be drawn that neatly. The Old Testament has a lot to say about personal faith, and the New Testament deals with social reality as well.

Yoder calls his own approach "the historical view," and he reads the Old Testament as the narrative of "a real word from the true Jahweh of hosts, speaking to His people in historically relevant terms."[53] Like Barth, Yoder emphasizes that the commands of God in the Old Testament were not ethical generalizations or principles but rather specific commands directed to people in a very different society from our own. To take the holy wars of Israel as an example, the point of those events was to teach the community that it did not need "any other crutches for one's identity

---

49. John Howard Yoder, *The Original Revolution: Essays on Christian Pacifism* (Scottdale, Pa.: Herald, 1971), 27.

50. Ibid., 28–29.

51. Kent Reames notes that, for Yoder, the two key elements of the Abrahamic covenant are: (1) that the people God is calling into existence through Abraham are to be separate from all the other nations and (2) that Abraham is able to trust God to provide in all things. See his "Histories of Reason and Revelation: With Alasdair MacIntyre and John Howard Yoder into Historicist Theology and Ethics" (unpublished Ph.D. diss., University of Chicago, 1997) 132; cf. Yoder, *Original Revolution*, 27.

52. For what follows in this paragraph, see Yoder, *Original Revolution*, 92–100.

53. Ibid., 107.

and community as a people than trust in Jahweh as king, who makes it unnecessary to have earthly kings like the neighboring nations."[54] Yoder contends that the holy wars, which were commanded by God, occurred early in Israel's experience and involved miraculous deliverance, as did the Red Sea experience itself. When the monarchy arose and the holy war pattern was replaced by standing armies commanded by foreign officers, foreign diplomacy, and power politics, war was one of the things condemned bitterly by the prophets, who saw the new developments as poor substitutes for standing still and watching the deliverance of the Lord.

2. The Roots of the Church in Diaspora Judaism. Since he reads the Bible historically, Yoder is able to identify a direction or a trajectory in which the Old Testament is moving and, therefore, is able to specify how the Old Testament is fulfilled in the New. In the exile, Jeremiah called the people to a new way of witnessing to monotheism, one that did not involve a nation-state, a monarchy, or the institution of war. The center of gravity shifted from the land to the Diaspora, from the monarchy to the synagogue and the rabbinate, and from war to pacifism. Even in the time of Jesus, Palestine was not the undisputed center of world Judaism. After the events of A.D. 135, rabbinic Judaism became the dominant form of Judaism until 1948, and it continues to exist side by side with Zionism and the secular state of Israel today.[55]

Yoder believes that the Jesus movement of the early 30s of the first century had far more in common with the Jeremianic vision of Diaspora, synagogue, and pacifism, which became the shape of rabbinic Judaism, than the Maccabean vision of nation, monarchy, and war. In fact, Yoder sees the church as the final step in the development of an alternative to a racially based, militaristic, violent, worldly people of God.[56] While Yoder sees real historical movement through the prophets and the monarchy to the exile and up to Jesus, that movement was not an evolution from primitive to higher ethical codes but an increasingly precise definition of the nature of peoplehood. Actually, Yoder sees the Old Testament as moving upward in the call of Abraham and the exodus, downward in the development of the monarchy, upward in the exilic vision of Jeremiah, and downward in the return under Ezra and Nehemiah. None of these stages,

54. Ibid.

55. Yoder notes that "after the end of kingship and the loss of the Jerusalem Temple, Jewry survived not by creating a surrogate for the Temple so as to keep using the priesthood, but by inventing a new role, that of the rabbi, steward of the Torah and a new social instrument, the synagogue, formed of any ten households with no religious specialists needed at all" (*Body Politics: Five Practices of the Christian Community before the Watching World* [Nashville: Discipleship Resources, 1992], 56).

56. See the introduction to John Howard Yoder, *The Priestly Kingdom: Social Ethics As Gospel* (Notre Dame, Ind.: University of Notre Dame Press, 1984), 10–12.

however, could be considered as either all bad or all good. God was at work in all of them, and obedience was imperfect in all of them.

The novelty of the new society created by Jesus was threefold: first, it was a voluntary society—one could not be born into it; second, it was mixed racially, religiously, and economically; and third, it was characterized by a new set of relationships in which sharing, forgiving, and suffering were prominent.[57] We have not understood Yoder's view of the eschatological character of the church unless we have understood it as the culmination of all that God had been doing throughout salvation history, and we have not understood the importance of pacifism until we have understood the mission of the church in its eschatological context. Yoder says:

> Once one's own national existence is no longer seen as a guarantee of Jahweh's favor, then to save this national existence by holy war is no longer a purpose for which miracles would be expected. Thus the dismantling of the applicability of the concept of the holy war takes place not by promulgation of a new ethical demand but by a restructuring of the Israelite perception of community under God.[58]

Yoder claims that this awareness of the new concept of peoplehood proclaimed by Jesus was not entirely new. The Old Testament exilic and postexilic prophecies were the inspiration for what Jesus taught and did, although there is definitely a sense of fulfillment in his proclamation, which is new. Yoder claims that, once the covenant is seen to be open to all people, then the outsider can no longer be perceived as less important than the insider and certainly cannot be seen as an object worth sacrificing for the sake of the nation.[59] No nation or state can now claim to be the bearer of the Abrahamic covenant, for that is the role of the church. But that claim, as we are about to see, is exactly what is entailed in Constantinianism.

57. Yoder, *Original Revolution*, 29.
58. Ibid., 108.
59. Ibid.

6

The Heresy of Constantinianism

In order to understand what Yoder means by Constantinianism, we must first note that his concept of Constantinianism is not simply a description of the historical career of the man, Constantine the Great, and his personal influence in history but rather a heresy named for a historical figure, like Arianism or Pelagianism.[1] Constantinianism is not, for Yoder, a complete description of any single church, movement, or figure in history. Nor was it embraced fully and absolutely by any particular part of the church. Nor has it ever characterized the entire church of any age.[2] Rather, Yoder means by Constantinianism a heretical eschatology, that is, one that is heretical precisely in that it denies or distorts all eight of the points made in the previous chapter's summary of New Testament eschatology.[3] Most important, Constantinianism proceeds as if the life,

1. John Howard Yoder, "The Disavowal of Constantine," *The Royal Priesthood: Essays Ecclesiological and Ecumenical,* ed. Michael Cartwright (Grand Rapids: Eerdmans, 1994), 245.

2. These three qualifications are necessary because Yoder is sometimes interpreted as being overly dismissive of too much of Christian history. For example, James Reimer criticizes Yoder's critique of Constantinianism as a "shibboleth for all that is bad." Reimer continues: "There were many serious Christians, including theologians, clerics and statesmen, who were attempting to address the profound issues raised by their cultures in the light of the gospel" ("Mennonites, Christ, and Culture: The Yoder Legacy," *Conrad Grebel Review* 16 [Spring 1998]: 10–11). It must be admitted that Yoder can sometimes sound this way, and the point is well taken. However, this would not be Yoder's considered opinion.

3. Zimbleman notes that at times Yoder appears to mean by *Constantinianism* the restructuring of the Roman Empire around the faith, but more often he means to refer to "the general tendency growing out of the alliance of church and state that rejects funda-

death, resurrection, and ascension of the Messiah had never occurred, and this leads to the repetition of many of the errors made by God's people in the Old Testament.

While it is true that Constantinianism has been prevalent within Christendom, it would not be quite accurate to say that Yoder simply and completely equates the two concepts. Oliver O'Donovan, in a book that defends the idea of Christendom, defines it as "a historical idea . . . the idea of a professedly Christian secular political order, and the history of that idea in practice."[4] O'Donovan interprets Stanley Hauerwas as equating Constantinianism with Christendom and as attacking both.[5] While I do not think that this is totally accurate even with regard to Hauerwas, it certainly would not be fair to interpret Yoder in this way because Yoder discusses the possibility of the ruler being converted and governing in a Christian way at several points in his writings.[6] He claims that such a possibility is highly unlikely but should not be dismissed *a priori*. It is not what O'Donovan refers to as "the obedience of rulers"[7] that is the problem for Yoder but rather the disobedience of rulers to the Lord Jesus Christ. Although Yoder does not rule out the Christendom idea *a priori*, he does believe that the historical period in which it was a real possibility has now passed. Therefore, he concludes that the vision of creating a fusion of church and state, a total Christian society, must be abandoned.[8]

---

mental elements of a proper eschatology" (Joel Zimbleman, "Theological Ethics and Politics in the Thought of Juan Luis Segundo and John Howard Yoder" [unpublished Ph.D. diss., University of Virginia, 1986], 219). The former would be just one particular historical instantiation of the latter.

4. Oliver O'Donovan, *The Desire of the Nations: Rediscovering the Roots of Political Theology* (Cambridge: University of Cambridge Press, 1996), 195.

5. See, for example, Stanley Hauerwas and William H. Willimon, *Resident Aliens* (Nashville: Abingdon, 1989), and Stanley Hauerwas, *After Christendom* (Nashville: Abingdon, 1991).

6. See, for example, Yoder's section entitled "What If There Had Been a Stronger Faith?" (*Christian Attitudes to War, Peace and Revolution: A Companion to Bainton* [Elkhart, Ind.: distributed by Co-op Bookstore, 1983], 53–54). Here he speculates about the hypothetical possibility that Constantine might have been converted and then obeyed Jesus Christ as Caesar: "would not the divine sovereignty be able to bless the believing obedience of a Caesar who, taking the risk of faith like any other believer, from his position of relative power, would love his enemies and do justice?" Yoder says that his enemies might triumph over him, but that often happens to rulers anyway. He might be killed or suffer or not stay in office all his life, but these things happen to rulers all the time. He might have to ask his followers to suffer, but emperors are accustomed to asking people to suffer for them. Yoder contends that it is not necessary, but in fact a denial of divine providence, to assume that nothing could have been achieved if Constantine had "taken on the substance of Christian discipleship rather than only the name and baptism." See also Yoder's discussion of the Pennsylvania experiment (ibid., 259–96).

7. This is the title of chapter 6 of O'Donovan's *Desire of the Nations*.

8. John Howard Yoder, "The Racial Revolution in Theological Perspective," *For the Nations: Essays Public and Evangelical* (Grand Rapids: Eerdmans, 1997), 107. Even many

Constantinianism As the Reversal of New Testament Eschatology

I am now ready to specify how Yoder views Constantinianism as departing from New Testament eschatology. Constantinianism denies or distorts all of the eight points listed in chapter 5 as summarizing Yoder's understanding of New Testament eschatology. It is thus, for Yoder, the reversal of New Testament eschatology.

1. The Lordship of Christ. Constantinianism denies the lordship of Christ by placing the human king, emperor, or other ruler(s) in the place of Jesus. This denial can happen in different ways and to different degrees. Yoder recognizes the right of governments to command the obedience of Christians except when such commands go against the will of God. But, he says, the state must be rejected when it demands "worship us" (as when early Christians were commanded to burn incense as an act of Roman emperor worship) or "kill for us" (as when the modern nation-state drafts Christians into the army and commands them to kill Christians from another nation-state).[9] Here is the point of testing, because here the state makes itself into an absolute value. When the concrete lordship of Jesus is modified, qualified, contradicted, or otherwise set aside by the state, then we have Constantinianism.

The glorification of the emperor qualifies the kind of lordship taught by Jesus in a more subtle manner as well. Yoder states that

> although the original message of Jesus was compromised in other ways, in the course of the process that created "Christendom," the most fundamental apostasy, which enabled and ratified the other kinds of betrayal, was the reversal of Jesus' attitude toward kingship in favor of the "Constantinian" glorification of imperial autocracy and wealth.[10]

of those who have thought that Christendom was a good idea in the past are now openly wondering if, perhaps, it is *passé*. See, for example, Paul Ramsey's questions along this line in *Speak Up for Just War or Pacifism: A Critique of the United Methodist Bishops' Pastoral Letter "In Defense of Creation"* (University Park: Pennsylvania State University Press, 1988). In this remarkable book, Ramsey wonders out loud if the time has not come to embrace the sectarian option and judges it to be "possible in principle" (128). He also states that the Niebuhrian charges of withdrawal and ineffectiveness against pacifism needs to be withdrawn and recognizes that Yoder is trying to find a way out of the "guilty responsibility" versus "irrelevant purity" dilemma (119). He asks: "Perhaps fidelity to Christ would have us, in this time and place, turn in that direction—and therefore away from speaking for the church to the church and to the nation and to one another as citizens of an armed power in the internationalism system" (142). Finding himself unable to pronounce a firm "no" to sectarianism, he finally says a halting, tentative "not yet" to the sectarian option (128).

9. Yoder, *Christian Attitudes to War*, 27.

10. John Howard Yoder, "Jesus: A Model for Radical Political Action," *Faith and Freedom* 1 (December 1992): 8.

Jesus taught his disciples that whoever wants to be great in the kingdom must become the servant of all (Mark 9:35). Furthermore, he taught them that they must not be like the kings of the Gentiles, who rule over people and let themselves be called benefactors. Instead, they are to be servants (Luke 22:25–27). Yoder comments:

> Why then should there be anything wrong with Christianity's becoming an official ideology? It must be because that change itself calls into question something definitional about the faith. Perhaps this would not need to be absolutely true. It nonetheless tends to be the case, in the experience of the Christianity community, that the only way in which the faith can become the official ideology of a power elite in a given society is if Jesus Christ ceases to be concretely Lord.[11]

The lordship of Christ means a new way of living for his disciples, the way of service, not power politics.

2. The Two Ages. In Constantinianism, the church basically lives in the old age, while the new age is either fused with the old age, pushed entirely into the future, or relegated to the realm of the ideal in some sort of metaphysical dualism.[12] All three views of what happens to the new age have been advocated by apologists for Constantinianism at different times and in different places. Yoder cites Eusebius of Caesarea, who was an advocate of the view that the two ages have come together.[13] Augustine relegated the kingdom to the realm of the ideal by means of his neoplatonic philosophy.[14] Many modern-day premillennialists would justify Constantinianism by making the kingdom a totally future reality. All of these strategies have in common the easing of the eschatological tensions between the "already" and the "not yet," which are so difficult to keep together.

3. The Powers. Kent Reames points out that, for Yoder, the structural denial of Christ's victory over the powers is a way of explicating the Constantinian error.[15] This can happen in two ways. First, if there is no consciousness of a need for such a victory, then the Constantinian error can be understood as a denial of the fall. This is a theological error. Second, there can be a recognition of the powers and a strategic decision to compromise with them in the name of "realism." This is a theological error

11. John Howard Yoder, "The Kingdom As a Social Ethic," *The Priestly Kingdom: Social Ethics As Gospel* (Notre Dame, Ind.: University of Notre Dame Press, 1984), 85. See also "The Christian Case for Democracy," *Priestly Kingdom*, 156–57.

12. John Howard Yoder, "The Constantinian Sources of Western Social Ethics," *Priestly Kingdom*, 140–41.

13. Yoder, *Christian Attitudes to War*, 43–44.

14. Ibid.

15. Kent Reames, "Histories of Reason and Revelation: With Alasdair MacIntyre and John Howard Yoder into Historicist Theology and Ethics" (unpublished Ph.D. diss., University of Chicago, 1997), 186.

and a moral error as well. The purpose of the church is to confront the powers and bear witness to Christ's victory over them, even if this involves suffering persecution, not to give credence to their claims to be absolute.

4. The Kingdom of God. The most blasphemous aspect of Constantinianism is the arrogation to a human construction the title of the kingdom of God. To identify the institutional church with the kingdom of God is to remove the ideal of the kingdom as a critical lever by which to judge the faithfulness of the church. As Yoder puts it,

> with the age of Constantine, Providence no longer needed to be an object of faith, for God's governance of history had become empirically evident in the person of the Christian ruler of the world. The concept of the millennium was pulled back from the future (whether distant or imminent) into the present. All that God can possibly have in store for a future victory is more of what has already been won.[16]

This kind of doctrine leads to the hubris expressed in empire, conquest, crusade, and persecution of religious minorities. Nationalism, however, must be rejected by those who live in the new age and look forward to the kingdom of God.[17]

However, it is still possible to have a form of Constantinianism in which the state does not go so far as to identify itself with the kingdom of God. As noted above, the kingdom can be spiritualized, made into a metaphysical ideal with no empirical reality, or pushed into the future. By not identifying itself as the kingdom of God, the Constantinian state can be much more humble and much more open to criticism. But Constantinianism always denies the power of the present reality of the kingdom in the name of "realism."

5. The Church. In Constantinianism, the church is no longer a body of people who have a different lifestyle; rather, it is merely an aspect of society. Yoder states:

> Before Constantine, one knew as a fact of everyday experience that there was a believing Christian community but one had to "take it on faith" that God was governing history. After Constantine, one had to believe without seeing that there was a community of believers, within the larger nominally Christian mass, but one knew for a fact that God was in control of history.[18]

The church becomes a part of culture. It becomes the institution that services the entire population with a certain category of "religious services."

16. Yoder, "Constantinian Sources of Western Social Ethics," *Priestly Kingdom*, 136–37.

17. John Howard Yoder, *The Original Revolution: Essays on Christian Pacifism* (Scottdale, Pa.: Herald, 1971), 61.

18. Yoder, "Constantinian Sources of Western Social Ethics," *Priestly Kingdom*, 137.

The church is the service station for the "crisis experiences" and for the "depth dimensions" of life. Christianity becomes a "religion," and religion is what holds a society together.[19] The church becomes the social institution that is concerned with the inward and the personal, while issues of power and justice are delegated to other institutions.[20] Thus, the church loses its ethical character.

6. The World. Constantinianism's basic failure is that of not distinguishing between the church and the world. The world comes to be in the church, and the church becomes worldly. The problem is not the engagement of the world by the church but rather the comfortable coexistence that results in the loss of witness. As Cartwright points out, the church's witness to the world in Yoder's thought takes the form of an evangelical nonconformity in and for the world.[21] In the title of the collection of essays by Yoder on ecclesiology, *The Royal Priesthood,* the term *royal* affirms the power of the servant community, and the term *priesthood* affirms the fact that the church does not exist for itself but to be the bearer of reconciliation. Yoder's view of mission is similar to Barth's in that he contends that the world needs the church in order to know itself as the world.[22] God allows the world the freedom to be the world, which in turn creates the necessary precondition for repentance and conversion. But Constantinianism does not give the world this freedom and, therefore, ceases to witness. In Constantinianism, all citizens are required to be a part of the church whether they wish to be Christians or not. Or, even if there technically is freedom of dissent, the state and the church are still so closely identified that being a Christian is closely bound up with being a loyal citizen.

7. The Meaning of History. According to Yoder, what happened in the life, ministry, death, and resurrection of Jesus altered history. Indeed, for Yoder, the lordship of Christ is what defines history.[23] As Zimbleman points out, history is incomprehensible for Yoder apart from the self-revelation of God.[24] Therefore, Yoder rejects all visions of history that lack

19. Yoder, *Christian Attitudes to War,* 52.

20. Yoder, "Constantinian Sources of Western Social Ethics," *Priestly Kingdom,* 141.

21. Michael Cartwright, "Radical Reform, Radical Catholicity: John Howard Yoder's Vision of the Faithful Church," in *Royal Priesthood,* 2.

22. See Barth's paragraph 72, "The Holy Spirit and the Sending of the Christian Community," in *CD* IV/3:2, 681–901, and, in particular, his correction of the Reformers' definition of the church in such a way that its mission is not its essence (767). This sense of the church being for the world distinguishes Yoder's position from that of Stanley Hauerwas and at least partly explains why Yoder entitled his last book *For the Nations: Essays Public and Evangelical,* a not-so-subtle reference to Hauerwas's book entitled *Against the Nations: War and Survival in a Liberal Society* (Minneapolis: Winston, 1985).

23. Michael Cartwright, "Practices, Politics, and Performance: Toward a Communal Hermeneutic for Christian Ethics" (unpublished Ph.D. diss., Duke University, 1988), 62.

24. Zimbleman, "Theological Ethics and Politics," 215.

a proper eschatological vision and that reflect a nonchristocentric fundamental orientation.[25]

Yoder critiques the Constantinian theory of causation, which presupposes a closed system of cause and effect in the universe and which therefore supposes that prediction and calculation are feasible. Zimbleman summarizes this critique in three statements.[26] First, Constantinianism tends to underestimate the effect of sin on human ego, rationality, and intellectual capacities.[27] Second, Constantinianism makes providence no longer a matter of faith but within the control of the ruler.[28] Third, Constantinianism holds individuals and collectives responsible for acts of omission in ways that contradict other important formulations of human agency and culpability.[29]

There are two problems with this theory of causation: its lack of realism and its constriction of vision. First, it is naive because, as Yoder puts it, "It has yet to be demonstrated that history can be moved in the direction in which one claims the duty to cause it to go."[30] This is ironic, since Constantinianism is usually defended by appeals to realism. But Yoder does not believe that the universe is a closed system, and even if it were, the Constantinian theory forgets that there is more than one moral actor. The calculation of one moral actor can be skewed by the unanticipated actions of other moral actors. The point is that human nature is not fully predictable.[31] Second, by assuming that if God wants something done, he is going to do it through the ruler, Christians tend to define what God wants by what it is possible for rulers to do. This leads Christians to forget that the church needs to do what only the church can do. But, says Yoder:

25. Ibid., 218.

26. Ibid., 222–23.

27. Yoder has been criticized for not having a more explicit doctrine of sin. See Robert M. Parham's comments in "An Ethical Analysis of the Christian Social Strategies in the Writings of John C. Bennett, Jacques Ellul and John Howard Yoder" (unpublished Ph.D. diss., Baylor University, 1984), 197–98. But Yoder's view of sin seems to be pervasive, given his suspicion of the function of ideologies of power.

28. Yoder, *Christian Attitudes to War*, 44.

29. Yoder notes that this is a Constantinian perspective because it thinks from the perspective of the one in power. But "the entire landscape looks different from a position of weakness. If you could not have stopped something, then you are not to blame when it happens" ("The Kingdom As a Social Ethic," *For the Nations*, 100).

30. John Howard Yoder, *The Politics of Jesus: Vicit Agnus Noster*, 2d ed. (Grand Rapids: Eerdmans, 1994), 230. Yoder notes that this is the phenomenon that Reinhold Niebuhr called "irony."

31. Alisdair MacIntyre writes convincingly of the lack of predictive power by the social sciences and the reasons for it in his chapter, "The Character of Generalizations in Social Science and Their Lack of Predictive Power" (*After Virtue* 2d ed. [Notre Dame, Ind.: University of Notre Dame Press, 1984], 88–108). The belief that bureaucratic managers and social scientists can predict future human behavior rationally is part of the myth of the Enlightenment that makes us comfortable in arrogating to ourselves, as a civilization, godlike characteristics and roles.

That Christian pacifism which has a theological basis in the character of God and the work of Jesus Christ is one in which the calculating link between our obedience and ultimate efficacy has been broken, since the triumph of God comes through resurrection and not through effective sovereignty or assured survival.[32]

A view of history that has no need of the miraculous is one that is sub-Christian, for Yoder, because "Christian ethics calls for behaviour which is impossible except by the miracles of the Holy Spirit."[33]

8. The State. In Constantinianism, the state becomes the bearer of the meaning of history and thus takes the place of the church eschatologically. Yoder notes that most Americans expect salvation in history to come from America, not from the church. In fact, the nation has become a substitute church.[34] Yoder thinks that it is possible to reject this extreme position and still have a relatively high view of the state: "In rejecting the idea that the norms for the social order are revealed in some order of creation, we do not mean to deny the foundation of human society within the creative intention of God."[35]

Of course, it must be remembered that, for Yoder, the ultimate intention for human society is revealed in the church and the role of the state is to provide order so that God's purposes can be revealed through the body of Christ.[36] Yet, the state can be affirmed as part of God's providential care for his creation and as the means by which social chaos can be restrained so that the preaching of the gospel can go ahead. Yoder says, "Vengeance itself, the most characteristic manifestation of evil, instead of creating chaos as is its nature, is harnessed through the state in such a way as to preserve order and give room for the growth of the church."[37]

But it must not be forgotten that vengeance, even when "harnessed" by the mysterious providence of God, is evil. Therefore, Yoder argues that no doctrine of the state is given in the New Testament and none is needed. He says:

32. Yoder, *Politics of Jesus*, 239.

33. Yoder, "Let the Church Be the Church," *Royal Priesthood*, 174.

34. Ibid., 176–77. Does not the reality of American, right-wing, civil religion constitute the strongest challenge to the defender of the viability of the Christendom idea today? Yoder thinks so.

35. John Howard Yoder, *The Christian Witness to the State* (Newton, Kans.: Faith and Life, 1964), 34.

36. Yoder, "Why Ecclesiology Is Social Ethics: Gospel Ethics versus the Wider Wisdom," *Royal Priesthood*, 126. Yoder puts it somewhat more colorfully in his lectures to his students: "What God wants of Christians is to love their enemies and suffer. What God wants of Caesar is to be decent and not persecute the Christians" (*Christian Attitudes to War*, 449).

37. Yoder, *Original Revolution*, 62.

It is thus formally wrong to look in the New Testament for specific guidelines for a good civil society. . . . We should look rather for a general orientation toward ultimate human values and the nature of redemption, and then ask for our time what those meanings have to say.[38]

A Christian view of the state will not expect redemption from the state and will be realistic in understanding the limits of how Christian the state can become. On the other hand, the historical situation varies enormously in terms of how much can be expected. The Christians in first-century Rome or contemporary China could expect far less from their government than could the Christians in England in the age of the Wesleys or in contemporary Canada, given the historical situations.[39]

A Constantinian view of the state is one that seeks to define the state and its function of restraining evil in terms of creation orders or natural law. Yoder denies that there is any such thing as a "state as such."[40] He points out that even theologians in the tradition of Karl Barth who reject the idea of natural law still tend to retain some conception of "the state as such" or "the legal state."[41] However, Yoder rejects all such "legitimist" theories of that state, that is, ones that claim to be able "to tell accurately the specific point at which a state would move from sobriety into idolatry."[42] As Yoder points out, Romans 13 does not qualify the Christian responsibility to be subject to the state by commanding subjection only to "legitimate" ones.[43] Very often, a comparison is drawn between the "legitimate state" of Romans 13 and the "illegitimate state" of Revelation 13. But no more is said about resisting or rebelling in Revelation 13 than is said in Romans 13.[44] The other view of the state, which arises at this point, is the "positivist" view, which says that "whatever is, is good."[45] Yoder rejects this view also as, perhaps, the height of Constantinianism. Between these two

---

38. John Howard Yoder and H. Wayne House, *The Death Penalty Debate: Two Opposing Views of Capital Punishment* (Dallas: Word, 1991), 146.

39. The view of David Hughes that Yoder is guilty of "demonizing the state with his Hobbsian reduction of the state to a monopoly on violence" must be rejected as too extreme ("The Ethical Use of Power: A Discussion with the Christian Perspectives of Reinhold Niebuhr, John Howard Yoder, and Richard J. Barnet" [unpublished Ph.D. diss., Southern Baptist Theological Seminary, 1984], 155). Yoder specifically refuses to "let fallenness define essence" and strongly denies that violence is the essence of the state. Rather, it is the *ultima ratio*, its outer edge. Yoder says that in taking this position he is siding with Barth and Biblical Realism against the Lutherans and Weberians (*Christian Attitudes to War*, 295).

40. Yoder, *Christian Attitudes to War*, 26–27.

41. Yoder, *Christian Witness to the State*, 79–80.

42. Ibid., 80.

43. Yoder, *Christian Attitudes to War*, 449.

44. Yoder, *Politics of Jesus*, 206.

45. Ibid.

views, Yoder carves out a third position. He urges subjection to whatever state exists but obedience only when the commands of rulers do not conflict with the will of God. Thus, the Christian may disobey but never rebel.[46] Suffering is always a possibility. The basis for the Christian witness to the state is not a theory of the state but the reign of Christ.

We have now examined how Constantinianism distorts or denies what Yoder understands to be the eschatology of the New Testament. It denies the lordship of Christ, dissolves the tension between the two ages created by the reign of Christ, fails to recognize Christ's victory over the powers, denies the power of the kingdom of God, causes the church to abandon its mission and to become the religious component of a particular culture, fails to recognize the freedom of the unbelieving world to rebel, operates with a naturalistic view of history by failing to acknowledge that the life, death, and resurrection of Christ has fundamentally altered history, and substitutes the state for the church as the bearer of the meaning of history. Yoder responds to Constantinianism by saying, first, "Let the church be the church," second, "Let individuals be reconciled to God," and third, "Let the state be the state."[47] Yoder's definition of eschatology is "a hope which, defying present frustration, defines a present position in terms of the yet unseen goal which gives it meaning."[48] Constantinianism is an attempt to have peace without eschatology or, perhaps one could say, an attempt to live as though this present world were permanent. As such, it represents a denial of Jesus Christ as he is testified to in the New Testament, that is, a denial of his death, resurrection, ascension, present reign, and future coming again in glory.

Constantinianism As a Return to the Solomonic Temptation

In spite of the fact that Roman Catholic, Orthodox, and Protestant theologians frequently have appealed to the Old Testament as the source of their Constantinian ideals, Yoder does not believe that the Old

46. Ibid., 198–209. For Yoder, the concept of revolutionary subordination (see ibid., chapter 9) means that the Christian should acknowledge the authority of the political authority and not be a revolutionary. But when the state commands something contrary to the will of God, then the Christian allows the state to punish him or her. An example would be civil-rights protesters committing civil disobedience and willingly going to jail as a means of appealing to the conscience of the wider society. But in Yoder there is less emphasis on calculating results and more on simply doing the right thing and leaving the outcome to God. A better example might be Daniel continuing his practice of praying three times daily even after the decree of the king that no one should pray to any god but the king (Daniel 6).

47. Yoder, *Original Revolution*, 75.

48. Yoder, "Peace without Eschatology," *Royal Priesthood*, 145.

Testament justifies Constantinianism any more than the New Testament does. Yoder claims that the thrust of the canon of Scripture as a whole is narrowed when, "as we have done it in the West from Augustine through Luther and Pietism to Kierkegaard, Bultmann and Billy Graham, its focus is upon a righteousness which is *coram Deo,* in 'the heart,' and not 'merely' civil."[49] This narrowing is potentially, though not necessarily, a betrayal. It is betrayal if it prevents us from seeing the fact that the canon of Scripture as a whole also involves the social embodiment of true faith: "To this challenge the canonical answer is clear, against all apoliticisms. From Abraham to the Apocalypse, the city God builds is on earth."[50] The focus on the inner and the personal becomes betrayal when it denies that "the newness of the gospel can take on flesh."[51] Yoder refuses to play off the supposedly outward-focused, socially concerned, institution-building Old Testament against the supposedly inward-focused, individual-oriented, anti-institutional New Testament. He sees the entire canon as being concerned for a faith that is both a matter of the heart and expressed in institutions and politics as well.

The "Solomonic temptation" is the same as the Constantinian one when it reduces the reordering demanded by the prophetic word and enables the hallowing of the present order. Speaking of both temptations, Yoder states: "It becomes betrayal when any power structure is identified as the order God desires."[52] The prophetic critique of the Davidic-Solomonic monarchy focused on the failure of the kings to conform to the Torah. The economic oppression, idolatry, power politics, class divisions, and standing army all combined to give the monarchy a stake in the maintenance of social order and the suppression of dissent. Since no social order in this sinful world can be perfect, to sacralize or sanctify or hallow one is always a form of idolatry in and of itself. Yoder notes that the Old Testament portrays the Davidic dynasty as a disappointment, not only to Samuel, but to God.[53]

Yoder argues that, under Jeremiah, the Jews came to see powerlessness as normal and Diaspora as a vocation given by grace and as permanent for the age until the Messiah comes.[54] He further holds that Jesus, as a prophet in the line of Jeremiah, reinforced this attitude:

> Jesus' impact in the first century added more and deeper authentically Jewish reasons, and reinforced and further validated the already expressed Jewish reasons, for the already well established ethos of not being in charge and not

49. Yoder, "The Bible and Civil Turmoil," *For the Nations,* 82.
50. Ibid.
51. Ibid.
52. Ibid., 83.
53. Yoder, "See How They Go with Their Face to the Sun," *For the Nations,* 60.
54. Ibid., 61–65.

considering any local state structure to be the primary bearer of the move-ment of history.[55]

Jesus founded a renewed Israel by choosing the Twelve. He founded a renewed and restructured people of God in which the key was faith, not ethnicity. The messianic congregations that sprang up around the Mediterranean basin during the first century were similar in structure and ethos to the synagogue-based rabbinic Judaism that had taken shape during the Diaspora. Yoder says, "Until the messianity of Jesus was replaced by that of Constantine, it was the only ethos that made sense."[56]

Constantinianism in Western History

Thus far I have examined Yoder's understanding of Constantinianism as an eschatological heresy that distorts the main points of New Testa-ment eschatology and have looked briefly at Yoder's critique of Constan-tinianism as constituting an inadequate reading of the Old Testament. The daunting task still remains, however, of attending to Yoder's reading of Western history as the story of the rise and fall of Christendom and the remarkable persistence of the Constantinian heresy up to the present.[57] Yoder has provided both brief overviews of Constantinianism in Western history and detailed investigations of specific episodes in that story that grapple with specific issues and situations.[58] This summary will follow the argument as it is developed both in the essays and in Yoder's studies in historical theology.

Yoder sees the events of the fourth century as having explicable histor-ical causes and not as the sudden appearance from nowhere of an en-tirely new attitude toward the state on the part of the church. As we saw above, Yoder contends that early Christianity assumed the shape and ethos of the Jeremianic vision of Diaspora, synagogue, and pacifism. As messianic Judaism quickly spread around the Mediterranean basin, in-evitably it encountered the Greco-Roman world. Yoder rejects both the view that the story of the church is one of constant, upward progress and the opposite extreme that the first-century Christians are the norm, from which Christendom later fell away. His own view is that no period of church history is absolutely authoritative and that the incarnation stands

55. Ibid., 69.

56. Ibid., 70.

57. The task is daunting because of the sheer volume of Yoder's historical writings. See the introduction to this book (n. 22).

58. See, in particular, the three essays in "Part B: History" of *Priestly Kingdom* and the early essays, "The Otherness of the Church" and "Peace without Eschatology," which have been reprinted in *Royal Priesthood*. See the works of historical theology cited above (introduction, n. 22) for the detailed study of specific episodes.

in judgment of all subsequent developments.[59] However, the early Christians at least had the advantage of reading the Bible in the same world and language as it had been written in, so their example must be taken with the utmost seriousness.[60]

Yoder locates the roots of the "fall of the church," or Constantinianism, as early as the second century in "the betrayal of the Jewishness of the early church, as the Christian apologetes of the second and third centuries moved into Hellenistic culture."[61] Yoder observes a "slow shift" in the second half of the second century as it becomes apparent that some Christians were beginning to do what the leaders still said was wrong, such as serving in the army.[62] He also points to what he terms "creeping empire loyalty,"[63] which develops as persecution recedes, more intellectuals join the church, and Christians find themselves occupying positions of authority, often due to their reputation for hard work and integrity. The number of Christians was also growing and is estimated by Yoder to be approximately 10 percent of the population by the year A.D. 300.

The upheavals between A.D. 300 and 410, which led to the fall of Rome, created the conditions for a drastic reversal of policy in which Christians went from being a persecuted minority to being tolerated in A.D. 311, to a favored status under Constantine, to legal establishment under Theodosius, who outlawed non-Christian worship in A.D. 390. In A.D. 420, Augustine called on the Roman government to bring the Donatists back into line, and the first persecution *by* Christians occurred. In A.D. 436, non-Christians were excluded from the army, and a two-century-long process can be said to have resulted in the birth of Christendom. The development of hierarchy and sacerdotalism, which gradually came to overshadow synagogue polity, are seen by Yoder as a "fall back into the pre-Jeremianic patterns of Hellenistic paganism."[64]

But Constantine did not change everything. The monastic movement may be seen as a protest against Constantinianism, a protest that preserves the memory of the earlier, pacifist community of disciples.[65] Yoder

59. See the discussion of this point in chapter 1.
60. Yoder, *Christian Attitudes to War*, 23–24.
61. Yoder, "The Authority of Tradition," *Priestly Kingdom*, 73. Yoder says that the apologists "are missionary in that they try to show the Gentiles that they can have the God of the Jews without the Jews." He goes so far as to say that, insofar as this is a sellout to Greek or Roman provincialism instead of Hebrew universality, this move can be identified as "the Fall of the Church" (Yoder, quoted by Gayle Gerber Koontz, "Confessional Theology in a Pluralistic Context: A Study of the Theological Ethics of H. Richard Niebuhr and John H. Yoder" [unpublished Ph.D. diss., Boston University, 1985], 218).
62. Yoder, *Christian Attitudes to War*, 30.
63. Ibid., 32.
64. Yoder, "See How They Go with Their Face to the Sun," *For the Nations*, 71 n. 48.
65. Ibid., 51.

points out that, in the Middle Ages, most of the church was still pacifist, even though the caesars, the princes, and their soldiers were permitted to kill in war. People who had shed blood *even in a just war* did not have access to the Eucharist without a period of penance[66] and could never become priests. There were several dissenting groups, such as the Franciscan penitents, the Brethren of the Common Life, the Waldensians, and the Czech Brethren, who rejected violence.[67]

Rabbinic Judaism, from A.D. 135 on, was "generally characterized as never justifying violence" and was able to keep its identity without possessing national sovereignty. In other words, says Yoder, "Judaism through the Middle Ages demonstrated the sociological viability of the ethic of Jesus. Judaism in terms of actual ethical performance represents the most important medieval sect living the ethic of Jesus under Christendom."[68] This is an intriguing point. I wonder if it has anything to do with the anti-Semitism of Christendom? It has always been difficult to explain the apparent felt need of so many Constantinian Christians to persecute Jews, and Yoder's observations at this point are suggestive. Could part of the explanation be a latent Christian consciousness of the moral superiority of the nonviolent lifestyle adopted by the Jews coupled with the moral questionableness of the Constantinian lifestyle with its compromise with violence? Is it possible that the witness of living out the lifestyle of Jesus cannot help but infuriate those who claim to follow him but who live by the sword? These are the kinds of questions raised by Yoder's analysis, even though Yoder himself does not raise them.

Once Christianity had become identified with empire, the concept of mission changed. Mission within the empire was basically education rather than evangelism, and the emphasis tended to be on enforcing outward conformity. Yoder refers to this development as "the Puritan misunderstanding."[69] Mission outside the empire was not common, except in tandem with political conquest. The era of Charlemagne was an era of annexation as "the name of Jesus is now intoned over a Germanic culture without changing its inner content, as it had been intoned over Graeco-

---

66. Yoder, *Christian Attitudes to War,* 115.

67. Ibid., 118.

68. Ibid., 125. Yoder summarizes the basis of Jewish pacifism in five points: (1) the sacredness of blood, for blood is life and belongs to God; (2) the messiah has not yet come; (3) the lessons of the Zealot experience, which did not result in righteousness even when partially successful militarily; (4) the wisdom in which God presides over the affairs of the Goyim is not revealed to us in any simple way; and (5) there is a place for suffering in the divine economy (127–28).

69. Yoder, "The Racial Revolution in Theological Perspective," *For the Nations,* 112. Yoder uses this expression because the Puritans have such a widespread reputation for forcing their Christian morality upon all members of their society. But, of course, it is not just the Puritans who have been guilty of doing this. So have Marxists, Muslims, Catholics, and Orthodox rabbis in the State of Israel.

Roman culture for half a millenium before."[70] The Crusades represented the apex of Constantinianism because they embodied the total reversal of regard for the outsider. Rather than seeing the outsider as "the test of one's love" (Matthew 5:43–48) or as "the proof of the new age's having come" (Ephesians 2), adherents to Constantinianism now saw the outsider as the "infidel" to be destroyed as proof of one's true faith without regard even for the usual rules for a just war.[71]

The Protestant Reformation brought about an intensification of Constantinianism in several ways. First, there could now be holy wars against other Christian nations.[72] Second, whereas at least a pretense of universality was possible with the Roman Empire, the nation-states of early modern Europe now took on a degree of autonomy never before seen in Western culture, and each nation-state had its own church to bless its actions. The decision of the Magisterial Reformers to call on local princes to defend the Reformation against its enemies created national churches. Third, since the wars of religion of the seventeenth century were fought for "the faith," the identification of the Christian population with the war aims of the government assumed a new level.[73] The foundation was laid for modern ideological and total war. As Yoder puts it, "the basic Constantinian vision remains, only on a much smaller, provincial scale."[74] This he calls neo-Constantinianism.

After the Enlightenment and the Age of Revolution, religious liberty and disestablishment weakened the ties between church and state as institutions. But "American patriotism remains highly religious," and the nation is seen as Christian. Yoder calls this neo-neo-Constantinianism. In our own century, we see religious persecution of Christians, for example, in Eastern Europe, yet Christians there remain patriotic. Their response is to claim that they should not be persecuted because their faith does not make them disloyal to the nation. In the case of the Soviet

70. Yoder, "Constantinian Sources of Western Social Ethics," *Priestly Kingdom,* 137. No doubt, defenders of Christendom would want to argue for a slow process of cultural change that would be seen as far more significant than Yoder would acknowledge. This is partly a historical and partly a theological debate.

71. Ibid., 138.

72. Ibid., 141.

73. This is why the just-war theory becomes a matter of doctrine for the first time in the Reformation confessions. Pacifism is thus a heresy for Protestants, although it has never been identified as such in the Roman Catholic Church (Yoder, "Constantinian Sources of Western Social Ethics," 144). See Mark Noll, *Creeds and Confessions of the Reformation* (Grand Rapids: Baker, 1991) for the Augsburg Confession, article 16: "Christians may without sin occupy civil offices or serve as princes or judges, render decisions and pass sentences according to imperial and other existing laws, punish evildoers with the sword, engage in just wars, serve as soldiers" (92) and the Thirty-Nine Articles of the Church of England, article 37: "It is lawful for Christian men, at the commandment of the magistrate, to wear weapons and serve in the wars" (226).

74. Yoder, "Constantinian Sources of Western Social Ethics," *Priestly Kingdom,* 142.

Union, the Orthodox Church was financed by a Marxist regime because of the resultant benefit to public relations on the world stage. Yoder calls this neo-neo-neo-Constantinianism. Finally, one more twist comes when God's cause (and the loyalty of Christians) is identified with some future "revolution" or hope that is yet to come. This is termed neo-neo-neo-neo-Constantinianism.

What is lost in Constantinianism? First, there is the loss of catholicity as the unit of loyalty becomes smaller and smaller. Second, there is the loss of the church's capacity to be critical of the regime. The power of the bishops and the pope to limit violence in the Middle Ages was considerable (rules of chivalry, the peace of God, the civil exemption of the clergy, the immunities of pilgrims, just-war criteria).[75] Third, there is the loss of connection to the example of Jesus. Yoder notes that "what the churches accepted in the Constantinian shift is what Jesus had rejected, seizing godlikeness, moving *in hoc signo* from Golgotha to the battlefield."[76] The proper response to this story, Yoder asserts, is repentance: the "disavowal" of Constantine.

The Charge of Sectarianism: An Evaluation

Having examined Yoder's view of Constantinianism as an eschatological heresy, I now turn to the charge of sectarianism that is often leveled against Yoder's theology and ethics. Is it possible to reject Constantinianism without cutting oneself off from moral discourse with those with whom one disagrees in fundamental ways? By adopting what appears (from a Constantinian perspective) to be a "sectarian" stance, does Yoder forfeit his right to critique the state or the wider community? Is it possible to take the kind of position that Yoder takes on natural theology and still have meaningful conversation about moral issues with non-Christians? Yoder does believe that the grounding of Christian ethics in God's self-revelation in Jesus Christ and the rejection of Constantinianism has implications for Christian ethical method, but he would not describe those implications as sectarian, except as a terminological concession made in order to facilitate the opening of dialogue.

1. Constantinian Moral Epistemology. Yoder rejects the need for meta-ethics or fundamental moral theology and identifies the attempt to formulate such systematic bases for Christian ethics as a Constantinian project. He rejects the idea that we must establish a set of agreed-upon axioms as the foundation for ethical debate. Instead, he suggests that the confession of rootedness in historical community is the place to start.[77] He also acknowledges that it is impossible to establish, either speculatively or from

75. Ibid., 144.
76. Ibid., 145.
77. Yoder, introduction to *Priestly Kingdom*, 7.

historical examples, a consistent anti-Constantinian model: "The denunciation of paganization must always be missionary and ad hoc; it will be in language as local and timely as the abuses it critiques."[78]

This means that Yoder is not committed to any one method in Christian ethics. He does not think ethical approaches can be categorized as either deontological or teleological or characterial if the point is to suggest that ethics can be done using one method alone.[79] He argues that deontological rigor is good for defending those absent from the decision-making process but wrongly used if taken to mean that in every situation there is only one imperative with no collisions. Consequential rigor is good as an acknowledgement of the length dimension of our actions but wrong if it is thought that it is possible to know all the costs and benefits in advance and also wrong if it is thought that cost/benefit analyses do not themselves involve prior deontological value judgments. The language of virtue is fine to acknowledge the depth dimensions of personality and culture and to negate punctualism, but it is wrong when it suggests that the virtuous person can operate without the resources of the other orders, as if there were a built-in moral compass, unfallen or easily repaired despite the fall. Yoder concludes: "Instead of seeking to settle on the one right idiom, the greater value will inhere in the skills of mixing and matching according to the shape of a particular debate."[80] Yoder contends that every moral decision involves elements of principle, character, due process, and utility.[81] He also states that no one can work in the Hebraic heritage and ignore the language of divine command. Nevertheless, "the life of the community is prior to all methodological distillations."[82]

Constantinianism needs to find a method that is above the particular because it needs authorization for the exercise of power over others. It sees institutions as the way to shape society according to the preferences of those in power, so the way to effect social change is to get control of the institutions of society. Yoder makes the point that even those who formally renounce Constantinianism can still be Constantinian in their moral thinking: "Ethics can continue to be seen as social engineering."[83] This kind of approach to ethics is basically a debate over what legitimately can be enforced on everyone or required of everyone. To put it in Yoder's terms, ethical discourse must now meet two tests: (1) Can you ask such behavior of everyone? (2) What would happen if everyone

78. Yoder, "The Disavowal of Constantine," *Royal Priesthood*, 250.

79. Yoder, "Radical Reformation Ethics," *Priestly Kingdom*, 113–14.

80. John Howard Yoder, "Walk and Word: The Alternatives to Methodologism," in *Theology without Foundations: Religious Practice and the Future of Theological Truth*, ed. S. Hauerwas, N. Murphy, and M. Thiessen Nation (Nashville: Abingdon, 1994), 87.

81. Yoder, "The Hermeneutics of Peoplehood: A Protestant Perspective," *Priestly Kingdom*, 36.

82. Yoder, "Walk and Word," *Theology Without Foundations*, 82.

83. Yoder, "The Racial Revolution in Theological Perspective," *For the Nations*, 104.

did it?[84] Constantinian moral epistemology thus appeals to the universal, natural law, common sense, a system, or a set of universally acknowledged axioms in order to justify the social order as it exists. But if it were not for the need to impose one's ethics on others, there would be no need for such claims to universality.

2. An Evangelical Moral Epistemology. Yoder contends that pluralism in epistemology is not a counsel of despair but part of the Good News. He says: "The divine command to walk in the communion of the Spirit is not in another compartment separate from procedural guidelines about how that communion works as an epistemology."[85] Yoder is not worried about having the right method for doing ethics before getting down to work because he views Christian ethics as being rooted "in revelation, not alone in speculation, nor in a self-interpreting situation."[86] He says: "The Christian loves his or her enemies because God does and commands his followers to do so; that is the only reason, and it is enough."[87] He also claims: "The good action is measured by its conformity to the command and to the nature of God and not by its success in achieving specific results."[88] Further, he claims: "Obedience means not keeping verbally enshrined rules, but reflecting the character of the love of God."[89] Again, he asserts, "The ethic of discipleship is not guided by the goals it seeks to reach, but by the Lord it seeks to reflect."[90]

This type of approach to Christian ethics is rooted in an evangelical epistemology, which is Yoder's alternative to a Constantinian epistemology. Chris Huebner perceptively observes that "while most commentators recognize the centrality of Yoder's account of 'political Constantinianism,' his discussion of what might be called 'methodological Constantinianism' is often overlooked."[91] I have attempted to describe Yoder's rejection of Constantinianism as involving a rejection of both its political and the epistemological implications. This rejection clears the

84. Yoder, "Constantinian Sources of Western Social Ethics," *Priestly Kingdom*, 139.

85. Yoder, "Walk and Word," *Theology Without Foundations*, 83.

86. Yoder, *Politics of Jesus*, 233.

87. John Howard Yoder, "Living the Disarmed Life: What Is Our Cross?" *Sojourners* 6 (May 1977): 17.

88. Yoder, *Christian Witness to the State*, 49.

89. Yoder, *Politics of Jesus*, 245. Richard Hays notes that Jesus as teacher of rules is minimized in Yoder's thought. He points out that Matthew 5:39 is never quoted in *Politics of Jesus* and only referred to once in a footnote. Yoder's arguments against violence are constructed along other, more hermeneutically sophisticated lines. The basic role of Scripture is not to provide rules for conduct but to serve as the "collective scribal memory" that the teacher draws on in teaching (Richard Hays, *The Moral Vision of the New Testament: Community, Cross, New Creation: A Contemporary Introduction to New Testament Ethics* [San Francisco: HarperSanFrancisco, 1996], 248–49).

90. Yoder, *Original Revolution*, 39.

91. Chris Huebner, "Mennonites and Narrative Theology: The Case of John Howard Yoder" *Conrad Grebel Review* 16 (Spring 1998): 23.

way for his constructive alternative to Constantinianism on the epistemological level, what we might call his evangelical moral epistemology.

Yoder defines the word *evangelical* as follows:

> What accredits news as good is that it enables or even commands wholeness
> or fullness, a validation or flourishing, not actualized in its absence. It cannot
> be imposed by authority, or coercively. It is rendered null when assent is im-
> posed. Nor can it be esoteric, reserved for specially inducted hearers.[92]

Yoder says that the Good News is *news* because those who hear it would
never have known it unless a messenger had told them. It is *good* news
because hearing it is liberating, not oppressive or alienating. Because it is
only such when *received* as good, "it can never be communicated coer-
cively; nor can the messenger ever positively be assured that it will be
received."[93]

Yoder is greatly misunderstood if his stance is interpreted as promoting either cultural relativism or a form of liberal individualism. His desire
to make it possible for the other person to reject his position is rooted in
the very center of his theology, the noncoercive love of God that is revealed in Jesus Christ.[94] As Gerber Koontz puts it:

> Fundamental to Yoder's theology is the faith that God is agape and that agape
> respects the freedom of the beloved. The idea that agape respects the freedom
> of the beloved "even to lose himself" is for Yoder the one solid point where no
> exceptions may be made: it is the starting point of theology, of history, of eth-
> ics, of church order, of every realm where agape matters.[95]

Yoder's evangelical epistemology does not authorize coercion or the
imposition of the truth on everyone whether they accept it or not. But he
does not need that kind of ethic because he is not interested in pursuing
a Constantinian project.

Gerber Koontz characterizes Yoder's alternative to Constantinian epistemology or apologetics as "heralding." She views Yoder as similar to
Barth in that both reject the idea that one can begin with human unbelief
and end up with God. She agrees that beginning somewhere other than
faith is not likely to bring unbelievers to faith. While Barth has been criticized for simply preaching to unbelievers instead of entering into dialogue with them, Gerber Koontz points out that, for both Barth and Yoder, the willingness to use the language of unbelievers may be a sign that

92. John Howard Yoder, "On Not Being Ashamed of the Gospel: Particularity, Pluralism, and Validation," *Faith and Philosophy* 9 (1992), 292.

93. Yoder, "'But We Do See Jesus': The Particularity of Incarnation and the Universality of Truth," *Priestly Kingdom*, 55.

94. Gerber Koontz, "Confessional Theology in a Pluralistic Context," 171–72.

95. Ibid., 71.

Christians are buying into non-Christian value systems.[96] She describes Yoder's concept of heralding as follows:

> The Christian herald must remain doubly vulnerable—vulnerable because he or she is reporting a particular relative historical event that itself may or may not speak to others, and vulnerable because the herald has disavowed those affiliations which might convince others to join the Christian movement for the wrong reasons. Defenceless confession of faith can only be "distinguished" from the colonial or crusader truth claim if the herald's double vulnerability is clearly perceived and willingly affirmed.[97]

The Christian mission involves bearing witness to Jesus Christ in both word and deed and renunciation of force, and the renunciation of the epistemological claims that justify force are part of that witness to the one who made himself vulnerable for us.

The strongest attack on this type of position comes from those who view pacifism as sectarian in the sense of condoning the suffering or death of innocent victims by refusing the path of violence.[98] To retreat from universal, moral truth claims can be seen as an abdication of responsibility to the neighbor. Yoder's response is to deny that this is a valid argument because, if it were, it would mean that God is complicit in all the evil of the world. It is part of the nature of agape to allow the other to rebel. The supreme example of this is God allowing his Son to be crucified.[99] Yoder also argues that there is a qualitative moral difference between allowing evil to occur, when the only way to stop it is to resort to lethal violence, and actually committing evil oneself. The reason there does not seem to be a difference to the Constantinian is that the Constantinian is asking a different question than the pacifist. The Constantinian is asking: What should the person in power do about this situation? But the pacifist is asking: How can a Christian testify to Jesus Christ in this situation? If using physical coercion and violence to enforce the rules is part of one's normal operating procedure, then refusing to intervene in just one specific case does look morally suspicious and even unfair. But if the use of violence has been ruled out in advance, then not using violence looks quite different.

One other critique of this epistemological position is the charge that this is a position of moral relativism. But we must separate the two questions of the truth claim itself and its justification. To reject foundationalism, as Yoder does, is to reject the possibility of finding a method that will

96. Ibid., 214.
97. Ibid. See Yoder's "Disavowal of Constantine," *Royal Priesthood*, 256.
98. Won Ha Shin, "Two Models of Social Transformation: A Critical Analysis of the Theological Ethics of John H. Yoder and Richard J. Mouw" (unpublished Ph.D. diss., Boston University, 1997), 179.
99. Yoder, *Original Revolution*, 64–65.

or should convince everyone that one's claim is right. But it is not to reject the conviction that one's truth claim is a universal truth. Yoder denies
the Constantinian notion that a claim must not be true for everyone if it
cannot be rationally justified to everyone. That notion is itself part of establishment thinking because it provides a way of distinguishing between "public" and "private" truth claims, that is, between the minority
ones, which can be overturned, and those of the power elite, which can
be imposed. Yoder rejects the idea that a claim must be rationally de-
monstrable in order to be true. He says, "there is the ontological problem. Does an epistemology of evangel presuppose some specific (remember that it need not be distinctive) understanding of what kind of
God can thus reveal himself? Of course it must somehow."[100] There is an
ontological basis to Yoder's moral claims, but he denies that that fact implies that they can be validated by means of a neutral process of moral
reasoning, because "the church precedes the world epistemologically."[101]

3. The Sectarian Character of Constantinianism. Yoder turns the accusation of sectarianism back on Constantinianism itself. Real sectarianism, in the biblical sense of un-Christian divisiveness, was "the formation of churches bound to the state and identified with the nation."[102] He
claims that sectarianism is a concept fostered and used by the Constantinian establishment for its own purposes:

> the initial intention of the "sectarian" communities which in the course of
> Western history have renewed a minority ethic has not been to be sects. Divi-
> sion was not their purpose. . . . They rather called upon the church at large to
> accept as binding for all Christians the quality of commitment which would in
> effect lead them all to be separated from the world once again in order to be
> appropriately in mission to the world.[103]

Many of the groups that have been branded "sects" are simply those that
have refused to buy into the Constantinian heresy.

William Placher has compared revisionist and postliberal theology
and has concluded that, in the postcolonial missionary situation, "the effort to ground Christianity in the broader tradition of Western culture
may make it less universally accessible."[104] He distinguishes between
three definitions of public theology. The first appeals to warrants available to any intelligent, reasonable, and responsible person; the second

100. Yoder, "On Not Being Ashamed of the Gospel," 295–96.
101. Yoder, introduction to *Priestly Kingdom,* 11.
102. Yoder, *Original Revolution,* 72.
103. Yoder, "Anabaptism and History," *Priestly Kingdom,* 85. See Chris Huebner
("Mennonites and Narrative Theology," 27) for an interpretation of Yoder at this point,
which parallels the one being advocated here.
104. William Placher, "Revisionist and Postliberal Theologies and the Public Character of Theology," *The Thomist* 49 (1985): 412.

understands religion as fundamentally a public, communal activity, not a matter of an individual's experience; and the third effectively addresses political and social issues.[105] Postliberal theology, including Yoder's, is clearly public in the second and third senses. With regard to the first sense, Yoder points out that every universe of discourse, although it is likely wider than some others, is also provincial in comparison to others.[106] The concept of a universal discourse is actually a myth perpetrated by the Constantinian establishment as an ideological justification of its political suppression of dissent. The point is not that there is no such thing as truth but rather that the contested nature of truth in a fallen world makes tolerance, dialogue, and pluralism both necessary and good. The anti-Constantinian, free-church tradition has led the way in the recognition of this insight in Western culture, and, in Yoder's thought, the free-church epistemology has been expressed systematically.

In this chapter, I have presented Yoder's understanding of Constantinianism as an eschatological heresy that distorts New Testament eschatology by denying the lordship of Christ, dissolving the tension between the two ages, failing to recognize Christ's victory over the powers, denying the power of the kingdom of God, causing the church to abandon its mission of witness, failing to recognize the freedom of the unbelieving world to rebel, operating with a naturalistic view of history, and substituting the state for the church as the bearer of the meaning of history. I have also noted that Yoder views Constantinianism as a revival of the Solomonic temptation, which misreads the Old Testament by giving priority to the Maccabean paradigm of nation, monarchy, and war instead of the Jeremianic paradigm of Diaspora, synagogue, and pacifism. This heresy has hindered the witness of the church throughout history, according to Yoder, and needs to be repented of and rejected by the church today.

Instead of acknowledging the Constantinian charges as to the sectarian character of pacifist dissent, Yoder describes Constantinianism itself as sectarian in that it identifies the church with particular nation-states and turns even fellow-Christians in other nations into enemies. In order for the true international, multiethnic, universal character of the church to be made visible, Yoder proposes repentance in the form of "the disavowal of Constantine." Only by separating itself from militaristic nationalism can the Christian church prepare itself for mission. Yoder not only rejects the notion that there is one universal method for accessing truth but also identifies the search for such a method as a typically Constantinian preoccupation. The Constantinian establishment needs so-called "universal" truth or "natural theology" in order to justify its imposition of the morality of the majority on the minority. The suffering, minority church needs no such epistemology. In fact, evangelical episte-

105. Ibid., 407.
106. Yoder, "'But We Do See Jesus,'" *Priestly Kingdom*, 47.

mology must be noncoercive in order for it to be experienced by those who hear it as *good news*. Yoder's opinion is that the gospel gains more credibility from the willingness of the church to suffer, and if need be die, for the sake of the gospel than it has ever received from the Constantinian willingness to kill for the sake of the gospel.

The connection between Yoder's Christology and his eschatology often has been overlooked, with the unfortunate result that his rejection of Constantinianism has been sadly misunderstood. Criticism of his concept of Constantinianism has often begged the question because it has been rooted in assumptions that themselves have been placed in question by Yoder's Christology. Unless critics come to terms with the eschatological grounds of his critique of Constantinianism and also with the rootedness of his eschatology in his Christology, they cannot engage Yoder's thought adequately. The most fundamental question raised by Yoder is that of the character of the God revealed in Jesus Christ. Furthermore, any critique of Yoder's rejection of Constantinianism that does not take seriously the loving character of the God who is revealed in the life, death, resurrection, and ascension of Jesus Christ is superficial.[107] No Christian view of history can ever be satisfactory that does not take seriously the implications of the fact that the incarnate Son of God died at the hands of the rulers of this world and of the fact that God has raised Jesus from the dead.

Yoder's rejection of Constantinianism, however, raises a question. If

---

107. The criticism of Yoder's position in Philip LeMasters's book is a case in point (*The Import of Eschatology in John Howard Yoder's Critique of Constantinianism* [San Francisco: Mellen Research University Press, 1992]). LeMasters appears to misunderstand Yoder on the central issue of the rejection of Constantinianism. He interprets Yoder as claiming that the reason we should not adopt the majority view, that the fusion of church and empire under Constantine was a blessing resulting from God's providence, is because God's providence is inscrutable (111). LeMasters then criticizes Yoder for being inconsistent in arguing that "God did not providentially bring Constantine to power" and for speaking "substantively on any question concerning God's action in history" (112). Actually, Yoder never says that providence is inscrutable in the sense attributed to him by LeMasters. His point is just the opposite. We *can* know that the identification of empire and church under Constantine is wrong because it causes members of the church to act against the revealed will of God in Jesus Christ by joining in imperial violence.

In chapter 2 of his book, LeMasters provides a good summary of Yoder's Christology (57–62) and correctly recognizes that "Yoder's Jesus is an eschatological Jesus" and that there is a general coherence between his eschatology and his Christology (62). But then LeMasters appears to forget these excellent conclusions in chapter 3, when he professes to be unable to comprehend why Yoder rejects Constantinianism (117). Is it the case that Yoder's thought is simply too counterintuitive to be grasped except by sustained concentration on the logic of his reasoning? Is it the challenge of suspending highly ingrained Constantinian thought patterns that defeats critics despite their best efforts? One thing is clear: it is the failure to come to terms with the logical connection between Yoder's Christology and his eschatology that, in the end, constitutes the inadequacy of LeMasters's book as a guide to Yoder's thought.

the state is not the bearer of the meaning of history and thus not the appropriate vehicle for Christians to use in implementing Christian social ethics, what concrete shape can Christian social ethics take in the world today? Given our Western, individualistic, liberal heritage, the temptation is to settle for a pietistic and inner response to the call of Jesus Christ and to abandon the world, structures, institutions, and politics to the devil. But Yoder contends that liberal individualism does not allow for an adequate witness to Jesus Christ any more than sectarianism does. Is there a way to have a non-Constantinian social ethic in this fallen world? Yoder argues that there is, but only if we begin to take the Christian community far more seriously than most of us are used to taking it. Therefore, in the next two chapters, we turn to Yoder's contention that the church is the shape of a faithful Christian social ethic.

Part IV

Ecclesiology as the *Shape* of Yoder's Social Ethics

The meaning of history is carried first of all, and on behalf of all others, by the believing community.

John Howard Yoder
"Why Ecclesiology is Social Ethics:
Gospel Ethics Versus the Wider Wisdom," 1980

The challenge to the faith community should not be to dilute or filter or translate its witness, so that the 'public' community can handle it without believing, but so to purify and clarify and exemplify it so that the world can perceive it to be good news.

John Howard Yoder
"Firstfruits: The Paradigmatic Role
of God's People," 1992

7

Yoder's Believers' Church Ecclesiology

In chapter 5, I noted Yoder's methodological innovation of beginning with the eschatological Jesus of the Gospels and then asking how our modern concept of history needs to be revised in order to make it possible to see the relevance of Jesus for Christian ethics, rather than setting Jesus aside as irrelevant for Christian ethics. I argued that the result was an understanding of the church as an eschatological community of disciples who follow Jesus in rejecting violence and the glorification of wealth and power and embracing love and servanthood. Ultimately, Yoder's ecclesiology is grounded in his Christology insofar as the church is the community brought into existence by the resurrection of Christ and that is, therefore, incomprehensible apart from the resurrection. The risen Lord continues to be present in his church by means of his Spirit, who fills the disciples who follow Jesus. Thus, the church is, as Yoder and McClendon put it, "an eschatological community grounded in Scripture."[1]

In this chapter, I wish to examine Yoder's believers' church ecclesiology in relation to other approaches to ecclesiology and to consider the ecumenical implications of his believers' church vision. Yoder's ecclesiology is one of an eschatological community, which is evangelical, ecumenical, catholic, and reforming. Then I will turn to a more detailed description of Yoder's vision of the Christian community as an alternative *polis,* a new society in which God's future intentions for human society in

1. John Howard Yoder and James Wm. McClendon Jr., "Christian Identity in Ecumenical Perspective: A Response to Layman," *Journal of Ecumenical Studies* 27 (1990): 571.

general can be discerned. The pivotal role of the Holy Spirit in the community will be emphasized. This chapter will lay the necessary foundation for the next one, when I will consider Yoder's views on how the Christian community can witness to the civil community. In that context, I will deal with the charges of withdrawal and irrelevance that have been made against Yoder's theology. At that point, I will be ready to give an account of the resources in Yoder's thought that can be deployed in response to these criticisms so that a proper evaluation of their validity can be made. Yoder has thought this issue through systematically in a way that will seem novel (and possibly intriguing) to many readers, especially those who have always taken for granted the assumption that the choice facing the church is always between purity and faithfulness, on the one hand, or compromise and influence, on the other hand.

Yoder's Believers' Church Ecclesiology Defined

What does Yoder mean by the term "believers' church," and why does he use it? The term "believers' church" was coined by Max Weber[2] and is closely related to the labels "the radical reformation," as used by George H. Williams,[3] and "the free church," as used by Franklin H. Littell.[4] Harold S. Bender attempted to define the term "Anabaptist" more precisely,[5] but, as we saw in the discussion of Reformation historiography in chapter 1, the precision of Bender's definition has been called into question by contemporary sixteenth-century historians. Recently, James McClendon has proposed the term "baptist" as a way of referring to "this 'free church' or 'believers' church' or baptist style of Christian thought" that is, he claims, "widely displayed but only haltingly voiced."[6]

The term "radical reformation" has a definite meaning with regard to sixteenth-century historiography. Its suitability for Yoder's use today, however, is limited by the fact that it includes movements that would diverge dramatically from his ecclesiology, such as the Evangelical Rationalists and the Spiritualists. The problem with the term "free church" is that it takes on very different definitions in various geographical locations. For example, in Great Britain, the free churches include all Protestant denominations other than the Church of England, which means that the Presbyterians are "free" in England even though they are the estab-

---

2. Max Weber, *The Protestant Ethic and the Spirit of Capitalism*, trans. T. Parsons (New York: Charles Scribner's Sons, 1958). Weber says that these groups sought a "community of personal believers of the reborn, and only these" (144–45).

3. George H. Williams, *The Radical Reformation*, 3d ed. (Kirksville, Mo.: Sixteenth Century Journal Publishers, 1992).

4. Franklin H. Littell, *The Free Church* (Boston: Starr King, 1957).

5. Harold S. Bender, *The Anabaptist Vision* (Scottdale, Pa.: Herald, 1944).

6. James Wm. McClendon Jr., *Ethics*, vol. 1 of *Systematic Theology* (Nashville: Abingdon, 1986), 7–8.

lished church in Scotland.[7] The term "Anabaptist," as defined by Harold Bender, is used quite often by Yoder, but it is really a historical term that applies to certain sixteenth-century reform movements rather than a description of any contemporary Christian group. McClendon's term "baptist" is useful as he seeks to describe a way of thinking rather than a historical movement or group, and Yoder is open to using it. One problem with it, however, is that it is so new that no one knows yet if it will become widely used or not. Another potential problem is that it can be confused with the term "Baptist," which is the name of a family of denominations, and it may not be possible to make the term "baptist" inclusive enough to cover non-Baptist believers' churches.

The term "believers' church" does have the advantage, from Yoder's perspective, of calling attention to some of the key distinctives of this ecclesiology, such as the voluntary nature of church membership and institutional independence from the state.[8] The disadvantage is that it seems presumptuous in its supposed implication that members of other churches are not believers. But need it imply this? Surely Roman Catholics do not mean to imply by using that denominational name that no other Christians are part of the catholic faith. The Christian Reformed Church, by its name, does not mean to imply that it is the only truly reformed church. The point of the term "believers' church" is not to make a negative judgment about the status of members of other churches but to affirm the distinctives held in common by this family of Christians in a descriptive way.[9] Clearly, this is how Yoder uses the term in his various writings, although, for the sake of dialogue, he is usually willing to start from the definitions set down by his dialogue partners and work from there. Thus, he sometimes uses the term "Anabaptist" to describe his position, sometimes "free church," and other times "believers' church," depending on the context.[10] In this chapter, I have chosen to use the term

7. John Howard Yoder, "Another 'Free Church' Perspective on Baptist Ecumenism," *Journal of Ecumenical Studies* 17 (1980): 149.

8. John Howard Yoder, "A 'Free Church' Perspective on Baptism, Eucharist and Ministry," *The Royal Priesthood: Essays Ecclesiological and Ecumenical,* ed. Michael Cartwright (Grand Rapids: Eerdmans, 1994), 279. Yoder notes that most of the people in these movements in the past preferred to call themselves simply "brethren."

9. This is the argument of Donald Durnbaugh in his classic work, *The Believers' Church: The History and Character of Radical Protestantism* (New York: Macmillan, 1968), ix, cf. 3–33.

10. See, for example, Yoder's use of "Anabaptist" in "The Anabaptist Dissent: The Logic of the Place of the Disciple in Society," *Concern* 1 (June 1954): 45–68; his use of "believers' church" in "The Believers' Church: Global Perspectives," in *The Believers' Church in Canada: Addresses and Papers from the Study Conference in Winnipeg May 1978,* ed. J. K. Zeman and W. Klassen (Waterloo, Ont.: The Baptist Federation of Canada and the Mennonite Central Committee, 1979), 3–15; and his use of "free church" in "A

"believers' church" as the best and most accurate (though by no means perfect) term to describe Yoder's ecclesiology.

Three Types of Ecclesiology

Yoder contends that there are three basic types of ecclesiology: the theocratic vision, the spiritualist reaction, and the believers' church.[11] These three types can be seen with clarity in the sixteenth-century continental Reformation, although they recur repeatedly in church history. To the theological left and geographical southwest of the Lutheran Reformation, we see the three types clearly distinguished in the movements relating to Zwingli in the 1520s. At one corner of a triangle, we see the Anabaptists, as exemplified most clearly in Michael Stattler and Pilgrim Marpeck. At a second corner of the triangle, we see the Spiritualizers, best exemplified by Casper Schwenckfeld. At the third corner of the triangle, we see the theocratic humanism of Erasmus as carried forward by Huldrych Zwingli. Each of these groups defined itself in relation to the other two and in relation to the Lutheran Reformation. Each group saw the other two groups as alike in their error.

From the perspective of Zwingli (and Calvin and the Roman Catholics), the Anabaptists and Spiritualists were alike in their divisiveness and their irresponsible willingness to undermine Christian government. They shared the Lutheran error of rejecting the theocratic vision and relegating government to a position outside the gospel. From the perspective of Schwenckfeld, the Anabaptists and the Magisterial Reformers in general were too concerned with outward forms. Both Zwingli and the Anabaptists had (like Luther) failed to carry to its logical conclusion their withdrawal from the Roman Church and its manifold ceremonies and forms. From the perspective of Pilgrim Marpeck, the Spiritualizers and Zwingli were quite similar insofar as they both denied the ultimate im-

---

'Free Church' Perspective on Baptism, Eucharist and Ministry," 278–88. In another setting he uses the term "free church," as assigned, but defines it to mean roughly the same as the term "believers' church" ("Another 'Free Church' Perspective on Baptist Ecumenism," 149.) Yoder, at another point in his writings, defines "free church" as the wider term, which includes "believers' churches" within it. Some "free churches" are not "believers' churches," as can be seen from the obvious fact that, in the United States, all the churches are "free churches." He then defines the Mennonites as one of the three "historic peace churches," which is a smaller subset of the "believers' churches," which, of course, includes nonpacifist denominations as well. So there are four concentric circles: (1) free churches, (2) believers' churches, (3) historic peace churches and (4) Mennonites (Yoder, *Christian Attitudes to War, Peace and Revolution: A Companion to Bainton* [Elkhart, Ind.: distributed by Co-op Bookstore, 1983], 165).

11. Yoder, "A People in the World," *Royal Priesthood*, 71–72. As Yoder notes, he is following Ernst Troeltsch and Franklin H. Littell in his typology of these groups. See Troeltsch's *The Social Teachings of the Christian Churches*, 2 vols., trans. O. Wyon (Chicago: University of Chicago Press), for his famous "church-sect-mysticism" typology.

portance of proper church order. Schwenckfeld, because he thought only spiritual reality matters, did not challenge the established worship and church structure of Christendom and thus suffered no persecution. Zwingli argued for the invisibility of the true church and so was able in good conscience to move as slowly in the reform of the church as public order required. Since faith is invisible anyway, Zwingli had no problem in continuing to baptize infants. Since faith is everything, Schwenckfeld attached no importance to baptism in any form.

Yoder views the theocratic type of ecclesiology as a "vision of the renewal of the church that hopes to reform society at large with one blow."[12] The locus of meaning is the movement of the whole society. It would be historically accurate to label this position "Puritanism," but Yoder does not do so because of the negative "emotional coloring" that this term has taken on in contemporary culture. Other advocates of this type of ecclesiology in history have included Roman Catholicism, Calvin, Knox, Cromwell, Christian Realism, and many segments of the World Council of Churches.

Yoder argues that the spiritualist type of approach to ecclesiology, which moves the locus of meaning from society to the spirit or the self, is a natural reaction to the theocratic type. Here the historically accurate term would be "Pietist," but this is an even more emotion-laden term. Also, it would be confusing to use this term because many groups with a believers' church type of ecclesiology historically have been labeled "Pietist," such as Methodist and Brethren groups. Spiritualism is able to function quite well within the framework of the theocratic society that it rejects, as a "church within the church." As Yoder puts it, "By giving no social form to its dissent, it leaves the established church in place."[13] It can even tolerate the structures of the theocratic ecclesiology, while insisting that outward forms are useless unless a "deep inward reality can be found."[14] Advocates of the spiritualist approach to ecclesiology have included Jacob Spener, much of contemporary evangelicalism, Rudolf Bultmann, and Billy Graham.

Yoder contends that the believers' church approach "stands not merely between the other two but over against both of them."[15] With spiritualism, the believers' church approach protests the coldness and formalism of the theocratic churches but insists that the answer is not to eschew forms altogether or to create parachurch organizations. Rather, this approach seeks to reform the church according to Scripture so that the forms can express the true character of the disciples' fellowship. Yo-

12. Yoder, "A People in the World," *Royal Priesthood,* 71.
13. Ibid., 72.
14. Ibid. An example of this would be the charismatic renewal movements within various mainline denominations today.
15. Ibid.

der's claim is that "the church is called to move beyond the oscillation between the theocratic and the spiritualist patterns, not to a compromise between the two or to a synthesis claiming like Hegel to 'assume' them both, but to what is genuinely a third option."[16] Yoder's believers' church approach is one that needs to be described in more detail, and we will turn to such a description in the second section of this chapter. However, before we do, it needs to be stressed that Yoder's ecclesiological vision is not one of justifying or sanctifying one, small, sectarian group or family of denominations as the only true church and condemning all the mainline Roman Catholic and Protestant denominations. His vision is an ecumenical one that is addressed to the entire church, and we turn to this ecumenical vision next.

Yoder's Ecumenical Vision

My goal in this chapter is to situate Yoder's ecclesiology in relation to other approaches to ecclesiology. Thus far we have seen that the best term to use in describing his ecclesiology is "the believers' church," and we have contrasted this type of ecclesiology with the theocratic vision and the spiritualist reaction. Now it is necessary to raise the question of the ecumenical relevance of Yoder's approach. It could be objected that he is merely the apologist for a small family of minor denominations, which he regards as true churches, as over against the mass of other Christian groups. Given his stern critique of Constantinianism as an eschatological heresy that obscures the message of the gospel and prevents the church from being a good witness to Jesus Christ, one might be inclined to suspect that Yoder thinks that the vast majority of Christian churches are beyond hope. One might suspect Yoder of being a separatist. But the diligent reader of Yoder's writings, especially as found in *The Royal Priesthood,* knows that such is not the case. In this section, I want to examine four motifs in Yoder's ecclesiology that make his ecclesiology evangelical, ecumenical, catholic, and reforming. The four motifs are the voluntary nature of membership, the conversational model of unity, the congregational focus of mission, and the unfinished character of the church. These motifs are not Yoder's outline but rather my analysis of what is going on in his various writings.

1. Evangelical. First, we draw attention to the *evangelical* character of Yoder's ecclesiology by considering the motif of the *voluntary nature of membership.* As we saw in our discussion of the charge of sectarianism in chapter 6, Yoder believes that the church-world distinction is essential in order for the gospel to be experienced as good news. He also believes that voluntary membership is essential to the proper ordering of the

16. Ibid., 72–73.

church for mission, because only if membership is voluntary can the necessary distinction between the church and the world be maintained. This distinction is also a prerequisite for the evangelistic task of the church because, unless the gospel is experienced as the call to join a new community, the social nature of the faith is obscured by individualism.

Oliver O'Donovan seriously misunderstands the significance of Yoder's concern for the voluntariness of church membership when he suggests that it is simply a matter of conformity to liberalism, "lining the church up with the sports clubs, friendly societies, colleges, symphony subscription-guilds, political parties and so on just to prove that the church offers late-modern order no serious threat."[17] For some reason, O'Donovan assumes that Yoder's defense of voluntary membership is in conflict with the idea that belief is foundational to church membership. He says: "I notice the emphasis John Howard Yoder lays upon *voluntariety* in his characterisation of the church, at the expense of *belief.* . . . A voluntary society is one that I could leave without incurring grave or irremediable loss."[18] But this is little more than a caricature of Yoder's position. Where does Yoder say that membership in the church is of such little importance that it can be dispensed with "without incurring grave or irremediable loss"? That attitude would characterize the spiritualist type of ecclesiology that Yoder rejects. And where does he say that belief is not the basis of church membership? It is, after all, not Yoder who is concerned to defend the tradition of infant baptism, which creates church members (Christians?) who have not even reached the point of being capable of belief. Rather, Yoder defends the tradition of believers' baptism as the mark of entrance into the believers' church. Why? It is primarily because, for him, the only logical reason to enter the church and accept the disciplines of the Christian life is that one has come to *believe* the gospel. Faith comes by hearing.

O'Donovan's defense of the Christendom idea and the state-church concept is strikingly eccentric in these days of religious freedom and separation of church and state, and it seems to be connected with his desire to affirm the truth of the gospel. But it is not his stout defense of the need to stand firmly for the truth of the gospel that is the problem. The problem, from a Yoderian perspective, is his method of doing so. Historically, the Christendom idea logically led to the Inquisition because, if the gospel is true and its truth is publicly accessible knowledge, then coercing people to accept it can be seen as perfectly justifiable. The debate is merely over the appropriate level of coercion, with the levels ranging from preferential taxation policies for church property to burning heretics at the stake. But Yoder is by no means suggesting that the alternative to authoritarianism is

17. Oliver O'Donovan, *The Desire of the Nations: Rediscovering the Roots of Political Theology* (Cambridge: University of Cambridge Press, 1996), 223–24.
18. Ibid., 223.

liberal individualism and religious pluralism. Rather, he is suggesting that "communities which are uncoerced can affirm individual dignity (at the point of uncoerced adherence of the member) without enshrining individualism," and "they can likewise realize community without authorizing lordship or establishment."[19] O'Donovan's theocratic vision does give substance to the Christian conviction that the gospel is true, but it does so at the cost of obscuring the uncoercive love of God that is at the heart of the gospel of Jesus Christ. What is needed is an ecclesiology that makes both the truth claims of the gospel and the loving God of the gospel equally visible. This is why Yoder affirms an epistemology of evangel, which rejects foundationalist methodology while affirming the truth claims of the gospel as proclamation. The voluntary, disciplined community of disciples is the logical result of an evangelical epistemology, which is why Yoder associates freedom of confession with the evangelical character of the believers' church ecclesiology.

2. Ecumenical. Second, we point out the *ecumenical* character of Yoder's ecclesiology by considering the motif of the *conversational model of unity.* Yoder claims that his ecclesiology is not "primitivist" or "fundamentalist" in the sense of claiming that nothing has happened since the first century.[20] He believes that it is possible to make choices that are more or less faithful at all points during church history and that the criteria of the self-revelation of God in Jesus Christ, as testified to in Scripture, is the criteria by which evaluative judgments can be made about the faithfulness of the church both in history and in the present.[21] Yoder is interested in a continuing conversation about the meaning of Christian faithfulness today.

All those who identify with the historic Christian faith are part of this conversation. In the introduction to *The Priestly Kingdom,* Yoder states:

> As these essays should be understood as addressed to Christians in general, and not peculiarly "sectarian," so also they should be understood not as "radical" in any modern sense of the term, which places a premium on the far out and unprecedented, but rather as classical or catholic.[22]

Yoder not only wishes to address all Christians, but he does so on the basis of that which all Christians claim to have in common, namely, Scripture. He speaks of his

---

19. John Howard Yoder, "The Hermeneutics of Peoplehood: A Protestant Perspective," *The Priestly Kingdom: Social Ethics As Gospel* (Notre Dame, Ind.: University of Notre Dame Press, 1984), 24.

20. John Howard Yoder, *Body Politics: Five Practices of the Christian Community before the Watching World* (Nashville: Discipleship Resources, 1992), 10.

21. See chapter 1 for a discussion of this point.

22. Yoder, *Priestly Kingdom,* 8.

claim that the vision of discipleship projected in this collection is founded in Scripture and catholic tradition, and is pertinent today as a call for all Christian believers.

. . . These pages do not describe a Mennonite vision. They describe a biblically rooted call to faith, addressed to Mennonites or Zwinglians, to Lutherans or Catholics, to unbelievers or other believers.[23]

Yoder sees his radical-reformation model as a paradigm "for all ages and communions, rather than an apology for a denomination claiming the last—or best—word."[24]

In spite of Yoder's strong views on the reality of apostasy, he is not, as Gerber Koontz points out, a separatist.[25] As the title of the article, "The Imperative of Christian Unity," clearly demonstrates, Yoder is deeply concerned about the need to express Christian unity, not for superficial reasons such as good manners or efficiency, but because it is a christological imperative. According to Yoder, the unity of the church is necessary for the fulfillment of the church's mission. With reference to the high-priestly prayer of Jesus in John 17, he says:

The function of the unity of the future believers is, therefore, to make credible the fundamental claim ("that the world might believe," said twice) and to reflect the nature of the unity between the Son and the Father, to render that credible witness substantial.[26]

Yoder also refers to Ephesians 2–3, which makes the same point. God's cosmic purposes are bound up with the visible unity of Jew and Gentile in the body of Christ. Religious pluralism, however, denies this gospel truth. By "pluralism" Yoder means "that pattern of independence and toleration whereby each group lets the others exist without coercion or unification, also without agreement."[27] The "lazy solution of pluralism" is founded on the false view that unity is based on agreement, so that every dispute calls for division. This reluctance to take the sin of disunity seriously is, in part, a reaction to centuries of Christians persecuting and killing each other in order to enforce unity. We know we cannot do this anymore, but we have given up on unity rather than finding different methods to pursue it.

23. Ibid.
24. Ibid., 4–5.
25. Gayle Gerber Koontz, "Confessional Theology in a Pluralistic Context: A Study of the Theological Ethics of H. Richard Niebuhr and John H. Yoder" (unpublished Ph.D. diss., Boston University, 1985), 154. See Yoder's argument that to say that all denominations or Christian propositions have equal validity is to be indifferent to questions of truth or ethics (John Howard Yoder and David Shank, "Biblicism and the Church," *Concern* 2 [1955]: 56).
26. Yoder, "The Imperative of Christian Unity," *Royal Priesthood*, 291.
27. Ibid., 291–92.

Yoder has no magic solutions for Christian unity. He calls for unity of discipleship and discipline on the congregational level and unity of conversation on the supracongregational level.[28] Yoder basically thinks that we should never stop talking and, therefore, never divide. His own life of involvement in the World Council of Churches, the Believers' Church Conferences, evangelical coalitions, and so on is ample evidence that he practiced what he preached at this point.[29]

3. Catholic. Third, we take account of the *catholic* character of Yoder's ecclesiology by considering the motif of the *congregational focus of mission*. Yoder gives a significant clue to his concept of how ecumenical progress can be made today when he points out that the modern ecumenical movement is a kind of believers' church in that it "begins by relativizing those definitions of unity that depended upon an established hierarchy, one particular body of authoritative creeds, or the rejection of a particular set of heretics."[30] It carries on a conversation in which those who choose to participate do so. The dialogical process, he points out, is thus self-defining rather than being made possible or restricted by an "inherited institutional, ritual, or creedal status."[31]

Yoder also is hopeful because unity at the congregational level is the most important kind of unity, and it is there that the barriers are least restrictive. For Yoder, the congregation, rather than the bishops or synods, is the basic unit of the church. All churches have congregations in common, and all congregations have a life of their own. Yoder argues that the most significant level of mission occurs at the congregational level and that, for this reason, the believers' church ecclesiology has something to say to congregations of all traditions and denominations.

4. Reformed. Fourth, we call attention to the *reforming* character of Yoder's ecclesiology by considering the motif of the *unfinished character of the church*. Yoder simply refuses to accept the idea that the Reformation is over. He points out that the divisions of the sixteenth century did not occur because some Christians left the catholic church to pursue their own visions of the faithful church. They occurred because the Magisterial Reformers appealed to local and provincial governments to help them in the conflict with the empire and the bishops. The institutionalization of the Reformation had the effect of freezing the process of reform: "They not only divided the Christendom which they had hoped to reform as a unit; they froze it into patterns of administration which were no longer reformable."[32] Since then, Western intellectual history has

28. Gerber Koontz, "Confessional Theology in a Pluralistic Context," 156.

29. See William Klassen's article for documentation of this point ("Yoder and the Ecumenical Church," *Conrad Grebel Review* 16 [Spring 1998]: 77–81).

30. Yoder, "A 'Free Church' Perspective on Baptism, Eucharist and Ministry," *Royal Priesthood,* 280.

31. Ibid.

32. Yoder, "The Hermeneutics of Peoplehood," *Priestly Kingdom,* 24.

been a pendulum swinging between the individual and the collective. But that was not the intended result as far as the Reformers were concerned. Yoder argues that now, in this post-Christendom era, it has become thinkable that this mistake could be undone. This is the significance of the believers' church strategy of ecumenical renewal.

The polite pluralism of much contemporary ecumenism is actually a hindrance, rather than a help, to genuine progress toward greater unity. There is a great reluctance in ecumenical discussions to face up to the reality of unfaithfulness in the past in such a way as to make genuine progress possible. Yoder sees no hope for progress in what he calls the "wider strategic tendency of inclusive agency leaders to believe that ecumenical unity can be achieved by going forward together without repentance."[33] Yoder points out that the sixteenth-century Anabaptists, like the later Puritans, believed that "the way God leads is that the Spirit gathers believers around the Scriptures."[34] This is the notion of "the hermeneutic community," a notion with its roots in 1 Corinthians 14:26ff. It is the conversation about what the Scriptures teach for the contemporary situation that should be the method by which the Spirit leads the community into making decisions, including decisions to repent and go in a different direction. This is how the church is to be continually being reformed. Yoder repeatedly insists on the "unfinished" character of the church and thus, as Michael Cartwright points out, articulates a vision of the church that is at the same time "radically reformed and radically catholic."[35]

Yoder's believers' church ecclesiology is evangelical in its emphasis on the voluntary nature of membership, ecumenical in its conversational model of unity, catholic in its emphasis on the congregation as the focus of mission, and reforming in its stress on the unfinished character of the church. Yoder contends that a believers' church ecclesiology is relevant to all branches of the church today because, to the extent that local congregations gather around the Word of God and under the guidance of the Spirit to make decisions that increase their effectiveness in mission through uncoerced conversation, they are implementing, at least to that extent, this ecclesiology.

The Believers' Church As a New Society

Having defined Yoder's ecclesiology, situated it with regard to other types of ecclesiology, and argued for its evangelical, ecumenical, catholic, and reforming character, I am now ready to flesh out Yoder's view of the church by

33. Yoder, "A 'Free Church' Perspective on Baptism, Eucharist and Ministry," *Royal Priesthood*, 281–2.

34. Yoder, "Radical Reformation Ethics," *Priestly Kingdom*, 117.

35. Michael Cartwright, "Radical Reform, Radical Catholicity: John Howard Yoder's Vision of the Faithful Church," in *Royal Priesthood*, 41. This is the point of Yoder's article "Catholicity in Search of Location," *Royal Priesthood*, 301–20.

looking at his view of those characteristics of the church that make it particularly relevant to social ethics. He views the church, first, as a new humanity created by the death and resurrection of Christ; second, as a new sociological entity with distinctive practices by which community is built up and maintained; and, third, as a foreshadowing of the future kingdom of God. We now turn to a discussion of these three aspects of his ecclesiology.

1. Justification As the Basis of the Church As a New Society. In Yoder's understanding of ecclesiology, the church is not merely a means by which an essentially individualistic message of salvation is delivered to the world but the new society into which the gospel invites those who believe to enter.[36] In *The Politics of Jesus,* Yoder deals with exegetical work in Pauline studies, done in the 1950s and 1960s, that suggests that the central message of Paul was not an individualistic message of the forgiveness of sins through faith but rather the message that Jews and Gentiles have been united into one body—the body of Christ, the church. I would like to consider his argument now.

Yoder begins by citing the well-known article by Krister Stendahl, "The Apostle Paul and the Introspective Conscience of the West," in which Stendahl demonstrates that "all of the constitutive elements of the classic 'Luther-type experience' are missing in both the experience and the thought of the apostle."[37] First, rather than being preoccupied with his guilt before a righteous God, Paul was actually "robust of conscience," and he never pleads with others to "feel an anguished conscience and then receive release from that anguish in a message of forgiveness."[38] Second, Paul's understanding of the law was not that its function was to make God's people aware of their guilt. Instead, he saw the law as "a gracious arrangement made by God for the ordering of the life of his people while they were awaiting the arrival of the Messiah."[39] Third, for Paul, faith was not a spiritual exercise of moving from self-trust through despair to confidence in God's mercy. Rather, faith is, at its core, the belief that Jesus is the Messiah. To become a Christian is to accept Jesus as the Messiah, which is what the Damascus road experience was all about.

The heresy Paul combated in Romans and Galatians was not that the Jewish Christians continued to keep the law; Paul was quite tolerant of those who did so. Rather, the heresy that he exposed was the failure of some Jewish Christians to accept the fact that "since the Messiah had come the covenant of God had been broken open to include the Gen-

36. Yoder says: "The church herself is a society" (*The Christian Witness to the State* [Newton, Kans.: Faith and Life, 1964], 17).

37. Krister Stendahl, "The Apostle Paul and the Introspective Conscience of the West," *Harvard Theological Review* 56 (1963): 199ff., quoted in John Howard Yoder, *The Politics of Jesus: Vicit Agnus Noster,* 2d ed. (Grand Rapids: Eerdmans, 1994), 215.

38. Yoder, *Politics of Jesus,* 215.

39. Ibid.

tiles."[40] Yoder comments: "In sum, the fundamental issue was that of the social form of the church."[41] Paul's concept of sin was not a matter of existential anguish about the righteousness and judgment of God but specifically his failure to recognize Jesus as Messiah and his persecution of the church.[42] Yoder argues that it was only later, in the context of anti-Jewish polemic, that Paul's language of justification was reinterpreted, particularly by Augustine, into "the terms of Western self-examination and concern for authenticity."[43]

The inclusion of Gentiles in the new covenant is the meaning of the one humanity spoken of by Paul in Ephesians. What had been for previous generations a mystery has now been made known to him (Ephesians 3:3, 9–10). The divine purpose is the reconciliation of Jew and Gentile in one community (Ephesians 2:11–22) as an eschatological sign of the renewal of all humanity in the new creation. Drawing on the work of scholars such as Markus Barth and Paul Minear, Yoder suggests that this understanding of justification is found in Galatians as well as Ephesians. Markus Barth, for example, argues that the issue at stake in Galatians 2 is whether Jewish and Gentile Christians were to live together in one fellowship. Moreover, "to be 'justified' is to be set right in and for that relationship."[44] Barth goes on to say:

> Sharing in the death and resurrection of Jesus Christ is the means of justification: only in Christ's death and resurrection is the new man created from at least two, a Jew and a Greek, a man and a woman, a slave and a free man, etc. . . . The new man is present in actuality where two previously alien and hostile men come together before God. Justification in Christ is thus not an individual miracle happening to this person or that person, which each may seek or possess for himself. Rather justification by grace is a joining together of this person and that person, of the near and the far; . . . it is a social event.[45]

Reconciliation to God and reconciliation to other human beings are thus not sequential, but two sides of the same event. Justification has a social meaning (not an implication) that is inherent in the doctrine and, in fact, inseparable from it.

Yoder says: "That men and women are called together to a new social wholeness is itself the work of God which gives meaning to history, from which both personal conversion (whereby individuals are called into this meaning) and missionary instrumentalities are derived."[46] Thus, Yoder

40. Ibid., 216.
41. Ibid.
42. Ibid., 217.
43. Ibid.
44. Ibid., 220. Cf. Markus Barth, "Jews and Gentiles: The Social Character of Justification in Paul," *Journal of Ecumenical Studies* 5 (1968): 241ff.
45. Barth, "Jews and Gentiles," 259, quoted in Yoder, *Politics of Jesus*, 220.
46. Yoder, "A People in the World," 74.

argues, "the distinctness of the church of believers is prerequisite to the meaningfulness of the Gospel message."[47] The church is the new humanity that God is creating as a witness to his ultimate intention for his creation. Yoder says:

> The identification of the church with a given society denies the miracle of the new humanity in two ways: on the one hand by blessing the existing social unity and structure that is a part of the fallen order rather than a new miracle, and on the other hand by closing its fellowship to those of the outside or the enemy class or tribe or people or nation.[48]

Yoder points out that what Paul was saying near the end of the evolution of apostolic Christianity about God reconciling classes of people in the new community is similar to what Jesus was saying at the beginning of the Christian movement about loving enemies, including outsiders, and drawing sinners into fellowship.[49] The love of God is displayed in the reconciliation in one body of those who are, by nature, enemies or separate. Thus, justification is the basis of the new society.

2. The Sociology of the New Society. The new society has, as part of its constitution in Scripture, certain practices that enable it to create and maintain community. Yoder's account of these practices occupies the place in his believers' church ecclesiology that would normally be taken up by a discussion of the "sacraments" in other accounts of ecclesiology. These practices include binding and loosing, the Lord's Supper, baptism, the universal ministry of believers, and the rule of Paul. Yoder originally developed his account of these practices in his Stone Lectures at Princeton and his Morgan Lectures at Fuller in 1980 and in a 1991 article, "Sacrament As Social Process: Christ the Transformer of Culture,"[50] before finally publishing a full account of these practices in *Body Politics: Five Practices of the Christian Community before the Watching World.*

Yoder's account of the "politics" of the body is his attempt to provide a constructive alternative to an account of politics drawn from natural theology, philosophy, or common sense. Rejecting the notion that politics is autonomous, Yoder takes Barth's "dogmatics is ethics" method to a new level by identifying politics with worship.[51] "Body politics," as we shall

47. Ibid., 74–75.
48. Ibid., 75.
49. Yoder, *Politics of Jesus,* 225.
50. John Howard Yoder, "Sacrament As Social Process: Christ the Transformer of Culture," *Theology Today* 48 (1991), reprinted in *Royal Priesthood,* 359–73.
51. Although Yoder does not explicitly acknowledge dependence on Barth at this point, what he is doing is methodologically similar to Barth's approach to ethics in *CD* IV/4, in which he structured the ethics of reconciliation around baptism, the Lord's Prayer, and the Lord's Supper and dealt with politics in his exposition of the Lord's Prayer.

see below, is not only the way in which members of the body relate to each other but also the basis for the church's role as an exemplary society, that is, as the presence of the coming kingdom.

I now need to analyze Yoder's account of the politics of the body, an account that extends and fleshes out the politics of Jesus. Yoder's thesis, stated formally, is: "The pattern we shall discover is that the will of God for human socialness as a whole is prefigured by the shape to which the body of Christ is called."[52] This "prefiguring" is incomplete, flawed, and inconsistent because it is done by sinful, imperfect human beings and it is done in a world that is not yet fully redeemed. Yoder has no interest in illusions of perfectionism either of individuals or congregations, but he is not willing to go so far as to say that the church is invisible or that the body of Christ is incapable, in the power of the Spirit, of bearing witness in both word and deed to the kingdom of God. Yoder discusses five sample ways in which the church is called to operate as a *polis*.[53]

The first is called "binding and loosing" or fraternal admonition. Matthew 18:15–18 contains the instructions on what to do when a brother or sister sins. A private attempt to resolve the matter is the first step. Taking a witness to a second encounter is the second step. If the matter is resolved, fellowship has been restored. The third step is to tell it to the church, and the expulsion of the offender from the community is the final resort.[54] Jesus says that whatever is bound on earth in this process will be bound in heaven and whatever is loosed on earth will be loosed in heaven. Yoder notes, first, that the initiative is personal (any member) and not a clergy function; second, that the intention is restorative, not punitive; third, that there is no distinction between trivial and major offenses; and fourth, the point is not to protect the church's reputation or to make a point about the seriousness of sin but rather to serve the offender by restoration of fellowship.[55]

Unlike most Protestants, Yoder would not limit the number of sacraments to two, and he is prepared to call this practice of binding and loosing a "sacrament." Yoder notes that the coming together of human and divine action is what some denominations call a "sacrament."[56] The anti-Catholic bias of most believers' churches leads them to deny that one human can forgive another in God's name, but exactly that is entailed in this passage.[57] So Yoder is prepared to see in one action both a church sacrament and a political practice, both a human and a divine act. One

---

52. Yoder, *Body Politics*, ix.
53. Yoder does not rule out the possibility that there could be more than five such practices.
54. Violence or coercion are never part of the picture.
55. Yoder, *Body Politics*, 2–3.
56. Ibid., 1.
57. Ibid., 3.

reason why the practice of church discipline, which is what this practice is usually called, has been distorted and turned into an instrument of oppression instead of liberation is that it only fits within a voluntary community to which the members have committed themselves personally and freely.[58] Outside of that context it becomes oppressive; it becomes the manipulation of the divine by humans. This practice aids the community in moral discernment because "conversation with reconciling intent is the most powerful way for a community to discover when the rules they have been applying are inadequate so that they may be modified."[59] The command of God is heard communally through prayer.

Yoder also stresses the ecumenical potential of this apostolic practice:

> Taking seriously this apostolic witness would seem to put us at the mercy of a number of ecclesiastical scarecrows. It gives more authority to the church than does Rome, trusts more to the Holy Spirit than does Pentecostalism, has more respect for the individual than does liberal humanism, makes moral standards more binding than did Puritanism, and is more open to the new situation than was what some called "the new morality" a quarter-century ago. If practiced it would radically restructure the life of churches. Thus the path of Christian faithfulness might lead through some positions contemporary Christian "moderates" have been trying to avoid.[60]

Yoder suggests that to take this practice seriously would mean asserting that the Lutheran view that the shape of the church does not matter is wrong and that the high Catholic views that the pope can promulgate new binding definitions that go beyond Scripture and that only a priest can give absolution are wrong as well. He also contends that it implies that the liberal Protestant tendency for the role of the pope to be taken over by educated, cultural elites is wrong and that the tendency of high scholastic Protestantism to affirm the a priori authority of the propositions contained in the Bible, but to neglect the actual reading of the Bible, is wrong. Yoder obviously is oversimplifying the positions of these groups in order to make his point here. His point is that these kinds of mistakes could be avoided by taking seriously a communal hermeneutic.

In terms of sacramentalism, he calls his view a moderately realistic view that could become a viable third way when it is assumed that there is no alternative to puritanical legalism or nondirective counseling. He asserts that the "sectarian" (or believers' church advocate) believes that, with the help of the Holy Spirit, the congregation can deduce from the New Testament a "set of instructions, commands, and prohibitions, which are objectively valid in that they translate the will of God ade-

58. Ibid., 5.
59. Ibid., 6.
60. Ibid., 6–7.

quately for all Christians at a given time and place."[61] Yoder says that for the Anabaptists (and for him) there can be no opposition between the scriptural text and the subjective conviction of the Holy Spirit.[62] "The agent of moral discrimination in the doxological community," says Yoder, "is not a theologian, a bishop or a pollster, but the Holy Spirit, discerned as the unity of the entire body."[63]

Yoder surveys the ways in which this practice has sporadically been applied in Christian history. Reformers such as Martin Bucer called it the "Rule of Christ." Balthasar Hübmaier wrote an order of service for fraternal discipline.[64] It can also be seen working in Scripture, as in the case of the Jerusalem Council in Acts 15. According to Yoder, the issue comes down to a willingness, or lack thereof, to trust the leading of the Holy Spirit. Yoder's proposal at this point may seem somewhat naive, given the inability of many congregations to agree on much of anything. But he would say that there is no shortcut to unity. Conversation may be slow, but at least it has the potential to bring about unity, whereas other more coercive or authoritarian methods may be more efficient in the short term but cannot bring real Christian unity.

The second social practice is the breaking of bread together, the Lord's Supper. Yoder rejects the premise upon which so many Protestant-Roman Catholic polemics have rested, namely, that the "sacraments" deal with a special realm of "religious reality" that is apart from the everyday world. Yoder claims that this concept of worship was taken over from paganism by Christians centuries after the New Testament, "when paganism had replaced Judaism as the cultural soil of the Christian movement."[65] He argues that the "synthesis of Christianity and empire beginning in the fourth century had to replace the economic meaning of breaking bread together with something else."[66]

According to Yoder, what Jesus meant in saying, "Whenever you do this, do it in my memory," was, whenever you have your common meal, remember me. The connection between food and the resurrection appearances of Christ would have reinforced the correlation between eating together and following Jesus that had characterized the formation of community in the ministry of Jesus. In Acts 6 we see that the economic sharing of the Jesus movement extended into the postascension life of the early church. The decision of the Jerusalem Council revolved around table fellowship, and many of Paul's injunctions to the Corinthians dealt with ta-

61. Yoder, "The Anabaptist Dissent," *Concern*, 61.
62. John Howard Yoder, "The Recovery of the Anabaptist Vision," *Concern* 18 (July 1971): 18–19.
63. Yoder, "To Serve Our God and to Rule the World," *Royal Priesthood*, 139; cf. Gerber Koontz, "Confessional Theology in a Pluralistic Context," 248–49.
64. Yoder, *Body Politics*, 7.
65. Ibid., 14.
66. Ibid., 15.

ble fellowship (1 Corinthians 8; 10; 11). Every meal in a Jewish household is an act of worship, and the word *Eucharist* identifies the meal with its prayer. The double meanings of meal fellowship and thanksgiving, and the placing of the supper in the context of the Passover celebration by the Gospels, means that in the Lord's Supper "we affirm our loyalty to the entire Hebrew heritage and to the understandings of God as liberator and creator of a people, which the Exodus memory celebrates."[67]

This new people is one in which there is economic sharing that is affirmed both symbolically and literally in the common meal.[68] Yoder thinks that it would be going too far to say that the Lord's Supper commits the church to social democracy because socialism is a modern theory that has become highly politicized. But it would be saying too little not to confess "some kind of sharing, advocacy, and partisanship in which the poor are privileged, and in which considerations of merit and productivity are subjected to the rule of servanthood."[69] The grounds for social justice are not in the original creation orders, which only need to be restored, but rather are the beginning of the age of fulfillment, the messianic age.[70] In Christian history, the monastic movement, the Waldensians, and the sixteenth-century Anabaptists are just a few examples of groups in which economic sharing was prominent. Yoder connects the theme of economic leveling to Jesus' proclamation of the Jubilee.[71]

Yoder's concept of the economic meaning of the Lord's Supper should not be taken to be a rationalistic reduction of a mystery to outward ethical performance, despite his polemics against pagan religiosity. He should not be interpreted so much as denying the spiritual aspects of the sacrament as seeking to retrieve its ethical meaning. It might help to get at his true intent to put it as follows: the "religious" or "spiritual" meaning of the Lord's Supper only becomes illegitimate when it obscures or replaces the ethical meaning. This interpretation would be in harmony with what Yoder says about the doctrines of justification by faith and the incarnation.[72]

The third social practice is baptism. Yoder says, "Baptism introduces or initiates persons into a new people. The distinguishing mark of this people is that all prior given or chosen identity definitions are transcended."[73] Paul stresses this point in Galatians, Ephesians, and 2 Corinthians. Yoder notes, "baptism celebrates and effects the merging of the Jewish and Gentile stories."[74] The primary narrative meaning of bap-

---

67. Ibid., 19.
68. Ibid., 20.
69. Ibid., 22.
70. Ibid.
71. Ibid., 24–25; cf. Yoder, *Politics of Jesus,* chapter 3.
72. See chapter 4 on the charge of reductionism for Yoder's comments on this point.
73. Yoder, *Body Politics,* 28.
74. Ibid., 30.

tism is the new society it creates. After the fifth century, there were no more outsiders to convert because the whole "world" had been declared Christian by imperial edict.[75] That made baptism a celebration of birth, and the same mistake of making ethnicity, rather than faith, the criterion for entry into the covenant was made all over again. Yoder advocates a form of sacramental realism that sees baptism as the actual creation of a new people.

The implications of baptism for interethnic inclusiveness are quite obvious. As Yoder states, "Little imagination is needed to see that affirming the oneness of humanity is one message which by its nature reaches beyond the church's membership."[76] Yoder affirms that Christian unity is the true internationalism and that Christian internationalism is the true unity.[77] Baptism is the sign that the messianic age has dawned and that a new phase of world history has begun in which sexual, ritual, ethnic, and economic statuses have been relativized.[78]

We must be careful, however, not to forget that the meaning of baptism is not exhausted by its character as the sign of entering into the new society made up of those who confess Jesus Christ as King. If Yoder were giving a systematic account of theology, instead of writing on the specific topic of the retrieval of the ethical meaning of Christian doctrines and practices, it would be a serious omission to leave out the meaning of baptism to the person baptized. For the individual, baptism means repentance, confession, and commitment. While I would not wish to accuse Yoder of reductionism, it must, nevertheless, be noted that his account of baptism is incomplete and needs to be incorporated into a systematic believers' church theology so that its implications can be worked out and clarified.

The fourth social practice described by Yoder is the practice of universal ministry or the fullness of Christ (Ephesians 4:11–13).[79] This is understood by Yoder to mean "a new mode of group relationships in which every member of a body has a distinctly identifiable, divinely validated and empowered role."[80] According to 1 Corinthians 12:7, every member of the body has a spiritual gift that is to be used for the common good. Yoder states that one of the reasons modern Protestants have difficulty taking seriously this doctrine is that we think we already understand it.[81] But it is not mere human potential or abilities that Paul is talking about. Rather, the gifts in question are supernatural enablements of the Holy Spirit.

75. Ibid., 32.
76. Ibid., 34.
77. Yoder, "Let the Church Be the Church," *Royal Priesthood*, 180.
78. Yoder, *Body Politics*, 37.
79. For a fuller exegetical discussion of the New Testament basis for this practice, see Yoder's, *The Fullness of Christ: Paul's Revolutionary Vision of Universal Ministry* (Elgin, Ill.: Brethren Press, 1987), 9–22.
80. Yoder, *Body Politics*, 47.
81. Ibid., 49.

The need for church order led the early church quite quickly in the direction of exalting the role of another kind of church officer, which became the purview of a few, as opposed to the many, males as opposed to females, and was based in ritual of installation or possession of a tradition. It would be naive to suppose that the direction this evolution took was not influenced by the patriarchal culture into which it fit so snugly. The countercultural Pauline vision was soon buried beneath the new, worldly view of leadership that reversed the servant model of Jesus and made the exercise of power central to the episcopal role.

The Reformation social theory of vocation was a needed correction for the developing idea that secular callings were not really Christian. But it was not the recovery of the Pauline vision. It is highly countercultural to question the role of the religious specialist.[82] The Reformation questioned it in theory with the doctrine of the priesthood of all believers, but in practice the religious specialist continued in a different form. But already in the exile, the role of the priest had become unnecessary to the survival of the people of God. The synagogue structure and the focus on the written Torah allowed the Jewish people to maintain their identity in the Diaspora. In Jesus' day, the temple had been restored, but he relativized it again, and Paul formed messianic synagogues in which there was no sacrificial worship. As Yoder puts it, "The specialized purveyor of access to the divine is out of work since Pentecost."[83] However, the alliance between the church and the sacral notion of kingship in Constantinianism has meant a return to the preexilic form of peoplehood and the reassertion of the centrality of the religious specialist. The Pauline vision has yet to be "consciously and consistently lived out," according to Yoder,[84] although the Plymouth Brethren, Salvation Army, and Friends have come close. Again, note that Yoder is not arguing for "restoration" but for the church to move forward and claim that which God is offering to it in this messianic age.

For Yoder, the reformation that has yet to happen will involve the elimination of the clergy-laity distinction and the restoration of the congregational practice of binding and loosing. In the process, there will also be the recovery of the economic meaning of the Lord's Supper and that of the inclusivist meaning of baptism. It is not so much a matter of recovering something that was lost in the past as it is a matter of moving forward into the fullness of what God has for the church. Part of the key to such a reformation would be to recover the rule of Paul, the fifth social practice of the body, which Yoder discusses next and which could itself be the means by which reform occurs.

82. For an expansion of this point, see Yoder, *Fullness of Christ*, 1–8.
83. Yoder, *Body Politics*, 56.
84. Ibid., 57.

In 1 Corinthians 14, Paul instructs his readers on how "to hold a meeting in the power of the Spirit."[85] Central to his advice here is the principle that everyone who has something to say should have a chance to have the floor. The mode of speech called "prophecy" should be taken with particular seriousness, and all members of the body should "weigh" carefully what the prophets have to say. The conviction underlying Paul's teaching here is that the Spirit will guide the community into consensus if there is a willingness to dialogue, wait, and trust the process. This process can be seen in action in Acts 15.

As churches were established around the Mediterranean world, they expressed their unity and sought to resolve their differences through synods or councils modeled on the pattern of Acts 15. Throughout church history, the vision of ecumenical councils has been held up as a method of achieving church unity. Today the World Council of Churches continues the tradition. At the time of the Protestant Reformation, the "disputation" format was borrowed from the university as a way for local councils or princes to settle theological disputes. Zwingli argued that the local church had the right to act to make changes concerning images, the mass, and other issues based on his interpretation of 1 Corinthians 14. Unfortunately, Zwingli "did not trust this vision fully," and, once he had the city fathers on his side, he equated them with the elders of the Jerusalem church and no longer felt it necessary to consult the community as a whole. From then on, the Reformation was carried out by the state.[86] There has always been a fear of anarchy on the part of the paternalistic hierarchy. But, says Yoder, "because Jesus Christ is always and everywhere the same, any procedure that yields sovereignty to the direction of his spirit will have ultimately to create unity."[87]

Yoder bases his concept of the universal ministry on the gifts of the Spirit and is careful to define the gifts as supernatural abilities, not natural, human abilities. However, his account of the universal ministry leaves many important questions not only unanswered but not even asked. For example, who discerns who has which spiritual gifts? Which spiritual gifts are in effect today, all or only some? What is the relationship of church offices to the gifts? What is the relationship of education for ministry to the gifts? What role does the pastor have in the congregation, for will there not continue to be pastors even if the clergy-laity distinction is eliminated? If each congregation is autonomous, should we expect different churches to develop varying structures of ministry and leadership? Would it be ethically wrong to have some models of congregational leadership that are more hierarchical than others? The com-

85. Ibid., 61.
86. Ibid., 65–66. Luther also appealed to 1 Corinthians 14 as the warrant for the congregation's taking its order into its own hands.
87. Ibid., 70.

pressed account of the universal ministry and the congregational model of decision making given by Yoder leaves too many questions unanswered. While it is suggestive and helpful, it needs to be systematically articulated.

3. The Exemplary Character of the New Society. All five of these biblical practices can be translated into nonreligious terms. Yoder elaborates:

> The multiplicity of gifts is a model for the empowerment of the humble and the end of hierarchy in social process. Dialogue under the Holy Spirit is the ground floor of the notion of democracy. Admonition to bind or loose at the point of offense is the foundation for conflict resolution and consciousness-raising. Baptism enacts interethnic social acceptance, and breaking bread celebrates economic solidarity.[88]

But is it right to "secularize" doctrine in this manner? Is it even appropriate? Yoder argues that it is right and appropriate because of the exemplary character of the church as the foretaste, herald, and model of the partially present, future kingdom of God.

In an important essay entitled "Why Ecclesiology Is Social Ethics: Gospel Ethics versus the Wider Wisdom," Yoder offers a reading of a section of Karl Barth's *Church Dogmatics* in which Barth makes the programmatic statement that "True Church law is exemplary law."[89] Barth denies that the church has a law that is to be imposed upon the world. But the gospel can be expressed to the world in terms of its particular law. Barth says:

> The decisive contribution which the Christian community can make to the upbuilding and work and maintenance of the civil consists in the form of the order which it has to give to it and to all human societies in the form of the order of its own upbuilding and constitution. . . . It is itself only a human society moving like all other to His manifestation . . . its cognitive basis, the lordship of Jesus Christ *ad dexteram Patris omnipotentis,* is the actual basis of all temporal law as well. Is it not to be expected therefore, that in its forms—however defective these may be . . . there will be at least some analogies or correspondences to ecclesiastical law?[90]

Yoder notes that what Barth has begun to do, by distinguishing between the civil and the Christian communities,[91] is to affirm, for the first time

---

88. Ibid., 72.

89. *CD* IV/2, paragraph 67, "The Holy Spirit and the Upbuilding of the Christian Community," 719.

90. Ibid., 721–22.

91. In his 1946 essay, "The Christian Community and the Civil Community," Barth goes so far as to refer to the "pagan State." See *Community, State and Church,* ed. W. Herberg (Gloucester, Mass.: Peter Smith, 1968), 163.

since Constantine in mainline Protestant theology, "the theological legitimacy of admitting, about a set of social structures, that those who participate in them cannot be presumed to be addressable from the perspective of Christian confession."[92] Barth's church-world distinction leads him toward what Troeltsch would call a "sectarian" approach to ecclesiology, or what Yoder would call a "believers' church" approach.

Yoder also notes that Barth emphasizes the narrative character of the church, since the meaning of Jesus is made known within the categories of ordinary, historical reality by means of the representation or reenactment of his story in the ongoing life of the church. This reenactment is what Barth means by speaking of the life of the church as "liturgical." In the eschatological context of the time between the resurrection and the return, Barth says, the community achieves "this representation provisionally but in concrete reality."[93] Barth is not ascribing perfection to the witness of the church at this point. He should be understood as making the minimalist claim that the witness of the church, while remaining imperfect, inconsistent, and flawed, nevertheless is *visible*.[94] It is the visibility of the witness that prevents a fall into ecclesiastical docetism. True church law is thus a proclamation of the gospel by the church to the world. The content of the proclamation is not mere words, however, but also the very life of the community itself.

Yoder stresses that, "when we speak with Barth of the Christian community as a liturgical or celebrating community we are accepting . . . our rootedness in the particularity of Judaism and Jesus."[95] But this is in no way a relativizing of the proclamation. Yoder makes this point strongly in his essay "To Serve Our God and to Rule the World," when he says of the worship of the early Christians as it is recorded for us in the New Testament: "For them, to say 'Jesus Christ is *kyrios*' was a statement neither about their subjective psychic disposition (as pietism would say) nor about their sectarian belief system (as scholasticism would assume) but about the cosmos, the way the world really is."[96] To reject the "wider wisdom" in favor of the historically particular story of Jesus does not condemn us to provincialism, Yoder argues, because the content of what we celebrate in the Christian community is not itself esoteric or provincial.[97]

92. Yoder, "Why Ecclesiology Is Social Ethics: Gospel Ethics versus the Wider Wisdom," *Royal Priesthood*, 108.

93. *CD* IV/2, 698–99.

94. For both Barth and Yoder it is true to say that, if the old age is characterized by rebellion and sin and the new age by harmony and shalom, the church in the present age should be thought of as participating in both ages and, therefore, as being characterized by both rebellion and harmony, sin and shalom. This is the result of the "already–not yet" eschatological tension of the presence of the kingdom of God.

95. Yoder, "Why Ecclesiology Is Social Ethics," *Royal Priesthood*, 113.

96. Yoder, "To Serve Our God and to Rule the World," *Royal Priesthood*, 131.

97. Yoder, "Why Ecclesiology Is Social Ethics," *Royal Priesthood*, 115.

Primal religion assumes the total known community as the bearer of the meaning of sacral history, but since Abraham that has changed. When the fourth-century Christians bought into the sacral kingship of Constantine and identified empire with church, they, in effect, reverted from their Jewish/Christian universalism into a pagan provincialism.[98]

Only as the church repudiates this narrowing of its vision and the sectarianness of Constantinianism can it regain its true universal message and display the truth of the message in its worship. This is why the subtitle of Yoder's book, *Body Politics* was *Five Practices of the Church before the Watching World*. Yoder believes that the church is the bearer of the meaning of history in that God is now doing something in the Christian community that he one day intends to do in all his creation. This is why to work on building community in the church is also mission. The church is the "new world on the way."[99]

One implication of the narrative and eschatological understanding of the social-ethical mission of the church is that "the story of the church is constantly redefined in the encounter of principle and place, of identity and situation."[100] Social ethics is always an encounter between the story of Jesus as it is unfolding in the church and the situation in which the church finds itself. Thus, it will not be systematic (any more than theology is systematic) but rather occasional and specific. What was wrong with the fad called "situation ethics" was not that it expected guidance in the situation but that it conceived of this guidance as arising from the situation in a "temporally punctual decision made all at once."[101] Yoder rejects what he terms "strong occasionalism" that abandons ethical accountability to intuition, but he affirms what he calls a "weak occasionalism" that insists on the leading of the Holy Spirit in the process of moral discernment, just as Jesus promised would happen (John 16:13).

Yoder's description of his believers' church ecclesiology as an alternative society is rich and full of suggestiveness for social ethics. He portrays the believers' church as a new society that is established by means of justification by grace through faith. It is characterized by social practices that demonstrate its eschatological character and reenact the story of Jesus: baptism, universal ministry, binding and loosing, the rule of Paul, and the Lord's Supper. It has an exemplary character as the new world in the process of being born or a foretaste of the kingdom of God. The eschatological Christian community is one in which the kingdom of God has become present, though not yet in its fullness. The Christian community thus lives in an eschatological tension, participating in both ages

98. Ibid., 116.
99. This is the title of Yoder's Stone Lectures, which were delivered at Princeton in 1980.
100. Yoder, "Why Ecclesiology Is Social Ethics," *Royal Priesthood*, 121.
101. Ibid., 122.

at once: the old age of sin and the new age of salvation. Thus, it is possible to view the church as not having a social ethic but rather as being itself a social ethic.[102] Yoder states: "The believing body of Christ is the part of the world that confesses the renewal to which all the world is called. . . . A church that is not 'against the world' in fundamental ways has nothing worth saying to and for the world."[103] The very existence of the Christian community is a sign of hope in the world. But how is that hope communicated, and what effect can we reasonably expect it to have on the wider world? To answer these questions, we now turn to a discussion of the social witness of the church.

102. I am borrowing this phrase, "The church is a social ethic," from Stanley Hauerwas, *The Peaceable Kingdom: A Primer in Christian Ethics* (Notre Dame, Ind.: University of Notre Dame Press, 1983), 99.
103. Yoder, *Body Politics,* 78.

8

The Social Witness
of the Church

We are now in a position to describe how Yoder conceives of the church as witnessing to the state. It should be clear by now that Yoder's social ethic is not public in the sense that non-Christians can hold to it just as well as Christians can but that it is public in the sense that it has relevance for all human beings and not just Christians. In this chapter I want to do two things. First, I need to flesh out the nature of Yoder's understanding of how the church witnesses to the state. Then, secondly, I will finally be in a position to address directly two charges often made against Yoder's approach to social ethics, namely, that it promotes the withdrawal of Christians from society and that it renders Christianity irrelevant. Neither of these charges has a solid foundation, and, in this chapter, I hope to show why this is so.

The Witness of the Church to the State

In order to understand how Yoder conceives of the Christian church witnessing to the non-Christian state, we need to focus on three crucially important characteristics of that witness: its basis in the lordship of Jesus Christ, its essentially *ad hoc* character, and its use of the doctrine of analogy. I will take some time to compare Yoder's use of the doctrine of analogy to that of Karl Barth, firstly, because Yoder develops his own thoughts on this topic in dialogue with Barth and, secondly, because Barth's more general use of analogy in his theology is relevant to an evaluation of the adequacy of Yoder's use of analogy. By the end of this section, I hope the reader is able to see that, to a very great extent, Yoder's position consists of the application of a Barthian theological method to social ethics.

1. Its Basis in the Lordship of Jesus Christ. For Yoder, the basis of the Christian witness to the state is not the doctrine of creation alone. Like Barth, Yoder rejects the possibility of knowing God's will by means of norms that are not subject to the norm of Jesus Christ and that, therefore, sometimes contradict the teaching and example of Jesus Christ.[1] A true Christian doctrine of creation would not only view creation christocentrically but also would speak of the goal of deriving norms for the present messianic age, not from the fallen creation or even from the original good creation, but rather from the creation as it is in the process of being transformed by the power of the resurrection that has been unleashed in the cosmos. This involves deriving norms for the present messianic age from the person of the Messiah.

Yoder thinks that Christians often make the strategic error of thinking that they can persuade people who reject the lordship of Jesus to accept the lordship of God the Father by means of a doctrine of creation that does not speak of Jesus Christ. If such a doctrine of creation exists, it is not biblical because John 1 (not to mention many other texts) identifies Jesus as the Word who was with God in the beginning. If such a doctrine is biblical, it is so to the extent that it is actually christocentric, whether or not this is admitted. Yoder stresses the necessity of beginning with "the confession of rootedness in historical community,"[2] but he does not see this as a handicap for Christians because everyone else must do the same thing, too. There is no such thing as a "scratch" from which one can begin. In a postmodern situation, Christians are at no disadvantage in this regard. But we are so used to being in the position of power that it *feels like* weakness to admit that our social ethics arises out of our historical community.

The basis for the Christian witness to the state, for Yoder, is not creation but rather the cosmic lordship of Jesus Christ. In his resurrection-ascension, Jesus Christ has triumphed over the powers and has ascended to the right hand of God the Father, the place of rule and authority. The church has been created by the power of the Holy Spirit in the teeth of the opposition from the powers of this world and represents the advance guard of the new creation. So, in a sense, the witness to the state is based on the doctrine of creation, as long as it is understood clearly that, first,

1. See Yoder's discussion of natural theology and natural law in *Christian Attitudes to War, Peace and Revolution: A Companion to Bainton* (Elkhart, Ind.: distributed by Co-op Bookstore, 1983), 46–49, and his discussion of "General Revelation" in *The Christian Witness to the State* (Newton, Kans.: Faith and Life, 1964), 33–35.

2. John Howard Yoder, introduction to *The Priestly Kingdom: Social Ethics As Gospel* (Notre Dame, Ind.: University of Notre Dame Press, 1984), 7.

the creation being spoken of is the new creation that God is bringing into being and, second, the church is the key to understanding the shape of this new creation.[3]

2. Its *Ad Hoc* Character. Next we examine the *ad hoc* character of the church's witness to the state. The witness is *ad hoc* in four ways: in the sense of not being systematic, in the sense of dealing with only one issue at a time, in the sense of usually taking a negative form, and in the sense of arising out of its own life as example. We now examine these four aspects of the church's witness to the state.

First, we note that Yoder has no positive doctrine of "the state as such."[4] The state, for Yoder, as we saw in the discussion of his eschatology, is one of the powers in creation that has been overcome by Christ in his resurrection but is still in rebellion. The lordship of Christ over the church and the state takes different forms as long as this age persists.[5] Romans 13 and 1 Peter 2 teach that the role of the state in this present age is the maintenance of order in society. Yoder argues that Romans 13:1 does not say that God creates, institutes, or ordains the powers that be but that he orders them.[6] So we can speak of an "order of providence," says Yoder, "where Christ reigns over man's disobedience, through the 'powers' including the state, side by side with the 'order of redemption' where Christ rules in and through the obedience of His disciples."[7] Both are orders of grace, and both are eschatological in nature, but they are different. Yoder says:

> Since we cannot say that God has any "proper" pattern in mind to which unbelief should conform, the Christian witness to the state will not be guided by an imagined pattern of ideal society such as is involved in traditional conceptions of the "just state," the "just war," or the "due process of law." An ideal or even a "proper" society in a fallen world is by definition impossible.[8]

The state is to punish evildoers and reward those who do good. The role of the state is limited and mostly negative in character; it is not of primary importance in achieving God's purpose in the world.[9]

---

3. For further discussion of Yoder's views of the lordship of Christ, the state, and the church see chapter 5, where I discuss Yoder's view of the state in the context of expounding his eschatology.

4. On this point, Yoder follows Barth, who, in speaking of the church, says: "It is not in a position to establish one particular doctrine as *the* Christian doctrine of the just State" ("The Christian Community and the Civil Community," *Community, State and Church*, ed. W. Herberg [Gloucester, Mass.: Peter Smith, 1968], 160).

5. Yoder, *Christian Witness*, 12.

6. John Howard Yoder, *The Politics of Jesus: Vicit Agnus Noster*, 2d ed. (Grand Rapids: Eerdmans, 1994), 201.

7. Yoder, *Christian Witness*, 12.

8. Ibid., 32.

9. Ibid., 13.

This understanding of the state explains why the New Testament does not provide a list of functions that are necessary for the state to perform and criteria for how to tell a good state from an evil state. It needs to be stressed that nowhere are we told to submit ourselves only to good states and to overthrow or rebel against tyrannical, despotic, or totalitarian ones. Instead, we are told to be subject to the state regardless of how good or evil it is.

Yoder points out that Romans 13:1–7 is found in the context of a block of material in Romans 12–13 that begins with a call to nonconformity to this world. This nonconformity takes the form of a new quality of relationships within the Christian community, and, outside the community, it takes the form of suffering. Yoder states that "any interpretation of Romans 13:1–7 which is not also an expression of suffering and serving love must be a misunderstanding of the text in its context."[10] Yoder points out the eschatological context of this passage (Romans 13:11–14), which looks forward in hope to "a salvation so concretely imminent and historical as to be 'nearer than when we first believed.'"[11] Yoder, following Oscar Cullmann, contends that the command to be subject to the powers in 13:1 is "motivated and exposited by the hope in 13:11–14."[12] Christians are told in 12:19 never to exercise vengeance but to leave that to God. Then, in 13:4 we are told that the ruler is God's agent who executes "the particular function which the Christian was to leave to God." Yoder concludes: "This makes it clear that the function exercised by government is not the function to be exercised by Christians."[13] Christians have a different and much more important calling, that is, the calling to be the church. I think that Yoder's argument here is very strong, primarily because it seems that to interpret Romans 13:1–7 in the traditional Lutheran and Calvinistic ways leaves Paul hopelessly confused and contradictory in this section.

Second, the church should speak prophetically to the state on one issue at a time. This is how real social progress has been made in the past. Yoder says: "The Christian social critique will always speak in terms of available, or at least conceivable, alternatives. It will not request from the state the establishment of a perfect society."[14] The church knows that all utopias are illusory and that romantic visions of perfection, which do not take the realism of sin into account, uniformly lead to social disasters. Therefore, the church will not advocate large-scale ideologies such as socialism or capitalism. Instead, it "will call for the elimination of specific visible abuses."[15]

10. Yoder, *Politics of Jesus,* 196.
11. Ibid., 197.
12. Ibid.
13. Ibid., 198.
14. Yoder, *Christian Witness,* 38.
15. Ibid.

Third, the church's witness to the state will usually take a negative form. Yoder notes that the message of the prophets always took a negative form: "In spite of all the ammunition which the social gospel theology took from the Old Testament prophets, those prophets do not propose a detailed plan for the administration of society."[16] Yoder's reason for this approach is important to note: "This is necessary in the nature of the case, for the state is not an ideal order, ideally definable; it is a pragmatic tolerable balance of egoisms and can become more or less tolerable."[17] To act courageously and take the lead in denouncing specific abuses is the role of Christians, who do not have to fear the power of the state because they know that Christ is Lord.

Fourth, the witness of the church to the state should arise out of its own exemplary character and should be backed up by action. The strength of Yoder's *Body Politics* is that the account of politics given there is described as operative in the life of the body of Christ before it is ever recommended to the state. If the church can practice equality of the genders, then perhaps the state, seeing this, can come to believe that such behavior is a real possibility. This has happened with public education, hospitals, and perhaps even democracy itself. Yoder says:

> The historian A. D. Lindsey is credited with giving wide currency to the idea that Anglo-Saxon democracy (different in important ways from the enlightenment democracy of Latin Europe) is an extension of the Puritan vision of the hearers freely gathered under the preaching of the Word and free to talk back to the expositor as he is their servant, not a mouthpiece of the king, the bishop or the university.[18]

So the church should not presume to speak on every issue, but only when it has some special expertise or reason to speak.[19]

If church leaders speak on issues on which there is no consensus in the church or on issues at which the church as body is failing to provide a viable alternative, their credibility is extremely low. There are few sights more pathetic (and few actions less effective) than denominational bureaucrats urging secular governments to take actions to enhance social justice that their own denominations are not able to take, or do not choose to take, themselves. The church does not have to express itself on every issue, but it should not be shy about expressing itself whenever it can say to the state: "Do such and such. We do it all the time, and it is, therefore, perfectly realistic. Here are the results of our work. Will you

16. John Howard Yoder, *The Original Revolution: Essays on Christian Pacifism* (Scottdale, Pa.: Herald, 1971), 79.
17. Ibid.
18. John Howard Yoder, *Body Politics: Five Practices of the Christian Community before the Watching World* (Nashville: Discipleship Resources, 1992), 67.
19. Yoder, *Christian Witness*, 21.

join us in addressing this problem?" The witness of the church to the state needs to be *ad hoc*, in Yoder's view, but it need not be without power and effect.

3. Its Use of Analogy. Yoder notes that Barth used the analogy of faith in his 1946 essay, "The Christian Community and the Civil Community," to describe the content of the church's message to, and evaluation of, the state.[20] Yoder says that "the very structure of this essay presupposes and explicates a denial that a state or civil community as such can be a self-aware moral agent so as to stand immediately before God" and points out that Barth appears to be uncomfortable about this fact.[21] In his earlier writings, Barth was thinking of Christian ethics as directly applicable to the state. But in the 1946 essay, he recognizes that the idea of Christian ethics for the civil community would "in a direct sense"[22] be a contradiction in terms.[23] In this essay, Barth develops twelve analogies between the state and various things: "The direction of Christian judgments, purposes, and ideals in political affairs is based on the analogical capacities and needs of political organisation," says Barth.[24] But he quickly adds: "Political organisation can be neither a repetition of the Church or an anticipation of the Kingdom of God."[25] This leaves one wondering what Barth means at this point. How are church, state, the kingdom of God, and Jesus Christ related by analogy?

Yoder speaks of a certain "exploratory whimsicality" at work in Barth's use of analogy in both the 1946 essay and in *Church Dogmatics* 4.2,[26] where he uses analogy with regard to the state.[27] Yoder resorts to the theory that the argument by analogy is probably offered "tongue-in-cheek" by Barth.[28] The analogies given in the 1946 essay certainly are a mixed bag. As Yoder points out, "Sometimes in Barth's examples the comparison was to the church as body: but other times it was to the nature of God about whom the church speaks ... sometimes to major doctrinal emphases and sometimes to less central descriptions of the church's

20. John Howard Yoder, *Karl Barth and the Problem of War* (Nashville: Abingdon, 1970), 100–1.

21. Ibid.

22. Ibid., 101.

23. Barth says: "There is therefore no such thing as a Christian State corresponding to the Christian Church" ("The Christian Community and the Civil Community," 160).

24. Ibid., 168.

25. Ibid.

26. Karl Barth, *Jesus Christ, The Servant As Lord*, ed. G. W. Bromiley and T. F. Torrance, trans. G. W. Bromiley, vol. 4, pt. 2 of *Church Dogmatics* (Edinburgh: T. & T. Clark, 1958), 719ff.

27. John Howard Yoder, "Why Ecclesiology Is Social Ethics: Gospel Ethics versus the Wider Wisdom," *The Royal Priesthood: Essays Ecclesiological and Ecumenical*, ed. Michael Cartwright (Grand Rapids: Eerdmans, 1994), 125.

28. Yoder, *Karl Barth and the Problem of War*, 126. This seems hard to accept, given the utter seriousness with which Barth usually takes social ethics.

work." Yoder's comment on this is: "If we are to take seriously the notion of the mission of the church as constituting the backbone of social ethics, it will need to be disciplined more firmly."[29] What will need to be disciplined more firmly? Certainly Yoder is not referring to the mission of the church, as the grammar of that sentence would imply; rather, he is referring to the use of the notion of analogy.

Yoder does not distinguish between Barth's use of analogy with regard to the state in the 1946 essay and his use of analogy in *Church Dogmatics* 4.2, but there is a major difference. In *Church Dogmatics* 4.2, Barth never draws analogies between the state and Jesus Christ or God or the kingdom of God, as he does in "The Christian Community and the Civil Community." In the later work, Barth consistently draws the analogy between the law of the Christian community and the law of the state. This is a highly significant move because it disciplines the use of analogy by refusing to move directly from the gospel to the state, as though he were doing Christian ethics for the state.

Yoder is correct to point out that Barth is the first major mainline theologian since Augustine to presume that the state is not directly addressable from a Christian perspective. Will Herberg contends that Barth rejects both the very positive Thomistic view of political order as rooted in natural law and the much more ambiguous Augustinian view of political order as an order of preservation.[30] Herberg correctly sees that Barth criticizes his own Reformed tradition for separating creation from redemption and thus falsifying the radically christocentric character of the faith.[31] John Webster's judgment that Barth's vision is "Augustinian-Calvinist in temper, though modified in favour of a greater sense of the range of human responsibility" and Webster's statement that, for Barth, "Jesus Christ relates to the human agent not only as substitute, rescuer, giver of status, but also as assigner of roles and model of performance" define the nature of Barth's modification of his tradition a bit more precisely.[32] Barth realizes that, if Christian ethics is to be both grounded consistently in Jesus Christ and applicable to the non-Christian state, then there must be a middle term. The "pagan state" (Barth's term) is not addressable by the gospel directly. But because the church, as the body of Jesus Christ, is the "earthly-historical form" of the existence of Jesus Christ,[33] it has bodily existence in history in common with the state. Thus, Barth can propose six ways in which church law can be a model for

---

29. Yoder, "Why Ecclesiology is Social Ethics, 125.

30. Will Herberg, "The Social Philosophy of Karl Barth," *Community, State and Church*, 24–29.

31. Ibid., 29.

32. John Webster, *Barth's Ethics of Reconciliation* (Cambridge: Cambridge University Press, 1995), 230.

33. *CD* IV/2, 719.

the state's law, even though he recognizes that the church can never make clear to the world its authority—Jesus Christ.[34]

I am making a twofold suggestion here. First, I would suggest that we need to see development in Barth's theology as his ecclesiology is developed christocentrically in volume 4 of *Church Dogmatics*. The development of Barth's ecclesiology in a christocentric manner results in the elucidation of the narrative and eschatological aspects of the doctrine of the church. This is rightly called a development, not a reversal or material alteration. But the later Barth definitely views the church as much more central to Christian social ethics than does the earlier Barth. The 1946 essay is a transitional point in which Barth's thought is not quite consistent, but by the time he has written *Church Dogmatics* 4.2 a refinement has taken place in that his ecclesiology now allows him to see the church as the model (exemplar) for the state. Second, I want to suggest that this refinement of Barth's social ethics brings him and Yoder into agreement on the ecclesiological shape of social ethics. What Yoder does in *Body Politics* is precisely an expansion and elaboration of the same insight that drives Barth's exposition of the statement "true church law is exemplary law."[35] The method is identical: the indirect use of the analogy of faith in the form of analogies between the state and the church as a means by which the church witnesses to the state.

Yoder's approach to the church's witness to the state needs to be understood in terms of Barth's ecclesiology. It is a development of Barth's christocentric method and a creative appropriation of Barth's method of analogy in Christian ethics. Yoder's development of themes in Barth's theology in a believers' church direction is one of Yoder's significant and original contributions to Christian social ethics. Yoder's appropriation of Barth at this point allows him to offer a third way besides the usual alternatives of either a doctrine of the state that is not specifically Christian because it is not derived from a christocentric account of the church or the inability of Christians to say anything to the state at all, which is the charge of irrelevance often made against those in the believers' church tradition. By understanding the church as an eschatological community, a new society in the process of being redeemed with an exemplary role as the foundation of its witness, it is possible to draw analogies from the nature of the Christian community to the will of God for human community in general. This is at least the beginning of a solution to one of the most important perennial questions of Christian social ethics and one worth further consideration by the ecumenical church. Although a foundation now has been laid for seeing how the frequently made charges of withdrawal and irrelevance are not valid with regard to Yoder's ecclesiology, it is still necessary to address

---

34. Ibid., 723.

35. For an essay in which Yoder does something similar, see "The Spirit of God and the Spirit of Men," *Journal of Theology for Southern Africa* 29 (December 1979): 62–71.

these charges explicitly and directly, and to this task I now turn in the final section of this chapter.

The Charges of Withdrawal and Irrelevance: An Evaluation

It is very much a matter of conventional wisdom among Roman Catholics and mainline Protestants that the charges of withdrawal and irrelevance, which are often made against the kind of ecclesiology defended by Yoder, are valid. Most of those who take this view for granted have simply never encountered a theologian of Yoder's ability defending the pacifist position. Speaking from personal experience, I observe that this encounter can be a somewhat unsettling experience! Before rejecting the pacifist position, one really should encounter it in its strongest form, and certainly Yoder presents a very strong case for peace.

Most of the time, however, critics of Yoder's position tend to jump to conclusions without really hearing him out. Usually the procedure is that the critic takes note of some of Yoder's pacifist statements and then, from the critic's own Christendom perspective, makes certain deductions about what then must be the case with regard to Yoder's social ethic. Sometimes the critics ask of Yoder's theology questions that assume Constantinian presuppositions and then label Yoder's position as deficient because it fails to answer questions to which their position requires answers. Yoder claims: "That discipleship means social withdrawal is a caricature projected by Troeltsch and the Niebuhrs, on grounds related to their own assumptions, not drawn from historical facts."[36] The procedure here will be to evaluate Yoder's claim at this point by asking if withdrawal and irrelevance are the logical implications of Yoder's theological position, considered as a whole, and of his ecclesiology in particular.

1. The Charge of Withdrawal. Throughout his career, Yoder engaged in debate with Christian Realism and with the thought of the Niebuhr brothers in particular. H. R. Niebuhr's classic work, *Christ and Culture*,[37] has been a highly influential apologetic for an Augustinian-Reformed approach to social ethics and a devastatingly effective refutation of the Anabaptist-Mennonite approach to social ethics that Yoder represents. Why has this book been so influential? What accounts for its wide appeal and significant staying power? Is there any way for Yoder to evade its force? These are the questions we address in this section. In order to do so, we will first examine Yoder's critique of *Christ and Culture* and then present Yoder's alternative perspective.

The well-known structure of *Christ and Culture* does not need to be rehearsed extensively in this context, so we will move directly to Yoder's

---

36. Yoder, introduction to *Priestly Kingdom*, 11.
37. H. R. Niebuhr, *Christ and Culture* (New York: Harper & Row, 1951).

analysis of Niebuhr's work. He points out that Niebuhr's two poles, around which he structures his typology, *Christ* and *culture*, are both defined in problematic ways. First, culture is defined sometimes as "everything people do, every realm of creative behaviour," but other times, the state is defined as prototypically the representative of culture.[38] So Tertullian, for example, could be an excellent Latin stylist, a lawyer, and a philosophical thinker, but he is considered to have been against culture because he refused to kill in war. Niebuhr calls him "inconsistent."[39] If one rejects the state, one is against culture, despite the fact that many aspects of culture have nothing to do with the state. If one rejects killing, one rejects the state, despite the fact that the state is much more than just violence. Yoder argues against Niebuhr by saying that the radicals do not reject language, education, culture, the arts, and urbanity. Rather, "What the radicals reject is the *uncritical* importation of value-laden substance that is extra-biblical or pagan."[40]

Niebuhr's tendency to define culture monolithically means that one must be against all of it, for all of it, hold it all in paradox, be above all of it, or transform all of it. This is unfair to the radicals because, instead of sticking to his definition of culture as everything people do, Niebuhr sometimes employs the definition of culture as the *majority* position of a given society. This allows him to portray people who discriminate between certain aspects of culture that are good and to be embraced and aspects that are evil and to be rejected as anticulture, as long as their position is a minority position.[41] Could one not easily find aspects of American culture (racist institutions, for example) that Niebuhr would be against? If Niebuhr took a stand against the Vietnam War or condemned the racism behind school segregation laws, would that mean he was against culture? Is it not more plausible to speak of all of us as being against culture in some sense? Of course, the answer to this question is the affirmative. It is possible to oppose even long-standing, firmly held, majority positions of the culture in which one lives without necessarily being against culture as such. So the problem of slippery definitions vitiates Niebuhr's argument.

However, Yoder is not content to make this point. He presses his case further by pointing out that "the historical fact that movements which at the outset use anti-cultural rhetoric turn out to be very culturally creative"[42] is a sign of inconsistency and hard for Niebuhr to explain. But it is quite under-

38. John Howard Yoder, "How H. Richard Niebuhr Reasoned: A Critique of *Christ and Culture*," in Glen H. Stassen, D. M. Yeager, and John Howard Yoder, *Authentic Transformation: A New Vision of Christ and Culture* (Nashville: Abingdon, 1996), 54–55.
39. Niebuhr, *Christ and Culture*, 55, 69–70.
40. Yoder, "The Disavowal of Constantine," *Royal Priesthood*, 249.
41. Yoder, "How H. Richard Niebuhr Reasoned," 56.
42. Ibid., 57.

standable if, in fact, being against significant aspects of culture is actually a prerequisite for transforming culture. Yoder says of the pacifism of consistent nonconformity, for example, "precisely because this type of pacifism takes culture seriously, it discerns worldliness as a cultural reality and identifies those practices which are to be avoided."[43] Yoder notes:

> Over against the depersonalizing effects of mass education, they have created not a cultural vacuum but an alternative pattern of transmission and value definition. In case of disaster, this just might be the only subculture capable of surviving in North America outside the mainstream or without the mainstream. Whatever is wrong with the Amish and Hutterian patterns, it is not that they are against culture.[44]

Yoder notes that, if the choice is between uncritical involvement and noninvolvement, then the radical-reformation person chooses noninvolvement.[45] But he denies that Christian involvement always has to be uncritical. This is especially true when it is focused on service to the poor rather than on governing the power structures.

Yoder's position is that Christians deny their Lord when they admit that there are certain realms of life in which it would be inappropriate to bring Christ's rule to bear.[46] But his contention is that it is the Christian Realists such as H. R. Niebuhr who do this by contending that Christians must conform to some of the evil aspects of culture because those aspects cannot be expected to change. As Cartwright notes, Yoder is critical of the degree of accommodation in American Protestantism that is justified by appeals to "realism."[47] The roots of this accommodation lie in Christology, so we now turn to a discussion of the definition of the other crucial term in Niebuhr's typology: *Christ.*

The real difference between Yoder and Niebuhr is theological because they have different understandings of revelation. Cartwright notes that H. R. Niebuhr's understanding of revelation is different from that of Barth. Cartwright follows Hans Frei in viewing Niebuhr's understanding of revelation as being rooted in Troeltsch's historicist vision of pluriform revelation.[48] For Barth, on the other hand, revelation must be understood in relation to the divine *perichoresis* of the Triune God, which

43. John Howard Yoder, *Nevertheless: The Varieties and Shortcomings of Religious Pacifism* (Scottdale, Pa.: Herald, 1992), 104.

44. Ibid.

45. Yoder, "Radical Reformation Ethics," *Priestly Kingdom*, 115.

46. John Howard Yoder, "Against the Death Penalty," in John Howard Yoder and H. Wayne House, *The Death Penalty Debate: Two Opposing Views of Capital Punishment* (Dallas: Word, 1991), 144.

47. Michael Cartwright, "Practices, Politics, and Performance: Toward a Communal Hermeneutic for Christian Ethics" (unpublished Ph.D. diss., Duke University, 1988), 427.

48. Ibid., 83.

means for Barth that revelation must be unified.[49] But Niebuhr exhibits little interest in the immanent Trinity and has "no integral conception of *perichoresis* operative in connection with God's revelation."[50] Yoder's concept of revelation, on the other hand, is Barthian in that it is christocentrically controlled and, therefore, unified. He says:

> To confess Christ as Lord differs from some other fundamental stances, in fact, in that its very structure does claim to incorporate other value data. It does this neither by affirming them all (which would be a mindless pluralism) nor by denying specifically any of them, but by a nuanced interlocking which understands other values as at once created, fallen, in the process of being judged, and in the process of being led toward restoration.[51]

Yoder's position is not christomonist in the sense of rejecting all sources of knowledge except Christ, but it is christocentric in the sense of testing all knowledge by the norm of God's self-revelation in Jesus Christ, which is always central.

Yoder notes that Niebuhr's definition of Christ is one-sided. He points out that Niebuhr's Jesus is a moralist who affirms the transcendence of the spiritual and therefore condemns concern for this world. He "points away" from the world and from himself to his Father, who alone is worthy of loyalty. He does not condemn culture as sinful; he simply points toward something incomparably more important.[52] But if we compare Niebuhr's portrait of Christ to the New Testament or to the mainstream of Christian thought, we find that it leaves out a great deal. The orthodox tradition teaches that Jesus was the Son of God incarnate who died an atoning death for sin and rose from the dead. If we compare Niebuhr's portrait to that of the New Testament, we find that Niebuhr ignores Jesus' role of an exemplary human who calls people to discipleship, as well as Jesus' lordship over nature as seen in his miracles and his lordship over history as seen in his resurrection. Also, the New Testament writers would not agree in contrasting the will of the Father or that of the Spirit with the teaching and example of the Son. Yoder concludes:

> he has excised from his picture of Jesus precisely those dimensions, clearly present in the biblical witness and in classical theology, which would have made impossible the interpretation of Jesus as "pointing away" from the realm of culture, and thereby as needing the corrective of a "more balanced" position.[53]

The "Christ" who is against culture is a straw man.

49. Ibid., 81.
50. Ibid., 81–82. See chapter 4 for further discussion of Niebuhr's doctrine of the Trinity.
51. John Howard Yoder, "How to Be Read by the Bible" (A Shalom Desktop Publication, 1996), 23. See the introduction to *Priestly Kingdom*, 11, for similar statements.
52. Yoder, "How H. Richard Niebuhr Reasons," 59.
53. Ibid., 60.

In Yoder's opinion, the real point of Niebuhr's book is to argue against the radical position. Ironically, this radical position is one that Niebuhr himself apparently held early in his career. In 1935, he published an article in a book entitled *The Church against the World*,[54] in which he said that the world has always been against the church. He spoke of the church as being in bondage to idolatry, capitalism, nationalism and the spirit of class, and to optimistic humanism.[55] He had already disagreed with his brother, Reinhold Niebuhr, in the 1932 article, "The Grace of Doing Nothing,"[56] but gradually came to modify his views in the direction of those of his brother. So Niebuhr, in *Christ and Culture*, is arguing against the position he himself had once held.

Ultimately, the crucial point on which Niebuhr's book stands or falls is christological. It is true that the doctrine of the church is as absent from H. R. Niebuhr's work as it is from his brother's work. But why? The reason is rooted in Christology and eschatology. The eschatological, Jewish, impossible-to-take-seriously Jesus of Albert Schweitzer haunts the thought of both of the Niebuhrs. In order to overcome the idealistic limitations of Christian Realism, it is necessary to retrieve classical, orthodox Christology by means of a more adequate Biblical Realism, and this is Yoder's project. Biblical Realism is an alternative to Christian Realism precisely in this respect. Barth, Yoder, and other Biblical Realists begin with the assumption that the reality portrayed in the biblical narrative is more real than the reality depicted in other narratives.

There is one further point that should be made in relation to the issue of withdrawal from culture. Today the main problem the Western church is facing is not that it has no involvement in culture but that it is too conformed to culture. Since the church has bought into the socially corrosive ideology of liberal individualism, the withdrawal from social responsibility actually is the result not of sectarian ecclesiology but of liberal individualism. As Gayle Gerber Koontz observes, in modern Western society, with its emphasis on individual rights, the breakdown of the family, high mobility, and an emphasis on personal fulfillment as the purpose of life, the real danger is not withdrawal into sectarian communities but into the world of privatized religion.[57]

---

54. H. R. Niebuhr, W. Pauck, and F. P. Miller, *The Church against the World* (Chicago: Willett, Clark, 1935).

55. Yoder, "The Kingdom As Social Ethic," *Priestly Kingdom*, 89. See also the comments by James Wm. McClendon Jr. in the foreword to Charles Scriven, *The Transformation of Culture: Christian Social Ethics after H. Richard Niebuhr* (Scottdale, Pa.: Herald, 1988), 10.

56. H. Richard Niebuhr, "The Grace of Doing Nothing," in *War in the Twentieth Century: Sources in Theological Ethics*, ed. R. B. Miller (Louisville: Westminster/John Knox, 1992), 6–11.

57. Gayle Gerber Koontz, "Confessional Theology in a Pluralistic Context: A Study of the Theological Ethics of H. Richard Niebuhr and John H. Yoder" (unpublished Ph.D. diss., Boston University, 1985), 252–53.

In their book, *Habits of the Heart: Individualism and Commitment in American Life*, Robert Bellah and his coauthors document the effects of individualism upon contemporary American life. One story stands out as, perhaps, the epitome of this trend. They actually interviewed one person, a young nurse who had received a great deal of therapy, who had named her religion after herself. Her "faith" (her term for it) is called "Sheilism."[58] She heard God speak, but the voice was her own. The authors make the point that the identification of self and the cosmos as a whole is not ridiculous nonsense; rather, it is a different worldview from the biblical one. It is an attempt to liberate oneself from what is perceived to be an oppressive set of social demands coming from society.[59] Yoder's ecclesiology is the affirmation of local community, modeled on the extended family, which has the potential to be a viable (nonoppressive because freely chosen) alternative to liberal individualism. Any contemporary Western ecclesiology that does not challenge liberalism is already conformed to the world around it.

The greatest strength of Yoder's believers' church ecclesiology is that it can oppose individualism without coercion. The voluntary nature of membership means that the discipline people take on when they join the community is self-imposed. But there is still discipline within the community. Individuals cannot make up their own rules for belonging. The community has its own standards, which it adopts on the basis of its communal hermeneutic under the guidance of the Spirit. The community is thus able to act as a force for social change without resorting to violence or coercion. In this way, the community is able to bear witness to the heart of the gospel, namely, the love of God as expressed in his sending his Son to die for the sins of the world and the free offer of salvation and new life to all who repent and believe. It is in this important sense that Yoder's ecclesiology is truly evangelical.

2. The Charge of Irrelevance. One objection still remains: although Yoder's project leads perhaps to faithfulness, it also results in the irrelevance of the church to the social problems of our day. It would seem that both Niebuhrs believed that the account of Jesus and discipleship ethics given by the tradition in which Yoder was raised is perhaps closer to the New Testament than was the liberalism in which they were raised. But they could not imagine how to make such an account relevant to social ethics, and, finding themselves caught between a choice of irrelevant faithfulness and less than totally faithful relevance, they viewed the latter as the lesser of two evils. Yoder disagrees with their choice for the very simple reason that, in this dilemma (a recurring one for Christians down through the centuries), unfaithfulness is ineffective in transforming cul-

---

58. Robert Bellah et al., *Habits of the Heart: Individualism and Commitment in American Life* (New York: Harper & Row, 1985), 221.

59. Ibid., 235.

ture anyway. So the choice is actually between being faithful to Jesus and seeing one's culture transformed partially sometimes or turning away from faithfulness and seeing culture gradually "squeeze you into its mold" (Romans 12:1 Phillips).

Yoder identifies the temptation to choose "responsibility" over faithfulness as the original temptation. Commenting on Philippians 2, he states:

> The renunciation of equality with God (v. 6) has been understood in later Christian doctrinal development as referring to the metaphysical meaning of deity and incarnation, but probably the first meaning in the hymn was the more concrete Godlikeness promised by the serpent to Adam in the garden, which would have consisted in unchecked dominion over creation. Or perhaps it refers as well to the kind of Godlikeness claimed by Caesar. What Jesus renounced was thus not simply the metaphysical status of sonship but rather the untrammeled sovereign exercise of power in the affairs of that humanity amid which he came to dwell. His emptying of himself, his accepting the form of servanthood and obedience unto death, is precisely his renunciation of lordship, his apparent abandonment of any obligation to be effective in making history move down the right track.[60]

So, the grasping of "responsibility" by Adam leads to condemnation and cosmic disaster, while the renunciation of "responsibility" by Jesus leads to exaltation to the right hand of the Father and the renewal of the cosmos. As Gerber Koontz points out, the issue ultimately is one of trust in God.[61]

But does this mean giving up on social change as a goal of Christian action in the world and becoming entirely passive in the face of evil? By no means, according to Yoder. The church has an effect on culture in several ways.[62] First, the very existence of the church as countercultural community will have an indirect effect on what can be conceived of as possible in the world. Second, the church takes the lead in providing services in areas such as health, education, refugee relief, and so on. Third, the church provides Christian education to some who do not choose to identify with the church as adults, and these individuals often reflect a higher form of morality that positively affects society. Fourth, the church can speak a prophetic word to the state on the basis of the lordship of Christ. A Christian community that seriously seeks to live out the gospel will not blend in with the wider society and, therefore, will inevitably affect that society. Thus, Yoder argues, choosing to spend one's energies in building up the church is not withdrawing from society or taking a defeatist attitude. The church is a lab for social experimentation, a pilot

---

60. Yoder, *Politics of Jesus*, 235.
61. Gerber Koontz, "Confessional Theology in a Pluralistic Context," 101.
62. Yoder, *Christian Witness*, 16ff.

project, a new paradigm, a nurturing ground for countercultural values, a live alternative to a society structured around retributive sanctions.[63]

Charles Scriven argues in *The Transformation of Culture: Christian Social Ethics after H. Richard Niebuhr*[64] that Yoder's approach is a more theologically adequate account of how Christ transforms culture than the Augustinian-Calvinist one advocated by H. R. Niebuhr. In my opinion, Scriven's thesis is essentially correct. But we would be misrepresenting Yoder if we were to go further and interpret him as holding to his position because he thinks it is the most pragmatically effective position. Yoder says: "Nonresistance is right, in the deepest sense, not because it works, but because it anticipates the triumph of the Lamb that was slain."[65] Yoder doubts that the criterion of effectiveness is ultimately coherent:

> The longer I look at the question of effectiveness the less I trust that way to put the issue to be of any help. . . . The person who says, "You must give up some of your scruples in order to be effective" is still saying that because the goal for the sake of which to be effective is in principle a good goal. So the argument which takes the clothing of "principle versus effectiveness" really means this principle versus that principle. . . . Likewise the people who say "You must simply be true to God" . . . and "let the heavens fall" . . . really say that because of a conviction about Providence, trusting that if the heavens fall God has another set of heavens ready, which is part of the process, so even this is not thumbing your nose at the results. It's trusting God who gave us the rules to know more about the results than we know. So I am increasingly convinced that the debate between the effectiveness ethic and the principle ethic is a false debate.[66]

For Yoder, what is needed is obedience to the revealed will of God and trust in him for the results. If he is sovereign, then he will use our obedience to glorify himself. If he is not, then the whole debate is beside the point anyway, and we might as well trust our own best moral insights in the situation. In the end, Yoder's whole social ethic stands or falls on the reality of the God of the Bible and the reliability of Jesus as a true revelation of his character and will.

In this chapter and the previous one, I have examined Yoder's ecclesiology and demonstrated its interconnection with his Christology and eschatology. We have seen that his believers' church ecclesiology, which can be contrasted with the theocratic vision and the spiritualist reaction, is evangelical, ecumenical, catholic, and reformed. His description of the

---

63. Yoder, *Original Revolution*, 131. Cf. idem, "Firstfruits: The Paradigmatic Public Role of God's People" and "The New Humanity As Pulpit and Paradigm," *For the Nations: Essays Public and Evangelical* (Grand Rapids: Eerdmans, 1997), 15–36, 37–50.

64. Scriven, *Transformation of Culture*.

65. Yoder, *Original Revolution*, 64.

66. Yoder, *Christian Attitudes to War*, 436–37.

Christian community as a new society, brought into existence by justification by faith, is characterized by practices that enable the community, in its communal life, to become exemplary in terms of what God's ultimate intention is for the whole of creation. He shows how it is possible to say that the church not only has, but is, a social ethic. The politics of the Christian community, by means of the doctrine of analogy, becomes the basis for the witness of the church to the state. Thus, the charges of withdrawal and irrelevance, which are often made against the believers' church tradition, are not well-founded, at least so far as Yoder's ecclesiology is concerned.

Conclusion

In this conclusion, I will attempt to do three things. First, I want to summarize the portrait of the thinker that emerges from my research on Yoder and state the main conclusions I have reached concerning the correct interpretation of his thought. Second, I want to point out what I think are three significant weaknesses in Yoder's theology. Finally, I want to give my views on the enduring relevance and value of Yoder's approach to Christian social ethics and reflect on the question of what it would mean for Christian social ethics to take Yoder's "politics of the cross" seriously. I am convinced that Stanley Hauerwas is right in saying that, a century from now, Yoder's work will be seen as a new beginning. It is neither a "final word" nor a complete "system." It is, rather, a new *beginning*, and in this conclusion I aim to show how and why this is so.

Conclusions Concerning the Interpretation of Yoder's Thought

During his lifetime, Yoder wrote literally hundreds of different works, including scholarly monographs in history, theology and ethics, translations of primary sources, scholarly journal articles and reviews in disciplines ranging from philosophy to biblical studies to history, popular articles in denominational publications, and close analyses of classic texts. In all of this writing, over a period of more than forty years, one notes a definite constancy of themes and a clear logical consistency between the various arguments. This is all the more impressive, considering that Yoder did not write one big book that could serve as an introduction to his thought and a reference point for the interpretation of his writings.

There are some developments in his thought, however, that should be noted. The prominence of rabbinic Judaism and the themes of Diaspora, synagogue, and pacifism certainly became more prominent in his thinking in the last third of his life. He spent 1976 living in Jerusalem and wrote the essay "The Disavowal of Constantine" during that year. From that point on, Yoder developed his alternate reading of the Old Testament and thereby deepened his critique of Constantinianism significantly. Some of the fruit of this study appears in his last book of essays, *For the Nations.* In reading Yoder's material on Judaism, one gets a definite sense of "unfinished business," and it is fascinating to speculate on what more Yoder would have had to say about Jewish-Christian dialogue had he had the opportunity to continue thinking and writing along this line.

Another development is a move from the "politics of Jesus" to "body politics." The material that eventually was published in *Body Politics* originated as one of the series of lectures given at both Princeton and Fuller in 1980.[1] Yoder's work on Jesus and Christian ethics in the early 1970s was highly significant, but one suspects that his work would be much easier to dismiss if he had not moved beyond the focus on individual discipleship to develop his ecclesiology in such significant ways during the last two decades of his career. His book of essays, *The Royal Priesthood,* shows that ecclesiology was hardly a new theme in his writings, but this book makes the originality and comprehensiveness of his ecclesiology apparent in a new way. Here we have a compelling believers' church ecclesiology not just described, but engaged in dialogue with mainline Roman Catholic and Protestant thought.

Yoder, then, was a clear, incisive, and consistent thinker who is not always perceived to be such because of the occasional and varied styles of his many writings. In the following section, I try to sketch the main outlines of his theological ethics. What kind of social ethicist was John Howard Yoder? I would point to eight characteristics as keys to the proper interpretation of his thought.

1. A Barthian, Anabaptist Social Ethicist. By creatively uniting aspects of his own Anabaptist-Mennonite theological heritage with the method and major themes of Karl Barth's theology, Yoder was able to build on and to develop social ethics in the tradition of Barth. A common caricature of Barth's theology is to see it as "scholastic" or "conservative" and detached from everyday life and the social and political problems confronting humankind. Yoder demonstrates the social-ethical relevance of Barth's theology by developing a social ethic that is as radically christocentric as Barth's theology. The result is not irrelevance, but a powerful and internally consistent system that forces us to rethink our whole approach to what it means to address social problems from a specifically Christian perspective.

Yoder's other main source of his ethical method and major themes, his own Anabaptist-Mennonite theological heritage, is also caricatured as one that is not relevant to, or involved in, social issues. But Yoder demonstrates that a separate, disciplined community is not only relevant to the wider society but also can be shown to be the intentional strategy of Jesus in the Gospels. Yoder is critical of his own denomination for not liv-

---

1. See *The Royal Priesthood: Essays Ecclesiological and Ecumenical,* ed. Michael Cartwright (Grand Rapids: Eerdmans, 1994), 381.

ing up to the "Anabaptist vision," which he believes is consistent with the New Testament. He seeks to employ a christocentric criterion for evaluating the social stance of all denominations. Thus he unites a Barthian method with themes from his Anabaptist heritage to create a social ethic that is both highly original and powerful. Yoder's social ethics cannot be understood unless both his indebtedness to Barth and his rootedness in the Anabaptist tradition are clearly understood.

2. A Postliberal Social Ethicist. I have argued that Yoder should be understood as a postliberal theologian in the sense of having rejected liberalism in both its nineteenth-century optimistic, culture-Protestant form and its twentieth-century, chastened, revisionist form and also in the sense of having been influenced by Barth. Yoder's thought also shows many similarities to that of the various postliberal theologians associated with Yale during the past thirty years. His clear commitment to theological realism is shared by the theologian George Hunsinger, and Yoder's emphasis on pacifism is shared by the ethicist Stanley Hauerwas. His extensive engagement of the biblical text is matched by that of the biblical scholar Brevard Childs, who shares many postliberal concerns with Yoder. Yoder's originality, however, consists in the way in which he combines these three emphases.

Yoder should, however, be distinguished from members of the "Yale School," precisely to the extent that their commitment to theological realism is doubted. In this book, I have not been able to take the time to give sustained attention to the thought of individual postliberal thinkers, although I did show in chapter 3 that there are definite parallels between what Frei and Yoder do with regard to the interpretation of the Gospels. I also noted in chapter 4 that there is some similarity between the ways that Lindbeck and Yoder treat the significance of the ecumenical creeds as rules for Christian speech. While Yoder and the Yale postliberals share many common concerns and a common appreciation for the theology of Barth, they nevertheless should not be interpreted as all affirming the same position.[2]

The biggest problem in Yoder interpretation arises with regard to Stanley Hauerwas. Since Hauerwas's work is better known than Yoder's, and since Hauerwas gives Yoder so much credit for influencing him, readers tend to interpret Yoder through the grid of Hauerwas's writings. But the degree of difference between the thought of Yoder and that of Hauerwas is still somewhat unclear. The really important question, more fundamental than issues of temperament or style,[3] is the issue of theological

2. It should be noted that this is as true for the relationship of various Yale theologians to one another as it is for the relationship of Yoder to any or all of them.

3. See Michael Cartwright's discussion of the relationship between Yoder and Hauerwas in "Radical Reform, Radical Catholicity: John Howard Yoder's Vision of the Faithful Church," in *Royal Priesthood*, 15 n. 25. Cartwright sees Yoder and Hauerwas as differing on the issues of ecclesiology, but he does not trace the origin of this difference back to their Christologies as I have done in this book.

realism. We know that Hauerwas and Yoder share a commitment to non-foundationalist epistemology. We may debate the issue of relativism with regard to Hauerwas, but Yoder makes it clear how and why he is not a relativist. What is less clear in the minds of many is the question of whether or not Hauerwas is prepared to embrace the classical realism of Yoder and Barth.

At this point, we cannot go into a detailed analysis of the thought of Hauerwas and we cannot settle the issue of whether Hauerwas's critics, such as Biggar,[4] for example, are being fair to him in doubting his theological realism. But the important point to note here is that, whether fairly or unfairly, *critics do in fact doubt it* and that, under the present circumstances, it is almost inevitable that the perception of Yoder by the scholarly world will be colored by this fact. One is reminded, to mention a perhaps somewhat more extreme example of the same phenomenon, of the way in which Barth's thought was (mis-) interpreted in the English-speaking world because of its having been read through the grid of Brunner's theology during the 1940s and 1950s. Since Barth's thought was only available in very large books, not yet translated from German, and since Brunner's thought was accessible in shorter works that were translated almost immediately after their publication in Europe, the very real differences between the two thinkers were ignored or minimized as Brunner was read as representative of something called "neo-orthodoxy," an entity supposed to include within its scope the thought of both Brunner and Barth. To the extent that it becomes common to speak of Hauerwas and Yoder together as representatives of something called "narrative ethics," some crucially important differences between the two thinkers are in danger of being overlooked. Yoder should be seen as a postliberal, but also as one of the postliberals who remained most faithful to Barth's theological realism and christocentric method.

3. A Theologically Orthodox, Radical Social Ethicist. Yoder's major challenge to the church today is his controversial contention that a discipleship ethic centering on pacifism and community is the logical implication of classical, christological orthodoxy. His social ethic is firmly rooted in a very coherent and orthodox theological system. Unlike many liberal theologians, who derive radical social-ethical conclusions from their radical, heterodox theologies, and many conservative theologians, who derive conservative social-ethical conclusions from their scholastic, orthodox theologies, Yoder derives a radical ethic, centering on pacifism and separation from all forms of nationalism, militarism, and hierarchy, from classical, christological orthodoxy. This makes Yoder's social ethic attractive to people who usually regard orthodoxy as an ideological tool of patriarchy, militarism, and capitalism.

4. See my discussion of Biggar, Hauerwas, and Yoder in chapter 2.

If Yoder is correct to argue that the pacifism of the messianic community is simply the logical implication of taking seriously what the church has always taught about Jesus, then the advocates of what might be termed "left-wing Constantinianism" and "right-wing Constantinianism" are both challenged to abandon their Constantinian social strategies. The right-wing Constantinians are those who see the nation-state as the bearer of the meaning of history and who, therefore, emphasize national security and the maintenance of the status quo. They are challenged by Yoder's critique of Christian Realism as lacking a doctrine of the church and as knowing nothing of the power of the Holy Spirit.[5] They overemphasize maintaining social order and underemphasize serving the poor. They are also suspect, from Yoder's perspective, because Jesus came into conflict with the "powers," including the state. Jesus' call to his disciples to take up their crosses is evidence of the fact that he expected the same destiny for them. Left-wing Constantinians, on the other hand, are those who see themselves as being against the maintenance of the status quo and as advocates of the poor, the oppressed, and those discriminated against by the conservative establishment. But their solution is to replace the current ruling party and ideology with a new and better ruling party and ideology. They are also challenged by Yoder's critique of Latin American liberation theology as not being radical enough.[6] Yoder contends that Constantinianism, not the current set of rulers or the currently dominant ideology, is the deeper problem. Yoder argues that those who seek the kind of power that is rooted in coercion seek something that is incompatible with a clear witness to the gospel of God's uncoercive love as it is expressed in Jesus Christ.

4. A Nonfoundationalist, Nonrelativist Social Ethicist. Although Yoder is nonfoundationalist in his epistemology, he nevertheless rejects moral relativism and clearly proclaims the ontological reality of God and the ability of Christians to know God's will. Yoder is often misunderstood at this point, because his critics often make their criticisms on the basis of Constantinian assumptions that he has already rejected. For example, Yoder strongly rejects the notion that one cannot proclaim as objectively true that which one cannot prove to be true by means of some sort of universal, neutral method. Yoder calls this "methodologism" and rejects it as part of the ideology of the Constantinian establishment.

5. See chapter 1 for Yoder's critique of Reinhold Niebuhr.

6. See Yoder's article, "The Wider Setting of Liberation Theology," *Review of Politics* 52 (Spring 1990): 285–96, and his sermon, "The Original Revolution," *The Original Revolution: Essays on Christian Pacifism* (Scottdale, Pa.: Herald, 1971), 13–33. Yoder's concerns for the Constantinianism of Latin American liberation theology were based on his experience in Latin America in 1970. As the possibility of successful social revolution has receded into the distance, Latin American liberation theology has had to learn how to think from a non-Constantinian perspective.

Yoder's epistemology is nonfoundationalist but not antifoundationalist. By this he means that his rejection of foundationalism is not itself a new foundationalism that subverts all meaning systems and thereby allows a social revolution to occur. His rejection of foundationalism consists of a recognition that all of us, Christians and non-Christians alike, begin our narratives from a historically particular perspective. All thought is rooted in historical communities. However, the ruling establishments of all civilizations have a need to legitimize their rule and justify their resort to violence and coercion. So the apologists for the ruling elite attempt to ground the authority of the state in religion, science, or whatever is taken to be of ultimate truth in their culture.

Yoder's epistemology is not relativist, even though he rejects the possibility of a neutral, scientific method by which any rational person can have access to the truth and can demonstrate the truth to any other rational person. The reason Yoder does not fall into an absolute relativism is that he roots his thought in the incarnation of Jesus Christ. He builds everything in his social ethics on the conviction that, in Jesus, we have the true revelation of the character of the living God of the Bible. Since the Christian church grounds its story in the biblical narratives centering on the life, death, resurrection, and ascension of Jesus Christ, its story is the true story of what God is doing in history. The good news of the gospel is that God has acted in history, in Jesus Christ, to reconcile and redeem his creation. So a social ethic that reenacts Jesus' story in the power of Jesus' Spirit bears witness to the forgiving love of God and is, therefore, true in the sense of being consistent with the ultimate meaning of the universe.

5. An Evangelical Social Ethicist. The fact that the gospel is rooted in a historical event and, therefore, consists of the proclamation of a historically particular narrative is not a liability from Yoder's perspective. Indeed, this is part of what makes it "good news." Yoder's "epistemology of evangel" is an original contribution to Christian thought and serves as an integrating concept for a distinctively Christian doctrine of God as love, a believers' church ecclesiology, and an eschatology characterized by a tension between the old era and the new era.

Yoder's "epistemology of evangel" can be defined as his noncoercive concept of the way in which God presents himself to his creatures, revealing his grace and yet doing so in such a way as to leave the creature with the option to accept that grace freely or to reject it. The pacifism of the messianic community is rooted in the loving character of God, who does not want mere obedience, but love and fellowship from his human creatures. Yoder views the message of the church to the world as consisting of heralding the message of Jesus Christ, not as proving the existence of God. He draws a connection between the Constantinian political coercion of membership in the church through the outlawing of unbelief and the Constantinian epistemological coercion of assent by means of a smothering and irrefutable argument for the existence of God.

Yoder's view of the church's mission as being primarily witness, his view of the nature of church membership as voluntary, and his view of the importance of the church-world distinction are all rooted in his evangelical epistemology. His social ethic, which he sees as one aspect of the church's mission and, therefore, primarily as a matter of witness to Jesus Christ, can never involve coercion or the use of violence. The point of social ethics, for Yoder, is not to do the task of the state, which is to maintain some basic semblance of order in a fallen world, but rather to bear witness to the gospel.

The context for this witness is the eschatological tension of the present age between the "already" and the "not yet" of the kingdom of God. Yoder's eschatology is partially realized and yet basically future oriented. He looks forward to a point in history when God will vindicate himself in judgment. This means that the messianic community does not need to vindicate itself here and now. Since God raised Jesus from the dead, the community need not fear even martyrdom and can, instead, trust fully in the God who is able to raise the dead. Yoder argues that part of the reason why Constantinianism feels the need to resort to violence is that it has lost this future hope and the freedom for obedience that it brings. The messianic community does not need to impose the truth on anyone, for God does not need to be vindicated by his creatures and, in any case, the truth of love cannot be communicated by violence. Yoder's epistemology is evangelical in the sense of emphasizing a noncoercive witness to the good news of God's love.

6. A Jewish, Christian Social Ethicist. By describing Yoder as "Jewish," I am making the point that Yoder's theology reaffirms the Jewish roots of the believers' church vision and the Old Testament roots of the messianic community's pacifism. Yoder's retrieval of, and appreciation for, the Jewish roots of Christianity and his "disavowal of Constantine" opens up significant possibilities for Jewish-Christian dialogue, particularly between the believers' church tradition and orthodox Judaism. Yoder's theology is original insofar as it lays a new foundation for dialogue between Christians and Jews in a post-Holocaust situation.

Unlike most approaches to Christian social ethics, which denounce the Holocaust yet remain within the Constantinian framework that led to it, Yoder "disavows" the Constantinian arrangements by which Christianity was identified with the power structures of Western culture. Yoder's epistemology of evangel leads him to reject forced conversion, the application of sanctions to non-Christians by government, and the exclusion of Jews from full citizenship, all of which have been common in the history of Western Christendom. No one knows if the Holocaust still would have occurred even if Christianity had not been the official ideology of the rulers of Western Europe, but it certainly would not have been possible to view Christian anti-Semitism as being at least partially responsible for it, had Christianity not been the official religion of Germany.

Yoder's disavowal of Constantinianism rejects not only the legitimacy of Christian persecution of Judaism but also the paganization of the church that caused it to lose much of its Jewish character. Yoder sees Constantinianism as a false reading of the Hebrew Scriptures, and he sees the reading developed by the rabbis of the exile, centering on Diaspora, synagogue, and pacifism, as a non-Constantinian reading that the non-Constantinian Christian church can affirm. By describing Judaism as the sect that most consistently lived out the ethic of Jesus in medieval Europe and by highlighting the story of the pacifism of rabbinic Judaism, Yoder finds much more common ground with Judaism than most other Christian theologians. Yoder believes that Jewish and Christian understandings of God have more in common with each other than either has with pagan concepts of God.

Yoder's reaching out to Judaism, therefore, should not be understood as a backing away from the affirmation of classical, christological orthodoxy. Rather, Yoder argues that Arianism was a more appropriate religion for the Empire, which is part of his explanation for why a court apologist like Eusebius of Caesarea would lean in that direction. The Nicene *homoousios* was a reaffirmation, in Greek philosophical categories, of the biblical teachings on the oneness of God and the deity of Jesus. Jewish historical particularity is preserved by Nicea, and pagan understandings of God as eternal and detached from the temporal are rejected.[7] The revelation of God in the history of Israel and in Jesus have in common the conviction that God's self-revelation is historical in nature. The concept of God as known by means of human reason is rejected as pagan by Nicea. Yoder's Barthian rejection of natural theology thus ties in with his retrieval of the Jewish roots of Christian faith and with his reaffirmation of classical, christological orthodoxy.

7. A Christocentric, Trinitarian Social Ethicist. Yoder does not emphasize the doctrine of the Trinity, if by emphasizing that doctrine one means speculating on the nature of God with no practical end in view. But Yoder's Christology presupposes the two-natures doctrine and the full deity of Jesus Christ, his eschatology presupposes the ontological re-

---

7. Here I have in mind the proto-Arian and Arian notions of God as so absolute and pure that no such concept as the incarnation is thinkable. This concept of God occurs throughout Western thought (for example, in Deism) and is incompatible with the biblical view of a God who speaks and acts. It is ironic that the Nicene Creed is sometimes viewed as the imposition of Greek metaphysical categories onto the "simple gospel." Something like the opposite is actually true. The biblical understanding of God as Creator, Revealer, and Redeemer is protected by the fences erected by the Nicene Creed around both monotheism and the divinity of Jesus Christ. Arianism was the rationalizing theology; Nicea confesses the mystery of the incarnation.

ality of God and his sovereignty over history, and his ecclesiology presupposes the work of the Holy Spirit in the Christian community. Yoder thus can be said to be a strong advocate of what could be termed "practical trinitarianism."

Yoder's trinitarianism is christocentric, as opposed to that of H. R. Niebuhr, which is a pluralistic type of trinitarianism. For Yoder, the deity of Jesus means that any view of God that is inconsistent with God's self-revelation in Jesus Christ is false. So the whole project of natural theology as a separate enterprise alongside a theology of revelation is rejected. Any knowledge of God we claim to get from reason, nature, or tradition must be tested with reference to the norm of Jesus Christ as he is attested in Scripture. This Barthian approach to the Trinity means that Yoder never has the kind of problem a theologian such as H. R. Niebuhr had, namely, that of trying to reconcile the tensions between the God of natural theology and the God of revelation. Whereas Niebuhr attempted to do this by locating the tensions within the Trinity itself, Yoder stressed the unity of purpose of the Father, Son, and Holy Spirit. In this respect, Yoder's doctrine of the Trinity may be seen to be more orthodox than that of Niebuhr.

In his eschatology, Yoder presupposed the sovereignty of God over history and the ability of God to act in history. This led Yoder to take history very seriously as the location of God's self-revelation and the arena of his redemptive activity. Yoder refused to set aside the eschatological Jesus or to minimize his importance for the messianic community. By resisting the temptation to idealize the kingdom or to make it either completely realized or completely future, Yoder maintained the eschatological tension that runs through the New Testament.

In his ecclesiology, Yoder presupposed the activity of the Holy Spirit in calling, building up, equipping, guiding, and empowering the messianic community. It is important to see that Yoder's understanding of the church's witness as being imperfect yet visible is only viable on the assumption of the reality of the Spirit's work in the community. The Spirit makes the witness of the community possible.

Yoder clearly treats the doctrine of the Trinity as a second-order doctrine, as a set of rules for proper Christian speech about God, much as Lindbeck does. He sees the doctrine of the Trinity as necessary for preserving the Christian doctrine of God from distortion by pagan notions of God that are ahistorical, rational, and nonbiblical. Yoder's view is not a form of Christomonism, in the sense that no other sources of knowledge are valid, but it is a form of Christocentrism, in the sense that no other sources of knowledge can be declared valid until they have been shown to be coherent with the center of Christian thought and worship, Jesus Christ. Yoder's social ethic is rooted in his christocentric trinitarianism.

8. A Biblical, Ecumenical Social Ethicist. The casual reader of Yoder's work should not be misled by Yoder's rejection of the scholastic doctrine of verbal inerrancy into thinking that Yoder has a low view of biblical authority or that his theology is unbiblical in any substantial sense. Yoder actually believes that the Bible proclaims a coherent message, which is narrative in structure though diverse in expression. He uses historical criticism in the confidence that, if one can just get close enough to the original meaning of the author in the original context, one will have a baseline upon which to construct an application that can be both in harmony with the thrust of Scripture as a whole and also relevant to our situation today.

Yoder's historicism is limited by his confession that, in the person of Jesus, God has become incarnate. The incarnation is what gives the Bible authority, for it is precisely the testimony to the incarnation that makes the message of the prophets and apostles true. Yoder's communal approach to interpretation is not an evolving free-for-all in which the interpretation has no fixed reference points and biblical texts become hostages to ideologies and political powers. Again, the reason for that is his commitment to the truth of the incarnation. It would be conceivable, for Yoder, to have a hermeneutic community coming to decisions about the proper interpretation of biblical texts, proceeding to enact those interpretations in its communal life, and still to be wrongly interpreting the text and living unfaithfully. More important, in Yoder's perspective, it would be possible to critique such an unfaithful community both from within and without that community on the basis of Scripture. In fact, Yoder does precisely that in his critique of Constantinianism.

Here is where the ecumenical potential of Yoder's theology becomes apparent. He offers a way forward in ecumenical debate that is more realistic than simply saying that no one is wrong and that we can all go forward happily together into a pluralistic future that does not take seriously the possibility of apostasy. Yoder's appeal is not on the basis of institutional indefectability, which, after all, is just as problematic a concept for advocates of the believers' church doctrine of the church as it is for the advocates of apostolic succession. Ecumenical unity cannot be built on the foundation of the wood, hay, and stubble of human institutions, human performance, or human faithfulness. It can only be built on the gold, silver, and precious jewels of the person of Jesus Christ, the work of Jesus Christ, and the faithfulness of Jesus Christ. In appealing to the Bible as witness to the self-revelation of God in Jesus Christ, Yoder is appealing to that which all Christians have in common. Therefore, insofar as all Christians acknowledge this norm of faith and practice, ecumenical debate has a starting point. Unity is not guaranteed, but it is at least conceivable, providing there can be repentance and reformation by all parties to the discussion.

Criticisms of Yoder's Theology

Yoder's theology is, of course, far from perfect, and at this point I need to make mention of a few of the areas in which his theology is open to considerable criticism. In the concluding sections of chapters 4, 6, and 8 we have seen that there are adequate resources within the theology of Yoder itself to invalidate the criticisms of reductionism (4), sectarianism (6), and withdrawal from cultural engagement and or irrelevance to social issues (8). We will now examine three points of valid criticism.

1. The Rejection of System. Yoder's critique of "methodologism" has a point, but he probably pushes it too far. In rejecting the call to systematize his thought by writing some sort of major book on Christian ethics, Yoder has left his thought open to misinterpretation and caricature. The point is that one does not, and cannot, evade the systematic questions by refusing to write a systematic book. Yoder's "system" is implicit, unarticulated, and very much in the background of his writing—but that he has a system is undeniable, and part of the purpose of my book has been to bring this fact to the surface. The high degree of consistency in his thought is evidence of the existence of a logical system of thought that governs his approach to various topics.

What happens when the systematic challenge is refused, as is so often the case with Anabaptist-Mennonite theologians, is not that systematic questions and problems go away but that they are dealt with in a more *ad hoc* and dialogical manner. Yoder would undoubtedly say that that is all for the best and that theology works better when done that way. No doubt there is far too much preoccupation with method in contemporary theology, and we ought to be thankful that Yoder did not neglect the task of constructive, situational theology in order to indulge himself exclusively in that sort of preoccupation. But is it not possible to have a better balance? And, more important, can a systematic presentation of a believers' church ethic not itself be part of a larger, ongoing conversation?

In suggesting that Yoder should have given more attention to a systematic presentation of his thought, I am not saying that Yoder should have created a neutral, scientific method that would be able to generate universally accessible truth. What I am saying is that Yoder's Barthian, christocentric method of relating all theological statements to their center, Jesus Christ, would not prevent the articulation of a believers' church systematic theology or theological ethics any more than Barth's christocentric method prevented him from writing *Church Dogmatics*. Richard Mouw's point that Anabaptists have left themselves open to misunderstanding by their refusal of the systematic challenge is well taken.[8] What is being called for here is not the creation of a rationalistic metaphysic to replace the biblical, christocentric theology Yoder developed. Rather,

8. Richard Mouw, foreword to *Royal Priesthood*, viii.

what is being called for is the systematic unfolding of Yoder's theology in such a way as to display its inner logic, consistency, and breadth. This type of theological writing need not be any different from the occasional type of writing that Yoder undertook throughout his career, as far as method is concerned. But it would make misunderstanding and caricature more difficult.

Perhaps one of the reasons why Yoder did not feel the need to pursue the large-scale systematic questions is that he believed that there was work enough to do in unfolding the social-ethical implications of the systematic work done by Karl Barth. The problem with this hypothesis is that Yoder was never explicit enough about this to be sure that it was a conscious strategy on his part. But the suggestion is not without merit, especially when one considers the high degree of agreement between Yoder and Barth on issues of method and system.

2. The Resurrection of Christ. Yoder believed in the bodily resurrection of Jesus Christ as an event in history. It would be hard for any serious reader of his writings to conclude otherwise. However, Yoder talked a great deal about the cross, especially in *The Politics of Jesus*, without so much as mentioning the resurrection. One supposes that if he had known how widely read that book was to become and to what extent he was to be judged by its contents and emphases, he might have considered giving more prominence to the resurrection of Jesus. But then again, given his commitment to emphasizing what was currently being denied or underemphasized, he might not have changed a thing.

We need to remember that Yoder's main work in biblical, historical, and systematic Christology, *Preface to Theology: Christology and Theological Method*, was only published informally and has never received a wide readership. The publication of this work would certainly help create more appreciation of the balanced and orthodox view of Jesus that underlay his other writings. It is unfortunate that Yoder's orthodoxy has been called into question, not simply because it is unfair to him personally, but because his main point is thereby obscured. Yoder's main challenge to the church was that, to the extent that the church takes seriously the two-natures doctrine and the doctrine of the Trinity, the life of discipleship characterized by pacifism and servanthood must also be taken seriously. His main challenge to the church is his claim that pacifism is implied by Nicene orthodoxy.

This criticism is really a concrete example of the first criticism above. If the resurrection had been treated as part of a systematic presentation of the theology underlying his social ethics, then not only would it have received treatment in such a way that no one would doubt the importance of this doctrine to Yoder's system but it would also have made the orthodoxy of Yoder's pacifism of the messianic community more obvious. If Yoder and those who follow him want the pacifism of the messianic community to be taken seriously as Christian social ethics, then the systematic challenge of presenting the orthodox, biblical, theological basis for that approach to social ethics must be taken up. Fortunately, Yoder has provided much of the raw material for such a believers' church systematic theology in his writings.

3. Prayer and the Spiritual Life. Richard Hays makes a fascinating observation when he points out that, of the five moral theologians he has surveyed on the issue of methodology (Barth, Hauerwas, R. Niebuhr, Schüssler Fiorenza, and Yoder), "only Barth, in his account of moral decision-making, requires—at least implicitly—a constant reliance on prayer and listening for the guidance of God."[9] This is an indication of a serious gap in Yoder's account of Christian ethics and one area in which he did not work out the implications of his strong implicit emphasis on the Holy Spirit in ecclesiology. Yoder's system needs an emphasis on the Spirit, the new birth, prayer, spiritual disciplines, and worship as praise of God.

The fault cannot be attributed to Yoder's Anabaptist heritage any more than to the influence of Barth. Arnold Snyder points out that, for the sixteenth-century Anabaptists, the spiritual life preceded and nourished the ethical life:

> The work of the Spirit provided the essential underpinning for biblical interpretation, for conversion and rebirth leading to baptism, and for discipleship (as the enabling power which made discipleship possible). Anabaptist ethics and ecclesiology rested on the living presence of the Spirit.[10]

Snyder puts forward the important thesis that those Anabaptists who emphasized the inner life of the Spirit tended to emphasize love, healing, and reconciliation as the goal of pastoral discipline, while those who lacked this emphasis tended to emphasize unity, purity, and obedience to the Word. Snyder attributes the lack of emphasis on the spiritual life to the growth, over time, of a more literal, legalistic, "outer" emphasis.[11] So the issue is the nourishment of the church as a body by the Holy Spirit. Without an emphasis on the inner life of the disciple, the outer life of the community can degenerate into legalism and even coercion. Yoder's theology is not incompatible with an emphasis on prayer and the spiritual life; in fact, his theology is incomplete without it. Yet, I find these emphases inadequately dealt with in Yoder's writings.

9. Richard Hays, *The Moral Vision of the New Testament: Community, Cross, New Creation: A Contemporary Introduction to New Testament Ethics* (San Francisco: HarperSanFrancisco, 1996), 233.
10. Arnold Snyder, *Anabaptist History and Theology: An Introduction* (Kitchner, Ont.: Pandora, 1995), 96.
11. Ibid., 339.

Conclusion

Yoder and the Future of Christian Social Ethics

It is my opinion that, despite its defects and shortcomings, Yoder's theological social ethics will become more and more relevant as we slowly and painfully enter into the post-Christian phase of Western culture. If we cannot simply accept his social ethic, neither can we avoid debating it as one of the live options for the church after Christendom. Paul Ramsey's animated wrestling with the pacifist and sectarian option in his final book is an example of the kind of interaction with Yoder's thought that can be expected in the future.[12] The full potential of Yoder's rich and complex thought has yet to be appropriated by the ecumenical church. But in the years ahead, it would appear that the importance of the thought of this wide-ranging, creative, logical thinker will grow. Ultimately, his legacy is the simple challenge that to be a disciple of Jesus means following him by taking up one's cross. Appreciating the complexity of this simple challenge, however, is the task of those who would appropriate this legacy.

I would now like to suggest five aspects of Yoder's theological social ethics that I believe must be embodied in any Christian social ethic that is adequate for the twenty-first century. These five aspects of Yoder's thought are not only relevant but crucially important for those who wish to practice Christian faithfulness in this area of theology. I do not claim that Yoder has invented these theological moves or is the only one to work with them, but I do claim that he has shown us how to integrate them into social ethics in a creative and exemplary manner. He himself would not want anyone mindlessly to repeat his words or ideas; he would hope that others would find what he has written to be helpful to them as they seek to be faithful in their own time and place. I find these aspects of Yoder's thought to be helpful in that sense.

1. The Triune God As the Starting Point. First, in Christian, theological, social ethics we must be sure that when we use the word *God* we are speaking of the God of Abraham, Isaac, and Jacob, the God and Father of our Lord Jesus Christ, the Triune God worshiped by the church for twenty centuries, the living God and not the god of the philosophers or a projection of our own imaginations. Much modern theology is ambivalent in its use of the word *God.* Yoder would have none of that ambivalence. He was explicit in his theological realism and relentless in exploring the implications of following the living God who has acted in history.

Like Barth, Yoder regards the Trinity—Father, Son, and Holy Spirit—as the proper name of God, and he presupposes the Trinity in his theology and social ethics. Yoder did not spend enough time explicitly exploring

---

12. See Paul Ramsey, *Speak Up for Just War or Pacifism: A Critique of the United Methodist Bishops' Pastoral Letter "In Defense of Creation"* (University Park: Pennsylvania State University Press, 1988).

the rootedness of his thought in trinitarian doctrine, but, one could argue, he did something even more important: he did trinitarian theology. But the rejection of systematic reflection is a weakness in Yoder's theology that should not be repeated by those who wish to learn from him and build on his thought. Radical Christian ethics must root itself intentionally in trinitarian theology. If it does not, then what Yoder presupposed could be forgotten and neglected by future generations.

The kind of trinitarianism Yoder presupposed was classically orthodox and christocentric. I am convinced that it was Barth's rejection of natural theology in favor of a christocentric trinitarianism that was key to Yoder being able to root his discipleship ethic in the doctrine of the Trinity. Only when we confess that all our knowledge of God is judged, controlled, and purified by the biblical account of Jesus Christ can we hope to do justice to what the early church called the *perichoresis* of the persons of the Godhead. And only when we see a true unity of action within the Godhead is it possible to develop a social ethic that is unified and not contradictory. The essential point is that the actual character of God is revealed in Jesus' renunciation of violence and willingness to go to the cross in order to defeat evil by means of love. This is who God is. This is who the Triune God is in the depths of God's self. This is not the discovery of human reason or a deduction from a system; this is the revelation of a mystery, a mystery that contains the key to the meaning of life and the ultimate nature of reality.

2. The Incarnation As the Focal Point. Second, in Christian, theological, social ethics we must focus on the incarnation of Jesus Christ as that which provides the content for our reflections. If Jesus was the incarnation of God in a human being, if he was the Word of God dwelling among us, if he was the Son who reveals the Father, then several conclusions are clear. First, Christian theology that is not focused on him is deficient to one extent or another. Second, the biblical narratives centering on the life, death, resurrection, and ascension of Jesus Christ must somehow be basic to our description of the moral life. Third, any importation into Christian social ethics of values such as culture, responsibility, or necessity in such a way as to make such values more important than Jesus is not permissible. Fourth, any Christian social ethic concluding that Jesus is irrelevant to the question of Christian faithfulness today is less than Christian. How could God be irrelevant to anything? How could Jesus be confessed to be both divine and irrelevant at the same time?

The focus on the incarnation will result in any Christian ethic being an ethic of discipleship. Following Jesus is the essence of the Christian life. But in an age of extreme, even pathological, individualism, we must be careful to define Christian discipleship as a patterning of lives on the example of the one who, himself, was the Second Person of the Trinity. The Trinity is a community of persons who relate to each other in love and who are one in being. To attempt to imitate Jesus by a radical withdrawal from community or by a self-centered ethic of fulfillment is therefore inconsistent. To turn freedom into an idol and to exalt it as the highest good, as is done in contemporary liberalism, is the temptation of the Western church today. Yoder's thought is sadly misinterpreted if it is thought to sanction or to justify this trend. To focus on the incarnation is to focus on what it means to be a person in community whose entire life is ruled and characterized by self-giving love.

3. Openness to the Leading of the Spirit As the Goal. Third, in constructing a faithful Christian, theological, social ethics we must build into the system a dependence upon the leading of the Holy Spirit. To do this, of course, is to reject the Enlightenment emphasis upon rationalism. Christian social ethics cannot hope to express itself in a fully rational system in which ethical decision making becomes a mechanical matter of using the right method. Much of the skill in doing ethics in a Christian manner is that of knowing where the boundaries of rational reflection are, that is, knowing when to press on with rational reflection and when to stop. For a truly Christian ethic, obedience is an indispensable element, and obedience is, in the end, partially but never totally rational. Rational reflection on God's self-revelation in Jesus Christ, which is what Christian theology is, need not degenerate into rationalism.

Yoder provided tantalizingly brief but nevertheless solid suggestions for discerning the will of God in his description of body politics. The communal hermeneutic he proposed has great potential for development. Conversation, worship, and communal discipline all have a role to play in the process of discerning the will of God, and Christian ethics is all about knowing and obeying the will of God. True Christian theology is a form of prayer, and, although Yoder did not emphasize prayer in his writings, his system is incomplete without this emphasis. But it is not prayer that is disconnected from community. For Yoder, the local Christian congregation is the context for doing Christian social ethics, and it is in that context that the guidance of the Holy Spirit may be expected. Like Barth, Yoder viewed ethics primarily as preparation for the ethical event, and no Christian ethical system that fails to recognize that the goal of all Christian ethical reflection is preparation for being led by the Holy Spirit will be adequate in the future.

4. Rootedness in Historical Community As the Alternative to Methodologism. Fourth, in doing Christian, theological, social ethics today, we have to begin from our situation of historical rootedness. The basic move is from the particular to the general, not the reverse. This means that Christian ethics must be ethics by and for Christians. Many modern theologians worry that this will lead to the marginalization of Christian ethics, to a kind of provincialism that disavows universal relevancy. But the various attempts to do universal ethics using a rationalistic method developed by Western Europeans in the past three centuries have now been exposed as being themselves both provincial and pretentious. In the postmodern situation, relevancy is not something that can be imposed; it must be recognized. What I mean is that to claim that one's perspective is relevant to all just because it is the perspective of the powerful has been exposed as illegitimate. An ethical perspective is only relevant if it is perceived or recognized to be so. This means that Christian ethics must concentrate on being Christian; if others recognize its relevancy, then Christians will be glad and celebrate.

This perspective means that the focus of the Christian theologian is not on discovering what might appeal to the non-Christian or the wider society and attempting to restate the Christian position in such a way as not to offend the wider culture. This apologetic approach usually leads to compromise and to the watering down of distinctive Christian claims, which, ironically, often only serves to lessen the appeal of the Christian position. This pattern has occurred repeatedly in Western culture whenever Christianity has been perceived as the ideology of the ruling elite and the basis of the "establishment." The remarkable repositioning of the Roman Catholic Church in Latin America from apologist for the ruling elite to defender of the oppressed, which has occurred in the second half of the twentieth century, is an example of how a Christian group has realized that it cannot speak for "all" if it wishes to be faithful. The Christian church must indeed take sides, rather than attempting to adopt a position of universal neutrality. The amazing thing is how relevant the Latin American Roman Catholic Church looks today, after choosing to take the side of the poor and daring to say that, in this place, at this time, the gospel means opposing specific injustices and being in solidarity with certain persons rather than others. The truth and relevance of Christianity is displayed best when the particular implications of the gospel for here and now are played out without regard for developing a universal ethic for all.

5. The Minority Perspective As the Alternative to Constantinianism. Fifth, doing Christian, theological, social ethics faithfully today requires us to begin with a minority perspective. Yoder does two things in developing his theological position that are instructive. First, he keeps the church-world distinction clearly in view. He constantly remembers that the church is not the world and the world is not the church. Second, he knows that the church is the minority and, as such, must rely on argument rather than coercion. The potential implication of faithful Christian witness is always martyrdom because of this minority position. Christian ethics focuses on what it means to bear a faithful witness to Christ in a world that has not bowed the knee to Christ rather than on how to govern the world from a position of power.

This minority perspective, Yoder argues, enables creativity and innovation in a way that an ethic of responsibility cannot. The disavowal of Constantine results in freedom for Christian faithfulness and a stronger witness. Sometimes it also results in greater influence on the wider society, but that is a byproduct rather than a primary goal. The minority perspective allows Christianity to be set free from the baggage of authoritarian control and violent coercion. This freedom enables faithful witness to the world, which is the primary goal of Christian life and scholarship. Postmodern, post-Constantinian Christians could learn much from the Jews about how to survive as a minority within a larger culture.

Yoder's approach to social ethics is so highly counterintuitive and so much against the grain of contemporary Christian social ethics that his position is difficult for many people to take seriously. However, this book has demonstrated that James Gustafson's assertion that "theological integrity more than moral distinctiveness is the challenge of the traditional radical Protestant view"[13] is accurate with respect to Yoder's thought. The undeniable christocentric focus and the high degree of logical coherence of the theological foundations of Yoder's social ethics make it extremely difficult simply to dismiss him. One difficulty in coming to terms with Yoder is that it is hard, in the end, to take bits and pieces of his thought and to leave behind the hard-to-digest parts, because of the logical coherence of his theological system. Yoder's work thus stands as a whole and invites either acceptance or rejection. This frustrates those who would seek to let him be a "corrective" without accepting his core affirmations about the concrete meaning of following Jesus. This absoluteness, one strongly suspects, is not accidental or incidental but rather integral to the central logic of Yoder's position, which is consciously developed from his conception of the lordship of Jesus Christ.

13. James Gustafson, *Theology and Ethics*, vol. 1 of *Ethics in Theocentric Perspective* (Chicago: University of Chicago Press, 1981), 75.

A Beginner's Guide To Reading
John Howard Yoder

In this book, I have tried to do justice to the main points of the theological foundations of John Howard Yoder's social ethics. But there is so much more that could have been said and so many more aspects of his complex and intriguing thought that could have been explored. My greatest desire for this book is that it will encourage readers to put my book down and begin reading Yoder himself. But where is one to start? That is a good question and, in this brief beginner's guide to reading Yoder, I want to make some comments which might be helpful to the person who wishes to start to read Yoder for the first time or, perhaps, more extensively and in greater depth.

By far the most famous of Yoder's writings is *The Politics of Jesus*[1] and there are good reasons why this is so. It is a book that even those who disagree with Yoder's conclusions find to be well-argued and difficult to refute. Its thesis is deceptively simple: Jesus is not only relevant to, but also normative for, Christian social ethics and contemporary, mainstream biblical scholarship supports this claim. The first half of the book focuses on the Gospel of Luke, the second half turns to the New Testament epistles, and one chapter is devoted to the Apocalypse. Yoder's use of biblical scholarship is an outstanding model for theologians who wish to be biblical in doing theology and ethics. Anyone interested in Christian social ethics or the witness of the church in a postmodern world who has not yet read this book should do so without delay.

In a sense, the rest of Yoder's work is devoted to two main tasks: first, working out the implications of the thesis of *Politics* for various aspects of social ethics and second, demonstrating that the thesis of *Politics* has, in fact, been taken seriously by many lesser-known movements in church history, especially by the sixteenth-century Anabaptists and

1. (Grand Rapids: Eerdmans, 1972, 1994). See the Introduction of this book, p. 15, n.3 for more information.

those influenced by their witness. Where it has not been taken seriously, the results have been grim for the witness of the gospel.

Yoder published four books of essays dealing with theology and ethics. The first one, *The Original Revolution: Essays on Christian Pacifism*[2], was published in 1971, when Yoder was, as yet, relatively unknown beyond Mennonite circles. It is now out of print. However, of the seven chapters in this book, five have been reprinted in later books. Chapter 3 of Part I, "If Christ is Truly Lord," and all three of the chapters in Part II, have been reprinted in *The Royal Priesthood* (see below). Chapter 1, "The Original Revolution," has been reprinted in *For the Nations*. That only leaves chapter 2 and 4 of Part I that have not been reprinted.

Chapter 2, "The Political Axioms of the Sermon on the Mount," however, is especially important because it deals with a major biblical text not treated in *Politics*. In *Politics*, Yoder was concerned to avoid the stereotype of legalistic perfectionism, which is thought to base the case for pacifism on a literal and rather simple-minded interpretation of commands such as Matthew 5:44. Motivated by a desire to present a broader and theologically deeper case for pacifism, he chose to read the entire New Testament in a holistic manner rather than focusing on the command of Jesus. Yoder's treatment of the Sermon in this essay as a catechism for those who choose to live under Jesus' lordship in the new society called the church is rich and suggestive. Chapter 4, "If Abraham is Our Father," deals with the problem of war in the Old Testament.

The second book of essays, *The Priestly Kingdom: Social Ethics as Gospel*,[3] was published as a follow-up to *Politics* in 1984, the first year Yoder taught full-time at the University of Notre Dame. Unlike *The Original Revolution,* this book has been widely read and cited in the social ethics literature. In this remarkable collection of essays, Yoder attempts to set forth a case for the "sectarian ecclesiology" which is now beginning to be taken seriously in the mainstream Christian communions. He emphasizes the ecumenical nature of his claims by saying: "my claim that the vision of discipleship projected in this collection is founded in Scripture and catholic tradition, and is pertinent today as a call for all Christian believers." (p. 8)

Yoder contends that the free-church tradition has a both a distinctive ethic and a distinctive, evangelical epistemology. For Yoder, the church precedes the world axiologically and so the lordship of Christ must be taken into account in all value choices, even those which the world pressures Christians to seal off from Christian faith. An important theme of this book is that faith in the incarnation requires nonrelative truth claims and, at the same time, a nonfoundationalist epistemology.

2. (Scottdale, Penn.: Herald Press, 1971).
3. (Notre Dame: University of Notre Dame Press, 1984).

The middle section, in which Yoder begins to make the case histori-cally for the credibility of the non-Constantinian approach to social eth-ics, is especially significant. In "The Constantinian Sources of Western Social Ethics," in particular, he argues that Constantinianism is an escha-tological heresy that either denies the future hope or turns it into some-thing interior to the believer in a Gnostic fashion. This book is the second most important book to read after *Politics.*

The third book of essays, *The Royal Priesthood: Essays Ecclesiological and Ecumenical,*[4] is a very important collection of work from four de-cades of writing on these themes. The fifty-page introduction by Michael Cartwright, "Radical Reform, Radical Catholicity: John Howard Yoder's Vision of the Faithful Church," is an excellent introduction to Yoder's ec-clesiology. The essay "Why Ecclesiology is Social Ethics: Gospel Ethics Versus the Wider Wisdom" is important as an interpretation of the ec-clesiology of Karl Barth and also as a statement of Yoder's view of the es-chatological nature of the church as the believing community that, on behalf of all others, bears the meaning of history and is, therefore, "the new world on the way."

The fourth book of essays, *For the Nations: Essays Public and Evangeli-cal,*[5] again brings together various writings from throughout Yoder's ca-reer. This book is designed to convey Yoder's sense of how the church is meant to exist as a witness to Jesus Christ in the Diaspora. Here Yoder is concerned to expose the Jewish roots of the free-church vision, specifi-cally the Jeremianic vision of life in the exile. Yoder states that his pur-pose in this book is to make explicit his claim in "Why Ecclesiology is So-cial Ethic" that "the very shape of the people of God in the world" is "a public witness" and "good news" rather than constituting a rejection of or withdrawal from the world. This is also an important book, especially the essays in Part I.

Another book, which deals with the public witness of the church, is the early, brief work entitled *The Christian Witness to the State.*[6] This book demonstrates that Yoder's concern for the church having a viable witness in the wider world is one that has been important for Yoder throughout his career. It also clearly shows the influence of Oscar Cull-mann on Yoder's eschatology and thus anticipates themes in his later writings. It would not be as important to read as the last three books of essays mentioned above.

One other book that needs to be taken into consideration by anyone wishing to evaluate the claims of Yoder in *The Priestly Kingdom* is the

---

4. (Grand Rapids: Eerdmans, 1994).

5. (Grand Rapids: Eerdmans, 1997).

6. (Newton, Kan.: Faith and Life Press, 1964). This book was published as part of a series sponsored by the Institute of Mennonite Studies of the Associated Mennonite Bib-lical Seminaries.

slim but profound work entitled *Body Politics: Five Practices of the Christian Community Before the Watching World.*[7] This book deals with practices internal to the church that can become part of its witness to the world around it. This account fleshes out the claims Yoder made earlier about the church being the "new world on the way."

The other major part of the Yoder corpus consists of the writings on historical theology and church history, which seek to show both the historical roots of the free-church vision and the inadequacy of the Constantinian approach to social ethics. The three most important works in this category are *Preface to Theology: Christology and Theological Method;*[8] *War, Peace and Revolution: A Companion to Bainton;*[9] and *Nevertheless: Varieties of Religious Pacifism.*[10] The case for the ethical authority of the life and teachings of Jesus being based in orthodox Christology is made in depth in *Preface*, which deals extensively with the relationship between New Testament Christology and developments in the first five centuries. There is a surprising amount of theology in the six hundred pages of church history in *War, Peace and Revolution* and there Yoder develops his case in dialogue with other traditions extensively. *Nevertheless* is vintage Yoder, an analytical *tour de force* organized around lists and sublists. Yoder's own "pacifism of the messianic community" is carefully distinguished from over twenty other types of pacifism. The reader who questions Yoder's commitment to orthodoxy should consult *Preface*, while the reader who wishes to reflect on the history of the church in the light of Yoder's biblical case for the social ethical relevance of Jesus should tackle *War, Peace and Revolution.* However, in either case, I recommend that the widely available *Nevertheless* be read first as an introduction to Yoder's impressive analytical skills.

Speaking of analytic skills, anyone interested either in the ethics of war or the thought of Karl Barth should not neglect Yoder's excellent book entitled *Karl Barth and the Problem of War.*[11] This is one of the best early introductions to Barth's ethics and shows that Yoder is, in some interesting ways, more Barthian than Barth! Yoder's treatment of Reinhold Niebuhr is also well worth examining, both in the article, "Reinhold Niebuhr and Christian Pacifism"[12] and also in *War, Peace and Revolution,*

---

7. (Nashville, Tenn.: Discipleship Resources, 1992).

8. (Elkhart, Ind.: Co-op Bookstore, 1981). A photocopied version is available from the Cokesbury Book Store at Duke Divinity School in Durham, NC. However, I am pleased to be able to say that Brazos Press intends to bring this important work to publication with an introduction by Stanley Hauerwas in 2002.

9. (Elkhart, Ind.: Co-op Bookstore, 1983). A photocopied version is available from the Cokesbury Book Store at Duke Divinity School in Durham, NC. Unfortunately, there are no plans as yet to publish this work.

10. (Scottdale, Penn.: Herald Press, 1971, 1976, 1992). The third (1992) edition is revised and expanded.

11. (Nashville: Abingdon, 1970).

12. *Mennonite Quarterly Review* 29 (April 1959).

chapters 16 and 17. Yoder's brilliant and devastating critique of H. R. Niebuhr's *Christ and Culture* is found in the book *Authentic Transformation: A New Vision of Christ and Culture*.[13]

The comprehensive bibliography published by Mark Thiessen Nation[14] includes several hundred works by Yoder in French, German, and Spanish, in addition to English. In this brief guide to beginning to read Yoder, I have only mentioned a few of his most important writings. Hopefully, those who want to learn from Yoder will find these central works helpful, and critics who wish to argue against his conclusions will find that the works I have mentioned prevent them from drawing false conclusions on the basis of insufficient evidence. Scholars interested in doing research in Yoder's writings are encouraged to consult Thiessen Nation's bibliography.

This is not the place to get into an extended discussion of the quickly-growing body of secondary literature on Yoder's thought, but I cannot resist just mentioning a couple of important collections of writings about Yoder's thought. One interesting collection of essays, tributes, and literary refractions appeared in a special memorial issue of *The Conrad Grebel Review* (Spring 1998). The essays contain very different interpretations of the importance of Yoder's thought, the tributes from Yoder's funeral are illuminating, and the literary refractions by Rudy Wiebe and others are moving. A *festschrift*, which was to have been presented to Yoder but was not because of his sudden death, has now been completed. It is called *The Wisdom of the Cross: Essays in Honor of John Howard Yoder*.[15] It contains a biographical sketch of Yoder by Mark Thiessen Nation, as well as a range of essays on Yoder's work by approximately twenty scholars. It also contains a supplement to Thiessen Nation's comprehensive bibliography. But my advice is not to dip into these collections until you have first read Yoder extensively. When you do read him, be prepared to have your life changed. It could occur before you even realize what is happening.

---

13. G. H. Stassen, D. M. Yeager and J. H. Yoder, eds. (Nashville: Abingdon Press, 1996). Yoder's essay is entitled "How H. Richard Niebuhr Reasoned: A Critique of *Christ and Culture*" (31–90).

14. "A Comprehensive Bibliography of the Writings of John H. Yoder" *Mennonite Quarterly Review* 71 (January 1997): 93–145.

15. S. Hauerwas, C. K. Huebner, H. J. Huebner, and M. Theissen Nation, eds. (Grand Rapids: Eerdmans, 1999).

Subject Index

249

Author Index